THE H.G. WELLS SCRAPBOOK

THE H.G. WELLS SCRAPBOOK

Articles, essays, letters, anecdotes, illustrations, photographs and memorabilia
about the prophetic genius of the twentieth century

EDITED BY
PETER HAINING

Foreword by
Jack Williamson

Clarkson N. Potter, Inc./Publisher

For

Philippa

– my Time Traveller

Art Editor: Deborah Miles
Designed by Nykola Stoakes

Library of Congress Card Catalog Number 78-73102

Printed in Great Britain by Thomson Litho Ltd,
East Kilbride, Scotland
Bound by Hunter & Foulis, Edinburgh
0-517 53722

ACKNOWLEDGEMENTS

The Editor is firstly and foremost grateful to Messrs A. P. Watt and the Estate of H. G. Wells
for permission to use material by H. G. Wells which is covered by copyright in this book.
Without their kindness this work would not have been possible. Sincere thanks are also extended
to Jack Williamson, Ken Chapman, Denis Gifford, Basil Copper, George Lawrence, Gerald
McKee, Mrs. I. D. Edrich, Jorge Luis Borges, P. H. Alexander, George Pal and Reg Smith.
Similarly to Canavaral Press, Opera Mundi, Popular Publications, *Marvel* Comics, *Amazing
Stories*, the *Illustrated London News*, the *Evening Standard*, *Evening News*, *The Times*, *Times Literary
Supplement*, *Punch*, *The New Yorker*, *New York Times*, the British Museum Newspaper Library,
New York Public Library, London Library, British Film Institute and Universal Pictures,
MGM and Paramount Pictures.

For the writer of fantastic stories to help the reader to play
the game properly, he must help him in every possible
unobtrusive way to *domesticate* the impossible hypothesis.
He must trick him into an unwary concession to some
plausible assumption and get on with his story while the
illusion holds. And that is where there was a certain slight
novelty in my stories when they first appeared. Hitherto,
except in exploration fantasies, the fantastic element was
brought in by magic. Frankenstein, even, used some
jiggery-pokery magic to animate his artificial monster.
There was trouble about the thing's soul. But by the end
of the century it had become difficult to squeeze even a
momentary belief out of magic any longer. It occurred to
me that instead of the usual interview with the devil or a
magician, an ingenious use of scientific patter might with
advantage be substituted. That was no great discovery.
I simply brought the fetish stuff up to date, and made it
as near actual theory as possible.

H. G. Wells

June 1934

JACK WILLIAMSON

Jack Williamson is an ideal person to be introducing this book for he is not only one of the most respected names in the field of science fiction, but actually wrote his PhD thesis on the work of H. G. Wells. He was appointed the second Science Fiction Grand Master (a year after Robert Heinlein) and this year celebrates fifty years since the publication of his first story, 'The Metal Man' in Amazing Stories in 1928. Of his many outstanding books, 'The Legion of Space', first published in volume form in 1947, is regarded as a classic. He now lives in retirement in New Mexico.

H. G. WELLS offers a golden lode for the scrapbook editor and a fabulous treasure chest for the scrapbook reader. In his own daring way, he was our first world citizen, discovering our future before it happened. Certainly he was one of the giant minds of modern times, his true greatness too seldom recognised.

He is sometimes slighted, I think, just because he is too much like the famous elephant described in six different ways by the six blind men. He lived through so many periods, showed so many dazzling facets, left such a vast and varied volume of work, that few people have ever tried to see the whole of him.

Physically, he was a small man with a squeaky cockney voice. He was prone to ill health, especially during the hard times of his youth. Yet he seems to have been full of nerve and life and wit, a great friend, an absorbing talker, a brilliant if unsystematic thinker. Many women found him charming.

To my regret, I never met him. Yet, growing up five thousand miles from London on a little sandhill farm in New Mexico, I felt his electric impact. He offered more than exciting entertainment. He opened unexpected new horizons. He helped me find my own life career.

For me – as for many thousand others – that first vital impact came from his early science fiction. I recall with a special fondness the big, green-bound volume of *Seven Famous Novels* and the thick red book of his complete short stories. Those wonderful books revealed new worlds almost incredible to a country boy who had lived somewhat below what is now the official poverty line. They carried me from the sand-hills to London and all around the Earth, back to the far past and on to the farther future, out to the stars. They changed my whole way of thinking. As inspiration, they taught me what to write. As literary models, they helped teach me how to write.

Wells was born in Bromley, Kent, in 1866. Looking at the child, nobody could have foreseen the literary giant, the first futurologist, the world historian and educator, the international statesman, the social philosopher.

His parents were former domestic servants, trying to squeeze a living from a little crockery shop. His pious mother accepted the creaky Victorian social system and tried hard to get him into it as a draper or a chemist. His father was larger-minded and more critical of the dismal status quo, but it was a series of lucky misfortunes that set him free.

Strange creatures beset the Time Traveller – an illustration by the brilliant Virgil Finlay for 'The Time Machine' in 'Famous Fantastic Mysteries,' 1950.

A broken leg gave him time to read. A second broken leg, his father's, helped break up the unhappy household behind the china shop and let him escape a disastrous apprenticeship. A haemorrhage from tuberculosis forced him to give up an ill-paid teaching job and his first unsatisfying marriage. He ran away with one of his students to become the author we remember.

In *Experiment in Autobiography*, he tells the absorbing story of his intellectual liberation. Plato's *Republic* gave him the idea that social systems can be rebuilt – that we can discard oppressive institutions and remake our world. An inspiring teacher, Thomas Henry Huxley, taught him biology at the Normal School of Science in London, and reshaped his whole philosophy.

Huxley had been the foremost champion of Charles Darwin when the theory of evolution was still new and controversial. From him, Wells learned to see our universe as a process, not as something fixed and static; he also learned to see the human race as just another animal species, still evolving and perhaps in danger of extinction, not as a perfected special creation.

In Wells' mind, this evolutionary insight became a powerful tool. Men had always been attempting prophecy, but now he could bring new and better rules to the game. His early science fiction is full of biological extrapolation. In his first great novel, *The Time Machine*, published in 1895, he projects the whole future evolution of the human race.

Above: The Earthman radios his strange story of life on the moon: a picture by an unknown artist for an early American edition of 'The First Men in the Moon'.
Below: The crucifixion scene from Harper's edition of 'When the Sleeper Wakes' published in 1899.

Through the next few years, he was not only writing his best science fiction but also pioneering the intellectual discipline we now know as future studies. In a little book published in 1902, *The Discovery of the Future*, he outlined the principles of futurology. This discovery shaped the rest of his life, because he was alarmed by the future he saw.

For several centuries before him, in spite of a few such dissenters as Jonathan Swift, men had generally been optimists about the usefulness of science and the shape of the future. It had been an 'age of reason'. With knowledge growing, social progress would become automatic. Man and his society could be perfected by well-planned change – the American Revolution and the French Revolution had been historic attempts in that direction, as the Russian Revolution was to be in Wells' own lifetime.

Swift had written *Gulliver's Travels* as savage satire on such ideas – on what he thought was man's misplaced pride in his own reason. Wells had always admired Swift, and several of the early novels, among them *The Island of Dr Moreau* and *The First Men in the Moon*, may be read as further voyages of Gulliver.

In a little book of my own, I call Wells a 'critic of progress'. His great early science-fiction stories are more than compelling adventure narratives: they dramatise three major hazards to the human future. Our universe isn't always friendly to life in *The Time Machine*, all life ends with the death of our sun. As an animal species, we have inherited traits that now threaten civilisation – that's the main theme of *The Island of Dr Moreau*, and one that Wells never forgot. He points out, too, that progress limits itself. The Martians in *The War of the Worlds*, for example, are victims of their own high science. They have destroyed the germs on Mars and lost their own natural immunities; when they meet the germs of Earth, they decay.

The invention of futurology led Wells away from fiction. Writing *When the Sleeper Wakes*, he found that serious forecasting got in the way of his fictional creation. And, with a growing interest in the actual future he was finding, he became more and more impelled to do something about it.

One thing he did was to join the Fabian Society, a socialistic reform group, where he tried and failed to take the leadership away from George Bernard Shaw and Beatrice and Sidney Webb – they defeated his efforts to reform the Fabians themselves.

Something else he did was to turn his novels into arguments for social causes. One cause was women's liberation, where he was practically a century ahead of his time. The ideal woman of his dreams was a perfect sexual partner and his intellectual equal, strong and beautiful and free. The search for such a woman led him through many love affairs – the most memorably successful being that with the brilliant Rebecca West – and supplied him with characters and themes for a whole cluster of novels about sex and marriage, so daring at the time that they caused him trouble with his publishers, though they seem quite tame now.

He had made his first reputation in the closing years of the nineteenth century with his dazzling science fiction. In the opening years of the twentieth, he earned a wider reputation as a major comic

novelist with such books as *Kipps*, *The History of Mr Polly*, and *Tono-Bungay*. Sometimes called a second Dickens, he became one of the most popular and highly paid writers of the time.

But he was not content with that. He had seen the future too clearly and found too much to fear. In the course of a famous literary quarrel with Henry James, an old friend who had admired his early work, he announced that he was giving up literature as art to work for the great social causes that absorbed him.

His greatest concern was world peace. As early as 1913, he had been writing about uranium bombs. Foreseeing world wars and atomic holocausts, he hoped to help establish a world state that might avoid them. Critical of democracy, he tried to alert and warn and train an 'open conspiracy', an élite group of pioneer world citizens who would organise to keep us from global suicide.

As educator, he devoted years of his life to three great works, *The Outline of History*, *The Science of Life*, and *The Work, Wealth, and Happiness of Mankind* – books intended to reveal our past evolution in the direction of a peaceful world commonwealth and to help us create it now.

As a would-be global statesman, he should have more credit than he gets for creating the sense of needed unity in the face of danger that led to the League of Nations. In later years, he wrote and lectured steadily, he visited and lectured such world leaders as Roosevelt and Stalin, to push his long campaign to settle our suicidal quarrels.

He died in 1946, the year after the first atomic bombs exploded in World War II, believing he had failed. His last small book, *The World at the End of its Tether*, is a confession of despair. But perhaps he didn't fail. After all, our world is still very much alive. If we do survive to make peace with our atoms and

Above: The mysterious stranger who becomes 'The Invisible Man': an illustration by Robb for an early English edition of the novel.

Below and facing page: Three panels from the Marvel Comics picture strip version of 'The Island of Dr Moreau', 1977.

ourselves, a good part of our gratitude should go to him.

Always industrious, Wells averaged about two books a year for half a century. Most are now collecting dust on library shelves. His great textbooks, once so popular, are now out of date, and many of his social battles have been won and long since forgotten. Only the science fiction is still more widely read than ever, the action still gripping and the themes still arresting, even though our astronauts found no Selenites in the Moon and our Viking landers have photographed no actual blood-sucking Martians.

Certainly, Wells was the chief creator of modern science fiction. Mary Shelley and Edgar Allan Poe and Jules Verne had been able pioneers, but they lacked the futuristic insights he had gained with Huxley's aid and the deep concern for the human future he had learned in his hard childhood. In addition, he had humour and invention, a sense of adventure and immense literary skill. He not only created most of the standard science-fiction plots still

in use, but gave us examples that are still outstanding. *The Time Traveller* and *The War of the Worlds* are still the best of their genres. Edmond Hamilton called *The Island of Dr Moreau* the best novel of its length in the English language.

Teaching my own science-fiction course, I used to divide the authors we read into optimists and pessimists, into those who believe we can use science and

reason to build a better future and those who fear we are inventing our own destruction.

As Mark Hillegas shows in a fine study called *The Future as Nightmare: H. G. Wells and the Anti-Utopians*, Wells holds a central place among the pessimists. He is the heir to Jonathan Swift, and he influenced many followers: Zamyatin, the Russian author of *We*; George Orwell and Aldous Huxley; Frederik Pohl and the once-debated 'New Wave'. Even me.

But he also wrote *A Modern Utopia*. Through the last half of his writing life, he was a spokesman for what C. P. (Lord) Snow calls the culture of science – the people who understand science and try to use it constructively. Not, I think, because he had discovered any sudden optimistic faith that technology equals automatic progress, but rather because he had foreseen early in his life that our technology could and probably would destroy us unless we learned to use it well. He did his best to teach us how to use it well.

Though he has been too much neglected, multitudes of readers still love his science fiction and academic researchers keep discovering and rediscovering him. His papers and letters are stored in the English Library at the University of Illinois in Urbana, and scholars there have been producing fascinating fragments: *Henry James and H. G. Wells, Arnold Bennett and H. G. Wells, George Gissing and H. G. Wells, H. G. Wells and Rebecca West*. No definitive life and letters has yet appeared, but there are fine recent biographies by Norman and Jeanne MacKenzie and by Lovat Dickson, besides a briefer book by Patrick Parrinder. W. Warren Wagar has published *H. G. Wells and the World State*. Bernard Bergonzi's *The Early H. G. Wells* is a revealing exploration of the great science fiction. My own little book is *H. G. Wells: Critic of Progress*. Much of this academic interest was touched off by an important essay by Wells' own son, Anthony West, in *Principles and Persuasions*. Robert Bloom's recent *Anatomies of Egotism* is a look at Wells' last novels, showing that even in the 1930s, long after the literary establishment had decided to forget him, he was still a very major novelist, writing skilful and absorbing fiction on a major theme – the selfish individual egotism that he had come to see as the most dangerous barrier to the happy human future he had fought for all his life.

Jack Williamson

Introduction

H. G. Wells strides the science fiction genre like a colossus, in much the same way that his towering Martians bestrode the English countryside in his famous novel, The War of the Worlds. *His impact on literature, too, has been equally awesome, although as the idea of 'science fiction' did not exist at the time he produced his greatest works in the genre he was not to be seen as one of the founding fathers of a new genre until nearly a quarter of a century later.*

Today, of course, with the enormous world-wide popularity of science fiction, it is perhaps hard to appreciate the impact the writings of Wells had on the general public. To be sure, many readers had already discovered the 'scientific romance' as it had been pioneered by the great Frenchman, Jules Verne, a decade before Wells arrived on the scene; but while Verne's stories were unashamed adventures and entertainments, the work of Wells was firmly rooted in scientific fact.

It was probably the Daily Telegraph *in September 1897 which first appreciated and spelt out what the young writer (he had just turned thirty) had achieved when it wrote of his* The Invisible Man*: 'Wells [is] a promoter of what may be called the new fairy story, which differs from the old in taking science instead of the supernatural for its subject matter.' Contemporary writers were even more struck by the uniqueness of his early work – Joseph Conrad enthusing in a letter a year later in 1898, 'O Realist of the Fantastic! . . . If you want to know what impresses me it is to see how you contrive to give over humanity into the clutches of the Impossible and yet*

One of Warwick Goble's illustrations for the first publication of 'The War of the Worlds' in 'Pearson's Magazine', 1897.

Floating loose in the space ship: a picture by Claude A. Shepperson who illustrated the serialisation of 'The First Men in the Moon' in 'The Strand Magazine', 1900-1.

manage to keep it down (or up) to its humanity, to its flesh, blood, sorrow, folly. That *is the achievement!'*

Even as we can see from these early judgements how Wells burst like a shooting star on his times, in hindsight we can be even more specific about his accomplishments – vide Bernard Bergonzi writing in H. G. Wells: A Collection of Critical Essays *(1976):*

> *His early scientific romances captured the imagination of the English-speaking world and very possibly influenced the subsequent development of technology; not, indeed, by visible cause and effect, but by inspiring scientists to realise certain fascinating, if remote possibilities. Thus, the First Men in the Moon of 1969 might never have stood where they did if it had not been for Wells' fictional anticipation of the event some seventy years before.*

What sort of man was it, then, that earned such praise and whose impact is still so highly revered three-quarters of a century after his major works in the field were published? A man who utilised the facts of science and technology as they were then known and understood to prophecy the future with uncanny accuracy?

Herbert George Wells (1866-1946) was born in Bromley, Kent, the son of English lower-middle-class parents. From his childhood he was evidently a dreamer, and his writings are dotted with reference to youthful influences which stimulated his imagination and later his work. As early as seven, he tells us, he was caught up in the magic of books. 'I had just discovered the art of leaving my body to sit impassively in a crumpled up attitude in a chair or sofa while I wandered over the hills and far away in novel company and new scenes.' For all this stimulation, though, he was an undistinguished schoolboy, a less than successful draper's apprentice, and only a modestly accomplished science student. It was as a journalist imagining the future, and a novelist letting his mind loose among the wonders of science and the universe, that he made his phenomenal impact on the world of late Victorian literature.

Two of Wells' prophecies come true. Above: The first man in space, Yuri Gagarin, as reported in the London 'Evening News', Wednesday, 12 April 1961; and below: Neil Armstrong steps onto the moon, 'Evening Standard', Monday, 21 July 1969.

What, though, the young Wells may have lacked in intellect – and he freely admitted this in his autobiography – he had a consuming enthusiasm for all manner of literary activities and a questioning, open-minded approach to science as it then stood. It was, too, a time when the British people desperately sought change. For many of them, Queen Victoria's reign was seemingly endless, too many of the entrenched ideas looked set to be carried unchanged into the new century, and while there was this undoubted weariness about the past and present, there was equal foreboding about the future. The expression fin de siècle fitted the mood of the period exactly – and critic Bernard Bergonzi again sees most precisely Wells' place in this situation:

> Wells' early romances are minor myths . . . they reflect some of the dominant preoccupations of the fin de siècle period; and it is important to remember that this significance is more than simply historical. If the fin de siècle expressed the final convulsions of the Nineteenth Century, it also marked the birth pangs of the Twentieth, and many of the issues that concern mid-Twentieth Century Man first appeared during that period.

Although young Wells was not the most successful of students, it would be wrong to overlook the fact that his education and particular interest in science made him well qualified to write scientific romances. As Ingvald Raknem has written in H. G. Wells and his Critics (1962), 'His studies included the biological sciences as well as physics and psychology, and he was keenly interested in sociology and politics. This fact gave his scientific tales a wider scope and made them something more than brilliantly told science-stories.'

londoner's APO11 diary

"Now we know why they didn't show on the Apollo 10 photos!"

ONE of the most closely guarded rooms in London during the present Apollo 11 programme is the NASA communication centre at Electra House on the Embankment.

Its door is barred to all save the team of 15 Post Office engineers and the station manager, Mr. Phil French; "Mission in Progress; Keep Out," says the notice on its steel door.

Failure to pass on the constant stream of information received from the Madrid tracker station —one of three beamed onto the Apollo mission—could be vital to the three astronauts.

CLIMAX

There are several other traffic routes from Madrid to Houston Space Centre, but Phil French is taking no chances. As well as being a relay switching centre from Madrid to the space control, the London NASA room picks up the Houston Public Affairs Offices non-stop talkback with the astronauts and relays it for Eurovision and British viewers.

The centre opened at Electra House about three years ago and operates 24 hours a day, mission or no mission. Clearly, Apollo 11 is the climax of its work.

FOR all former railway enthusiasts who now want to be spacemen: the money is good

Astronaut Michael Collins earns 20,000 dollars a year; Astronaut Edwin Aldrin, 23,000 dollars a year. And Commander Neil Armstrong, a civilian, 27,000 dollars a year.

Armstrong's higher pay is to compensate for his later retirement and smaller pension at the age of 60. Military personnel retire after 20 years' service on half pay.

WELLSIAN METHOD

ALL this immense expense and fantastically complicated hardware in the moon rocket would have been saved

Wells, is a professor of zoology and a frequent broadcaster.) "I've done very little in films for some time," says Frank Wells. "But I've been involved in several theatrical disasters."

But Jule's Verne's grandson, M. Jean-Jules Verne, a retired chairman of the Toulon French

strategic hold over the rest of the world. This spiritual fault will mean that the moonshots will be attended by developments in physical activities on the moon. But more Mr. Holdaway would not say.

"We shall do our best to balance the repercussions re-

from Houston but I refused: to see the goal we had worked towards for those 11 years recede from my grasp was terrible.

"I have enough ego left," he continues, laughing, "to imagine that they chose July 20 as a

Stauffenberg had been executed for the plot against Hitler.

A significant item on page one reported that "a site in Northern France believed to be connected with the enemy's threatened use of long-range rockets" had been bombed by

12

Truly, then, the young man deserved his instant success and the wide-ranging discussion that went with it – though he was not untouched by controversy and criticism, nor were the predictable charges of sensationalism from certain quarters unexpected. According to that amazing late Victorian man-about-town and self-proclaimed sexual adventurer, Frank Harris, he achieved it all in the space of just a few years: 'Wells' first successes came to him when he was only twenty-nine and they were flattering enough to turn the steadiest head. His scientific stories had an extraordinary vogue, were translated into a dozen languages; by the time he was thirty-two or three, Wells was known from Kyoto to Paris.'

Just how H. G. Wells earned this recognition – and how it has continued to exert its influence to the present time – is one of the primary questions that is tackled in this book. Like the previous books in this series, the Scrapbook is a compendium of articles, essays, newspaper reports and reviews, pictures, photographs and souvenirs reflecting Wells' life with particular regard to his works of science fiction and fantasy. I must stress that the book is only concerned with these specific elements of his work, for after the romances he completely turned his back on the genre to write mainstream novels and then devoted himself wholeheartedly and almost exclusively to sociology and criticism. These further facets of his talent would, of course, justify books on their own, and consequently I have chosen just to consider the area in which – despite Wells' own fervent desire to be remembered as a social reformer – the public at large hold him in greatest esteem. I believe the text illuminates the Wells success story in a more immediate and diversified way than any biography might hope to do, and the illustrations, ranging from those which appeared with the first publication of the stories right through films to the modern comic book interpretations, highlight the inventiveness of his genius. I hope, too, that enthusiasts of the great man will welcome as special features the inclusion of one of the first of Wells' prophetic articles, 'The Man of the Year Million', one of his earliest short fantasies, 'A Tale of the Twentieth Century' and a completely forgotten and uncollected short story written in 1931, 'The Queer Story of Brownlow's Newspaper'. All are of considerable rarity.

That Wells turned science fiction (or 'scientific romance' as it was then called) into literature is beyond question – nor, in my opinion, is there much doubt that few young authors have written so much that was so new and unique in so short a time. For his part, though, Wells may well have started out to write 'entertainments' with no thought of any deeper implications, nor any idea that they might last and grow in influence with the passing years. Indeed, he commented to one of his biographers, Geoffrey West, about his early works, 'I see Sir J. C. Squire doubts if I shall "live" and I cannot say how cordially and unreservedly I agree.'

As this book will show – and time itself has proved – this was one of the few times in his life when the great pioneer of science fiction was absolutely and completely wrong!

PETER HAINING
Boxford, Suffolk
1978

A nice link between 'Gulliver's Travels' the book which delighted Wells as a child (this illustration (opposite above) is by T. Morten from the 1976 edition) and (opposite below) the gossip column from the London 'Evening Standard' on the day man first walked on the moon. An item from this column is reproduced below.

Below: Another picture from an early American edition of 'The First Men in the Moon' showing the astronauts approaching the moon in their space ship powered by the antigravity metal, Cavorite.

From Londoner's Apollo Diary – Monday 21 July 1969.

WELLSIAN METHOD

All the immense expense and fantastically complicated hardware in the rocket which has landed on the Moon would have been saved if the Americans had been as ingenious as H. G. Wells's hero in *The First Men in the Moon* which he wrote in 1901.

Wells's scientist, his son Frank Wells reminds me today, just invented a material which did away with the force of gravity. Simple when you think of it.

Fairly recently Mr Wells reread his father's book which was made into a film three or four years ago. "It followed the book quite closely, only they had to take a girl with them," he says.

In a varied career, Mr Wells has been author and film director. His elder brother, G. P. Wells, is a professor of zoology and a frequent broadcaster.

The Fables of H.G.Wells

JORGE LUIS BORGES

Over the years Wells has had many admirers and champions both among writers of fantasy and science fiction, and in the larger world of general literature, too. Few, though, have shown a greater understanding of his role in the evolution of science fiction, and a love of his work, than the masterful South American writer and poet, Jorge Luis Borges. In the following short essay, written at the time of Wells' death, he manages to say and explain more than many of the numerous lengthy biographies of Wells which have been published in the intervening years.

Frank Harris relates that when Oscar Wilde was asked about Wells, he called him 'a scientific Jules Verne.' That was in 1899; it appears that Wilde thought less of defining Wells, or of annihilating him, than of changing the subject. Now the names H. G. Wells and Jules Verne have come to be incompatible. We all feel that this is true, but still it may be well to examine the intricate reasons on which our feeling is based.

The most obvious reason is a technical one. Before Wells resigned himself to the role of a sociological spectator, he was an admirable storyteller, an heir to the concise style of Swift and Edgar Allan Poe. Verne was a pleasant and industrious journeyman. Verne wrote for adolescents; Wells, for all ages. There is another difference, which Wells himself once indicated: Verne's stories deal with probable things (a submarine, a ship larger than those existing in 1872, the discovery of the South Pole, the talking picture,

the crossing of Africa in a balloon, the craters of an extinguished volcano that lead to the center of the earth); the short stories Wells wrote concern mere possibilities, if not impossible things (an invisible man, a flower that devours a man, a crystal egg that reflects the events on Mars, a man who returns from the future with a flower of the future, a man who returns from the other life with his heart on the right side, because he has been completely inverted, as in a mirror). I have read that Verne, scandalized by the license permitted by *The First Men in the Moon*, exclaimed indignantly, '*Il invente!*'

The reasons I have given seem valid enough, but they do not explain why Wells is infinitely superior to the author of *Hector Servadac*, and also to Rosny, Lytton, Robert Paltock, Cyrano, or any other precursor of his methods. Even his best plots do not adequately solve the problem. In long books the plot can be only a pretext, or a point of departure. It is important for the composition of the work, but not for the reader's enjoyment of it. That is true of all genres; the best detective stories are not those with the best plots. (If plots were everything, the *Quixote* would not exist and Shaw would be inferior to O'Neill.) In my opinion, the excellence of Wells's first novels – *The Island of Doctor Moreau*, for example, or *The Invisible Man* – has a deeper origin. Not only do they tell an ingenious story; but they tell a story symbolic of processes that are somehow inherent in all human

Top left: Edgar Allan Poe and above: Jules Verne, the two great predecessors of Wells in the art of scientific prediction.

Facing page: A group of bystanders struggle with 'The Invisible Man' in an illustration by R. E. Lawlor for 'Amazing Stories', July 1928.

"Don't you leave go of en!" cried the big navvy, holding a bloodstained spade; "he's shamming."

destinies. The harassed invisible man who has to sleep as though his eyes were wide open because his eyelids do not exclude light is our solitude and our terror; the conventicle of seated monsters who mouth a servile creed in their night is the Vatican and is Lhasa. Work that endures is always capable of an infinite and plastic ambiguity; it is all things for all men, like the Apostle; it is a mirror that reflects the reader's own traits and it is also a map of the world. And it must be ambiguous in an evanescent and modest way, almost in spite of the author; he must appear to be ignorant of all symbolism. Wells displayed that lucid innocence in his first fantastic exercises, which are to me the most admirable part of his admirable work.

Those who say that art should not propagate doctrines usually refer to doctrines that are opposed to their own. Naturally this is not my own case; I gratefully profess almost all the doctrines of Wells, but I deplore his inserting them into his narratives. An heir of the British nominalists, Wells condemns our custom of speaking of the 'tenacity of England' or the 'intrigues of Prussia.' The arguments against that harmful mythology seem to be irreproachable, but not the fact of interpolating them into the story of Mr. Parham's dream. As long as an author merely relates events or traces the slight deviations of a conscience, we can suppose him to be omniscient, we can confuse him with the universe or with God; but when he descends to the level of pure reason, we know he is fallible. Reality is inferred from events, not reasonings; we permit God to affirm *I am that I am* (Exodus 3:14), not to declare and analyze, like Hegel or Anselm, the *argumentum ontologicum*. God must not theologize; the writer must not invalidate with human arguments the momentary faith that art demands of us. There is another consideration: the author who shows aversion to a character seems not to understand him completely, seems to confess that the character is not inevitable for him. We distrust his intelligence, as we would distrust the intelligence of a God who maintained heavens and hells. God, Spinoza has written, does not hate anyone and does not love anyone (*Ethics*, 5, 17).

Like Quevedo, like Voltaire, like Goethe, like some others, Wells is less a man of letters than a literature. He wrote garrulous books in which the gigantic felicity of Charles Dickens somehow reappears; he bestowed sociological parables with a lavish hand; he constructed encyclopedias, enlarged the possibilities of the novel, rewrote the Book of Job – 'that great Hebrew imitation of the Platonic dialogue'; for our time, he wrote a very delightful autobiography without pride and without humility; he combated Communism, Nazism, and Christianity; he debated (politely and mortally) with Belloc; he chronicled the past, chronicled the future, recorded real and imaginary lives. Of the vast and diversified library he left us, nothing has pleased me more than his narration of some atrocious miracles: *The Time Machine, The Island of Doctor Moreau, The Plattner Story, The First Men in the Moon.* They are the first books I read; perhaps they will be the last. I think they will be incorporated, like the fables of Theseus or Ahasuerus, into the general memory of the species and even transcend the fame of their creator or the extinction of the language in which they were written.

Baron Munchausen's Trip to the Moon

R. E. RASPE

One of the first books with any mention of interplanetary travel which the young H. G. Wells read (probably in his early teens) was The Travels and Surprising Adventures of Baron Munchausen *first published in 1786. The book was written at the time when many explorers were claiming the kind of discoveries which made certain people sceptical, and Baron Munchausen deliberately parodies and upstages the lot with a string of quite farcical claims. Although the work was published anonymously, it is believed to have been the work of 'a learned but unprincipled scholar, of the name R. E. Raspe, who had taken refuge in this country from the pursuit of justice' according to an enquiry conducted by the Gentleman's Magazine in 1857. In any event, Wells fell upon a later edition of the book, complete with illustrations by the famous Victorian artist George Cruikshank, and devoured it. So impressed was he – and in particular with the description of Munchausen's voyage to the moon – that when he was seventeen he wrote a fifty-page tale about his own*

Baron Munchausen

Munchausen, one Otto Noxious. Unfortunately, this tale is lost, but here, though, is the episode which may well have played an important part in drawing young Wells towards scientific romances:

I now come to the part in my discourse of my life to describe my trip to the moon and the several things which happened. I will endeavour to describe all as accurately as my memory will permit.

I went on a voyage of discovery at the request of a distant relation, who had a strange notion that there were people to be found equal in magnitude to those described by Gulliver in the empire of BROBDING-NAG. For my part I always treated that account as fabulous; however, to oblige him, for he had made me his heir, I undertook it, and sailed for the South Seas, where we arrived without meeting anything remarkable, except some flying men and women who were playing at leap-frog, and dancing minuets in the air.

On the eighteenth day after we had passed the Island of Otaheite, mentioned by Captain Cook as the place from whence they brought Omai, a hurricane blew our ship at least one thousand leagues above the surface of the water, and kept it at that height till a fresh gale arising filled the sails in every part, and onwards we travelled at a prodigious rate; thus we proceeded above the clouds for six weeks. At last we discovered a great land in the sky, like a shining island, round and bright, where, coming into a convenient harbour, we went on shore, and soon found it was inhabited. Below us we saw another earth, containing cities, trees, mountains, rivers, seas, &c., which we conjectured was this world which we had left. Here we saw huge figures riding upon vultures of a prodigious size, and each of them having three heads. To form some idea of the magnitude of these birds, I must inform you that each of their wings is as wide and six times the length of the main sheet of our vessel, which was about six hundred tons burthen. Thus, instead of riding upon horses, as we do in this world, the inhabitants of the moon (for we now found we were in Madam Luna) fly about on these birds. The king, we found, was engaged in a war with the sun, and he offered me a commission, but I declined the honour his majesty intended me. Everything in this world is of extraordinary manitude! a common flea being much larger than one of our sheep; in making war, their principal weapons are radishes, which are used as darts: those who are wounded by them die immediately. Their shields are made of mushrooms, and their darts (when radishes are out of season) of the tops of asparagus. Some of the natives of the dog-star are to be seen here; commerce tempts them to ramble; their faces are like large mastiffs, with their eyes near the lower end or tip of their noses: they have no eyelids, but cover their eyes with the end of their tongues when they go to sleep; they are generally twenty feet high. As to the natives of the moon, none of them are less in stature than thirty-six feet: they are not called the human species, but the cooking animals, for they all dress their food by fire, as we do, but lose no time at their meals, as they open their left side, and place the whole quantity at once in their stomach, then shut it again till the same day in the next month; for they never indulge themselves with food more than twelve times a year, or once a

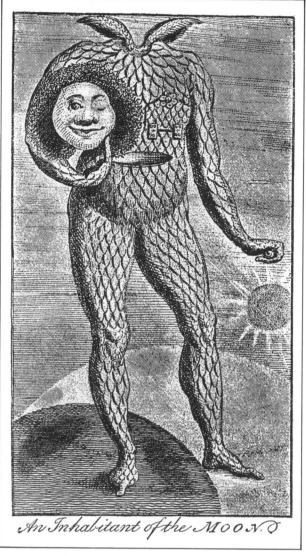

An Inhabitant of the MOON.

Above and facing page: Illustrations by George Cruikshank for 'The Travels and Surprising Adventures of Baron Munchausen' which H. G. Wells read.

month. All but gluttons and epicures must prefer this method to ours.

There is but one sex either of the cooking or any other animals in the moon; they are all produced from trees of various sizes and foliage; that which produces the cooking animal, or human species, is much more beautiful than any of the others; it has large straight boughs and flesh-coloured leaves, and the fruit it produces are nuts or pods, with hard shells at least two yards long; when they become ripe, which is known from their changing colour, they are gathered with great care, and laid by as long as they think proper: when they choose to animate the seed of these nuts, they throw them into a large cauldron of boiling water, which opens the shells in a few hours, and out jumps the creature.

Nature forms their minds for different pursuits before they come into the world; from one shell comes forth a warrior, from another a philosopher, from a third a divine, from a fourth a lawyer, from a fifth a farmer, from a sixth a clown, &c. &c, and each of them immediately begins to perfect themselves, by practising what they before knew only in theory.

An Inhabitant of the DOG STAR.

Another of Cruikshank's engravings for the Baron Munchausen adventures.

When they grow old they do not die, but turn into air, and dissolve like smoke! As for their drink, they need none; the only evacuations they have are insensible, and by their breath. They have but one finger upon each hand, with which they perform everything in as perfect a manner as we do who have four besides the thumb. Their heads are placed under their right arm, and when they are going to travel, or about any violent exercise, they generally leave them at home, for they can consult them at any distance; this is a very common practice; and when those of rank or quality among the Lunarians have an inclination to see what's going forward among the common people, they stay at home, i.e. the body stays at home, and sends the head only, which is suffered to be present incog., and return at pleasure with an account of what has passed.

The stones of their grapes are exactly like hail; and I am perfectly satisfied that when a storm or high wind in the moon shakes their vines, and breaks the grapes from the stalks, the stones fall down and form our hail showers and I would advise those who are of my opinion to save a quantity of these stones when it

hails next, and make Lunarian wine. It is common beverage at St. Luke's. Some material circumstances I had nearly omitted. They put their bellies to the same use as we do a sack, and throw whatever they have occasion for into it, for they can shut and open it again when they please, as they do their stomachs; they are not troubled with bowels, liver, heart, or any other intestines, neither are they encumbered with clothes, nor is there any part of their bodies unseemly or indecent to exhibit.

Their eyes they can take in and out of their places when they please, and can see as well with them in their hand as in their head! and if by any accident they lose or damage one, they can borrow or purchase another, and see as clearly with it as their own. Dealers in eyes are on that account very numerous in most parts of the moon, and in this article alone all the inhabitants are whimsical: sometimes green and sometimes yellow eyes are the fashion. I know these things appear strange; but if the shadow of a doubt can remain on any person's mind, I say, let him take a voyage there himself, and then he will know I am a traveller of veracity.

A Voyage to the Planets

SIR HUMPHREY DAVY

During his years as a student at the Normal School of Science in South Kensington, Wells read avidly, both his proscribed text books, and contemporary and classic imaginative literature. The text books of the great English chemist, Sir Humphrey Davy (1778-1829), formed part of his syllabus, and it was while he was idly thumbing through the professor's Collected Works, *that he came across the volume* Consolations in Travel *(1839) and a remarkable episode in which the author described a voyage in the heavens. Young Wells read spellbound at the unnamed traveller's journey among the planets in the company of an all-wise being known as 'Genius'. Here was speculation by a renowned man of science about the universe around us – and although dressed as fantasy, there was no denying that there were elements of it which rang true. Wells was undoubtedly impressed, and the episode – reprinted here – provided another important step towards the development of his talent for scientific speculation.*

I was in a dark, deep and cold cave, of which the walls of the Colosseum formed the boundary. From above, a bright and rosy light broke into this cave, so that whilst below all was dark, above all was bright and illuminated with glory. I seemed possessed at this moment of a new sense and felt that the light brought with it a genial warmth; odours like those of the most balmy flowers appeared to fill the air, and the sweetest sounds of music absorbed my sense of hearing; my limbs had a new lightness given to them, so that I seemed to rise from the earth, and to mount gradually into the bright luminous air, leaving behind me the dark and cold cavern and the ruins with which it was strewed. Language is inadequate to describe what I felt in rising continually upwards through this bright and luminous atmosphere. I had not, as is generally the case with persons in dreams of this kind, imagined to myself wings, but I rose gently and securely as if I were myself a part of the ascending column of light. By degrees this luminous atmosphere, which was diffused over the whole of space, became more circumscribed, and extended only to a limited spot around me. I saw through it the bright blue sky, the moon and stars, and I passed by them as if it were in my power to touch them with my hand; I beheld Jupiter and Saturn as they appear through our best telescopes, but still more magnified, all the moons and belts of Jupiter being perfectly distinct, and the double ring of Saturn appearing in that state in which I have heard Herschel often express a wish he could see it. It seemed as if I were on the verge of the solar system, and my moving sphere of light now appeared to pause. I again heard the low and sweet voice of the Genius, which said, "You are now on the verge of your own system: will you go further, or return to the earth?" I replied, "I have left an abode which is damp, dreary, dark and cold; I am now in a place where all is life, light, and enjoyment; show me at least, before I return, the glimpse which you promised me of those superior intellectual natures and the modes of their being and their enjoyments." "There are creatures far superior," said the Genius, "to any idea your imagination can form in that part of the system now before you, comprehending Saturn, his moons and rings. I will carry you to the verge of the immense atmosphere of this planet; in that space you will see sufficient to wonder at, and far more than

Sir Humphrey Davy – another early influence on Wells.

with your present organisation, it would be possible for me to make you understand." I was again in motion and again almost as suddenly at rest. I saw below me a surface infinitely diversified, something like that of an immense glacier covered with large columnar masses, which appeared as if formed of glass, and from which were suspended rounded forms of various sizes, which, if they had not been transparent, I might have supposed to be fruit. From what appeared to me to be analogous to masses of bright blue ice, streams of the richest tint of rose-colour or purple burst forth and flowed into basins, forming lakes or seas of the same colour. Looking through the atmosphere towards the heavens I saw brilliant opaque clouds of an azure colour that reflected the light of the sun, which had to my eyes an entirely new aspect, and appeared smaller, as if seen through a dense blue mist. I saw moving on the surface below me immense masses, the form of which I find it impossible to describe; they had systems for locomotion similar to those of the morse, or sea-horse; but I saw with great surprise that they moved from place to place by six extremely thin membranes, which they used as wings. Their colours were varied and beautiful, but principally azure and rose-colour; I saw numerous convolutions of tubes, more analogous to the trunk of the elephant than to anything else I can imagine, occupying what I supposed to be the upper parts of the body, and my feeling of astonishment almost became one of disgust, from the peculiar character of the organs of these singular beings; and it was with a species of terror that I observed one of them mounting upwards apparently flying towards those opaque clouds which I have before mentioned.

"I know what your feelings are," said the Genius: "you want analogies and all the elements of knowledge to comprehend the scene before you. You are in the same state in which a fly would be whose microscopic eye was changed for one similar to that of man; and you are wholly unable to associate what you now see with your former knowledge. But, those beings who are before you, and who appear to you almost as imperfect in their functions as the zoophytes of the polar sea, to which they are not unlike in their apparent organisation to your eyes, have a sphere of sensibility and intellectual enjoyment far superior to that of the inhabitants of your earth. Each of those tubes which appears like the trunk of an elephant, is an organ of peculiar motion or sensation. They have many modes of perception of which you are wholly ignorant, at the same time that their sphere of vision is infinitely more extended than yours, and their organs of touch far more perfect and exquisite. It would be useless for me to attempt to explain their organisation, which you could never understand; but of their intellectual objects of pursuit I may perhaps give you some notion. They have used, modified and applied the material world in a manner analogous to Man; but with far superior powers they have gained superior results. Their atmosphere being much denser than yours and the specific gravity of their planet less, they have been enabled to determine the laws belonging to the solar system with far more accuracy than you can possibly conceive, and any one of these beings could show you what is now the situation and appearance of your moon with a precision that would induce you to believe that he saw it, though his knowledge is merely the result of calculation. Their sources of pleasure are of the highest intellectual nature. With the magnificent spectacle of their own rings and moons revolving round them, – with the various combinations required to understand and predict the relations of these wonderful phenomena, their minds are in unceasing activity, and this activity is a perpetual source of enjoyment. Your view of the solar system is bounded by Uranus, and the laws of this planet form the ultimatum of your mathematical results; but these beings catch a sight of planets belonging to another system, and even reason on the phenomena presented by other suns. Those comets, of which your astronomical history is so imperfect, are to them perfectly familiar, and in their ephemerides their places are shown with as much accurateness as those of Jupiter or Venus in your almanacks. The parallax of the fixed stars nearest them is as well understood as that of their own sun; and they possess a magnificent history of the changes taking place in the heavens, – changes which are governed by laws that it would be vain for me to attempt to give you an idea of. They are acquainted with the revolutions and uses of comets; they understand the system of those meteoric formations of stones which have so much astonished you on earth; and they have histories in which the gradual changes of nebulae in their progress towards systems have been registered, so that they can predict their future changes. And their astronomical records are not like yours which go back only twenty centuries to the time of Hipparchus; they embrace a period a hundred times as long, and their civil history for the same time is as correct as their astronomical one. As I cannot describe to you the organs of these wonderful beings, so neither can I show to you their modes of life; but as their highest pleasures depend upon intellectual pursuits, so you may conclude that those modes of life bear the strictest analogy to that which on the earth you would call exalted virtue. I will tell you however that they have no wars, and that the objects of their ambition are entirely those of intellectual greatness, and that the only passions they feel in which comparisons with each other can be instituted are those dependent upon a love of glory of the purest kind. If I were to show you the different parts of the surface of this planet, you would see marvellous results of the powers possessed by these highly intellectual beings, and of the wonderful manner in which they have applied and modified matter. Those columnar masses, which seem to you as if arising out of a mass of ice below, are results of art, and processes are going on in them connected with the formation and perfection of their food. The brilliant coloured fluids are the results of such operations as on the earth would be performed in your laboratories, or more properly in your refined culinary apparatus, for they are connected with their system of nourishment. Those opaque azure clouds, to which you saw a few minutes ago one of those beings directing his course, are works of art and places in which they move through different regions of their atmosphere and command the temperature and the quantity of light most fitted for their philosophical researches, or most convenient for the purposes of life. On the verge of the

visible horizon which we perceive around us, you may see in the east a very dark spot or shadow, in which the light of the sun seems entirely absorbed; this is the border of an immense mass of liquid analogous to your ocean, but unlike your sea it is inhabited by a race of intellectual beings inferior indeed to those belonging to the atmosphere of Saturn, but yet possessed of an extensive range of sensations and endowed with extraordinary power and intelligence. I could transport you to the different planets and show you in each, peculiar intellectual beings bearing analogies to each other, but yet all different in power and essence. In Jupiter you would see creatures similar to those in Saturn, but with different powers of locomotion. In Mars and Venus you would find races of created forms more analogous to those belonging to the earth. But in every part of the planetary system you would find one character peculiar to all intelligent natures, a sense of receiving impressions from light by various organs of vision; and towards this result you cannot but perceive that all the arrangements and motions of the planetary bodies, their satellites and atmospheres, are subservient. The spiritual natures therefore that pass from system to system, in progression towards power and knowledge, preserve at least this one invariable character,

Above: The planet Saturn as it was pictured during Wells' youth.

Facing page: 'A Voyage to the Planets' – the spirit Genius conducts the traveller on a journey through the universe.

and their intellectual life may be said to depend more or less upon the influence of light. As far as my knowledge extends, even in other parts of the universe the more perfect organised systems still possess this source of sensation and enjoyment; but with higher natures, finer and more ethereal kinds of matter are employed in organisation, substances that bear the same analogy to common matter that the refined or most subtle gases do to common solids and fluids. The universe is everywhere full of life, but the modes of this life are infinitely diversified, and yet every form of it must be enjoyed and known by every spiritual nature before the consummation of all things. You have seen the comet moving with its immense train of light through the sky; this likewise has a system supplied with living beings and their existence derives its enjoyment from the diversity of circumstances to which they are exposed; passing as it were through the infinity of space they are continually gratified by the sight of new systems and worlds, and you can imagine the unbounded nature of the circle of their knowledge. My power extends so far as to afford you a glimpse of the nature of a cometary world." I was again in rapid motion, again passing with the utmost velocity through the bright blue sky, and I saw Jupiter and his satellites and Saturn and his ring behind me, and before me the sun, no longer appearing as through a blue mist but in bright and unsupportable splendour, towards which I seemed moving with the utmost velocity. In a limited sphere of vision, in a kind of red hazy light similar to that which first broke in upon me in the Colosseum, I saw moving round me globes which appeared composed of different kinds of flame and of different colours. In some of these globes I recognised figures which put me in mind of the human countenance, but the resemblance was so awful and unnatural that I endeavoured to withdraw my view from them. "You are now," said the Genius, "in a cometary system; those globes of light surrounding you, are material forms, such as in one of your systems of religious faith have been attributed to seraphs; they live in that element which to you would be destruction; they communicate by powers which would convert your organised frame into ashes; they are now in the height of their enjoyment, being about to enter into the blaze of the solar atmosphere. These beings so grand, so glorious, with functions to you incomprehensible, once belong to the earth; their spiritual natures have risen through different stages of planetary life, leaving their dust behind them, carrying with them only their intellectual power. You ask me if they have any knowledge or reminiscence of their transitions; tell me of your own recollections in the womb of your mother and I will answer you. It is the law of divine wisdom that no spirit carries with it into another state and being any habit or mental qualities except those which may be connected with its new wants or enjoyments; and knowledge relating to the earth would be no more useful to these glorified beings than their earthly system of organised dust, which would be instantly resolved into its ultimate atoms at such a temperature; even on the earth the butterfly does not transport with it into the air the organs or the appetites of the crawling worm from which it sprung. There is however one sentiment or passion which the monad or spiritual essence carries with it into all its stages of being, and which in these happy and elevated creatures is continually exalted, the love of knowledge or of intellectual power, which is in fact in its ultimate and most perfect development the love of infinite wisdom and unbounded power, or the love of God. Even in the imperfect life that belongs to the earth this passion exists in a considerable degree, increases even with age, outlives the perfection of the corporeal faculties, and at the moment of death is felt by the conscious being; and its future destinies depend upon the manner in which it has been exercised and exalted. When it has been misapplied and assumes the form of vague curiosity, restless ambition, vain-glory, pride or oppression, the being is degraded, it sinks in the scale of existence and still belongs to the earth or an inferior system, till its errors are corrected by painful discipline. When, on the contrary, the love of intellectual power has been exercised on its noblest objects, in discovering and in contemplating the properties of created forms and in applying them to useful and benevolent purposes, in developing and admiring the laws of the eternal Intelligence, the

destinies of the sentient principle are of a nobler kind, it rises to a higher planetary world. From the height to which you have been lifted I could carry you downwards and show you intellectual natures even inferior to those belonging to the earth, in your own moon and in the lower planets, and I could demonstrate to you the effects of pain or moral evil in assisting in the great plan of the exaltation of spiritual natures; but I will not destroy the brightness of your present idea of the scheme of the universe by degrading pictures of the effects of bad passions and of the manner in which evil is corrected and destroyed. Your vision must end with the glorious view of the inhabitants of the cometary worlds: I cannot show you the beings of the system to which I myself belong, that of the sun; your organs would perish before our brightness, and I am only permitted to be present to you as a sound or intellectual voice. *We* are likewise in progression, but we see and know something of the plans of infinite Wisdom; we feel the personal presence of that supreme Deity which you only imagine; to you belongs faith, to us knowledge; and our greatest delight results from the conviction that we are lights kindled by his light and that we belong to his substance. To obey, to love, to wonder and adore form our relations to the infinite Intelligence. We feel his laws are those of eternal justice, and that they govern all things from the most glorious intellectual natures belonging to the sun and fixed stars to

H. G. WELLS

I had reveries – I indulged a great deal in reverie until I was fifteen or sixteen, because my active imagination was not sufficiently employed – and I liked especially to dream that I was a great military dictator like Cromwell, a great republican like George Washington or like Napoleon in his earlier phases. I used to fight battles whenever I went for a walk alone. I used to walk about Bromley, a rather small under-nourished boy, meanly clad and whistling detestably between his teeth, and no one suspected that a phantom staff pranced about me and phantom orderlies galloped at my commands, to shift the guns and concentrate fire on those houses below, to launch the

the meanest spark of life animating an atom crawling in the dust of your earth. We know all things begin from and end in his everlasting essence, the cause of causes, the power of powers."

The low and sweet voice ceased; it appeared as if I had fallen suddenly upon the earth, but there was a bright light before me and I heard my name loudly called; the voice was not of my intellectual guide, – the genius before me was my servant bearing a flambeau in his hand. He told me he had been searching me in vain amongst the ruins, that the carriage had been waiting for me above an hour, and that he had left a large party of my friends assembled in the Palazzo F——.

The Battle.

WAR ON THE FLOOR, WITH LEADEN SOLDIERS. CAR

final attack upon yonder distant ridge. The citizens of Bromley town go out to take the air on Martin's Hill and look towards Shortlands across the fields where once meandered the now dried-up and vanished Ravensbourne, with never a suspicion of the orgies of bloodshed I once conducted there. Martin's Hill indeed is one of the great battlegrounds of history. Scores of times the enemy skirmishes have come across those levels, followed by the successive waves of the infantry attack, while I, outnumbered five to one, manoeuvred my guns round, the guns I had refrained so grimly from using in spite of the threat to my centre, to enfilade them suddenly from the curving slopes towards Beckenham. 'Crash,' came the first shell and then 'crash' and 'crash'. They were mown down by the thousands. They straggled up the slopes wavering. And then came the shattering counter-attack, and I and my cavalry swept the broken masses away towards Croydon, pressed them ruth-

Above facing page: On the planet Saturn – a fanciful view for Davy's 'A Voyage to the Planets'.

Below facing page: 'The Battle' a drawing by Wells for his earliest literary work, 'The Desert Daisy' which he composed when he was twelve years old. This profusely illustrated tale of warmongering has been described as a precursor of the present-day comic books, and undoubtedly played a part in shaping 'The Invisible Man' and 'War in the Air'. It also shows his interest in war games, and led directly to his publishing in 1913 when he was 46 a book entitled 'Little Wars'. The illustration below of Wells playing with model soldiers was by J. Begg for the 'Illustrated London News' of 25 January 1913.

AND SHRUB COUNTRY, AND GUNS FIRING WOODEN "SHELLS": MR. H. G. WELLS PLAYING LITTLE WARS.

lessly through a night of slaughter on to the pitiful surrender of the remnant at dawn by Keston Fish Ponds. . . .

For many years my adult life was haunted by the fading memories of those early war fantasies. Up to 1914, I found a lively interest in playing a war game, with toy soldiers and guns, that recalled the peculiar quality and pleasure of those early reveries. It was quite an amusing model warfare and I have given its primary rules in a small book 'for boys and girls of all ages', *Little Wars*. I have met men in responsible positions, L. S. Amery, for example, Winston Churchill, George Trevelyan, C. F. G. Masterman, whose imaginations were manifestly built upon a similar framework and who remained puerile in their political outlook because of its persistence. I like to think I grew out of that stage somewhere between 1916 and 1920 and began to think about war as a responsible adult should.

Experiment in Autobiography (1934)

A Tale of the Twentieth Century

FOR ADVANCED THINKERS

It was while Wells was at college that he began his first serious attempts at stories of scientific romance. He also played a part in founding the students' magazine, The Science Schools Journal, *and apart from being its editor for a time, also contributed numerous items to it, both under his own name and using pseudonyms such as Walter Shockenhammer and Sosthenes Smith! In 1888 he began a serial with the title, 'The Chronic Argonauts' about time travel which, though it was never completed, was in effect the first draft of* The Time Machine *for he later utilised the material in the writing of the great novel which made his name. Important though this story was, he had already written another item a year earlier when he was still twenty, 'A Tale of the Twentieth Century' which accurately views the coming century as one of enormous scientific possibilities – even though it is written in a farcical style. The story, perhaps the earliest of his efforts to see print, appeared in the* Journal

Another sketch by Wells caricaturing his search for work.

The high-spirited Wells photographed while a science student in 1886.

of May 1887 and was signed 'S.B.'. Even almost one hundred years later, this jocular tale of what happens when a device for perpetual motion is applied to the Underground railway in London makes fascinating reading and clearly shows several of the hallmarks which Wells made all his own.

CHAPTER I

Years had passed. . . . .

The Inventor had died in a garret. Too proud to receive parish relief, he had eaten every article of clothing he possessed, scraped off and assimilated every scrap of the plaster on the walls of his wretched apartment, gnawed his finger nails down to the quick, and – died.

His body was found a mere mass of bones, a result of the disproportionate amount of lime in his too restricted dietary.

But though the Inventor was dead, the Thought was not.

That commercial enterprise to which this nation owes its greatness, its position in the vanguard of the armies of progress, had taken the thing up. The pawnbroker, to whom the Inventor had pledged his patent rights for thirteen shillings and sixpence, this pawnbroker, Isaac Meluish, type of sustaining capital, organized a Youarenowgoingtobetoldwhatsodontgoa-gettingimpatient Company Limited, and made it a practical thing.

The idea was this –

A locomotive of a new type. The wheels rotated by electricity, generated by a dynamo-electric machine, worked by the rotation of the wheels. It will be obvious, that all that is required in such a machine is an initial velocity, to ensure an exceedingly efficient and durable motive force. This initial velocity was furnished by the agency of compressed air.

This idea Isaac Meluish developed: he took the underground railway, the idea, numerous influential persons, and a prospectus, and mixed them up judiciously, so that the influential persons became identified with the prospectus. Scrip was then issued, and the whole conception crystallized out as a definite tangible thing.

The 'Metropolitan and District' was to undergo a second birth from the Meluish brain. No longer were AS_2O_3 and SO_2 to undermine the health of London. Ozone was to abound exceedingly. Invalids were no longer to repair to and at the seaside: they could train on the Underground.

The tunnels were to be illuminated and decorated.

Moreover, the shares of the companies connected with the enterprise were to go up to infinity and stay there – like Elijah.

August persons took shares, and in part paid for them.

It was resolved to make the adoption of the new idea a Britannic festival. A representative cargo of passengers was to travel in the first train round the Inner Circle. The sole lessee and actor of the Lyceum Theatre was to perform all at once every one of the parts he had ever previously taken, admission gratis. There was to be a banquet to the British great ones at the Crystal Palace, and an unsectarian national thanksgiving at the Albert Hall.

July 19th, 1999, approached.

All was lissomness of heart.

It was July 19th, 1999. The nave of the Crystal Palace was brilliantly lit and gorgeously adorned. All the able, all the eloquent, all the successful, all the prosperous, were banqueting below. In the galleries, clustered unnumbered mediocrity: innumerable half guineas had been paid to secure the privilege of watching those great men eat. There were 19 Bishops in evening dress, 4 Princes and their interpreters, 12 Dukes, A Strong Minded Female, the P.R.A., 14 popular professors, 1 learned ditto, 70 Deans (assorted), the President of the Materialistic Religious Society, a popular low comedian, 1,604 eminent wholesale and retail drapers, hatters, grocers, and tea dealers, a reformed working man M.P., and honorary directors of well nigh the universe, 203 stockbrokers, 1 Earl (in a prominent place), who had once said a remarkably smart thing, 9 purely Piccadilly Earls, 13 sporting Earls, 17 trading ditto, 113 bankers, a forger, 1 doctor, 12 theatrical managers, Bludsole the mammoth novelist, 1 electrician (from Paris), a multitude no man could number of electrical company directors, their sons and their sons' sons, their cousins, their nephews, their uncles, their parents, and their friends, the leading legal stars, 2 advertisement contractors, 41

patent medicine manufacturers, 'Lords, Senators, a Spirit Raiser, a Soothsayer, foreign Musicians, Officers, Captains, Guards, &c.'

A great man was speaking.

The people in the galleries could hear – 'twang, twang, TWANG, *twang*, twang'. Those around the great man heard 'little know whirrrrr erprise – daring energies of the race – (*great applause*) – wherrererer ergree with me in this marr that (*ssh!*) – scale inaccessible mountains, nay – MORE. Bore them through, nullify them – (TREMENDOUS APPLAUSE) – murr rr rrr rrr – (*loud and prolonged cheering*) – burr, burr, burr – (FRANTIC APPLAUSE. *Sssh!*) – daring yet calculating; bold yet rr, burr, burr, butt——'

Thus was the great man speaking apparently, when a telegram was handed to *Sir* Isaac Meluish. He glanced at it, and turning a pale lavender colour, sunk beneath the table.

Let us leave him there.

Ally Sloper, the rakish Victorian cartoon character that Wells liked and imitated.

CHAPTER II

This had happened. The representative passengers had assembled. There were an August Person, his keeper, the Premier, two Bishops, several popular actresses, four generals (home department), various exotics, a person apparently connected with the Navy, the Education Minister, 124 public service parasites, an idiot, the President of the Board of Trade, a suit of clothes, bankers, another idiot, shopkeepers, forgers, scene painters, still another idiot, directors, &c. (as per previous sample). The representative passengers had entrained. By means of the compressed air, a high velocity had been attained. The scientific manager had smilingly remarked to the august person, 'We will, an' it please you, first run round the Inner Circle and see the decorations.' All had gone as merry as a muffin bell.

Never had the conscientious desire of the august person to take an interest in everything been more conspicuous. He *insisted* – really *insisted* – on the scientific manager taking him on to the motor, and explaining it in detail.

'All that I have been showing you,' said the scientific manager (a small and voluble mechanism), concluding the display, 'is of English manufacture. You know the great firm of Schulz and Brown of Pekin (they removed there in 1920 in order to obtain cheap labour) – and it is consequently sound and strong in every particular. I must now explain the stopping action. I may mention here that the original inventor designed an engine carrying a considerable store of compressed air. *I* have improved on this. The rotary action not only works the dynamo, but also compresses air for the next start. Actually there is *no* force put into this thing from without, from this moment until it breaks, it costs us *nothing* in working. Talking of breaks, I must now show you them.' And the scientific manager, smiling with the approving consciousness of a joke, looked round him. Apparently he did not see what he wanted, his searching eye became more eager. He flushed somewhat. 'Baddelay,' said he, 'how are the brakes worked?'

'I *dun'* no,' said Baddelay; 'these here 'andils, wot *I* took for brakes broke orf, bein' touched; bein', apparently, plaster o'Paris deckerashuns.'

Thereupon the hues of the scientific manager's face hurried through the spectrum at a tremendous rate, from strontium red to thallium green. And he said to the august personage, 'The breaks are broke'; and he added, his voice assuming the while, that low, clear tone only heard from men struggling against overwhelming emotion, 'Look at that manometer.'

'I think,' said the august person, 'I won't see anything else, thank you; I would prefer not. I should like to get out now if you can manage it. The high velocity is unpleasant.'

'Sire,' said the scientific manager, 'we *can not* stop. And, moreover, that manometer warns me that before us is a choice of two things: to double our speed or to be blown to fragments by the ever-increasing tension of the compressed air.'

'In this sudden and unexpected emergency,' said the great one, with a vague recollection of Parliamentary first nights, 'it is perhaps advisable to increase the speed as suddenly as possible.'

The Crystal Palace meeting broke up in confusion, and the banquet became a battle for hats. Boanerges at the Albert Hall, uttering unsectarian platitudes on the heaven-sent prosperity of this land, received a telegram and preached thereafter on the text, 'Vanitas vanitatum'. The dismay slowly spreading from these foci, flashed over the entire land with the evening papers.

Chapter III

What was to be done?

What *could* be done?

The matter might have been raised in the Senate, had not the unexpected absence of the Speaker (he was in the train) prevented the meeting of the governing body. A popular meeting in Trafalgar Square to consider the matter was automatically suppressed by a new method.

Meanwhile the fated train whirled round the circle with ever-increasing velocity. Early on the 20th the end came.

It was slightly risque pictures such as this in 'Punch' magazine of 17 December 1874 which first stirred the sexual side of Wells's nature: a side which was to play a major part in later life and work.

THE TRANSIT OF VENUS.—December 9, 1874.

Between Victoria and Sloane Square the train left the lines, dashing violently through the walls of the track and throttling itself among a subterranean network of waterpipes, gaspipes, and drains. There was an awful pause, broken only by the falling in of the houses on either side of the scene of the catastrophe. Then a terrific explosion rent the air.

Most of the passengers were utterly destroyed. The august person, however, came down all right in Germany. The commercial speculators descended in foreign regions in the form of blight.

The Man of the Year Million

H. G. WELLS

Aside from his writing, the personable young H. G. Wells was also addressing his college debating society. In 1885 he read a paper to the members on 'The Past and Future of the Human Race' which most authorities see as his first experiment in prophecy. In this, as in 'A Tale of the Twentieth Century' two years later, he demonstrated that already he had hit on the formula of mixing romance, satire and scientific ideas, that eventually made him famous. When, in 1893, Wells was at last having his work published in mass-circulation magazines and journals, he decided to rework his paper into an article which he called 'The Man of the Year Million'. It was published by the popular Pall Mall Gazette *and enjoyed the distinction of public comment and being parodied with an illustration by* Punch. *The essay, despite its tone of cynicism, can still be seen as a prototype of his attempts to see 'the shape of things to come', and in its description of men eventually evolving into creatures with tiny bodies and huge brains is an anticipation of the Grand Lunar in* The First Men in the Moon *and the Martians in* War of the Worlds.

Accomplished literature is all very well in its way, no doubt, but much more fascinating to the contemplative man are the books that have not been written. These latter are no trouble to hold; there are no pages to turn over. One can read them in bed on sleepless nights without a candle. Turning to another topic, primitive man in the works of the descriptive anthropologist is certainly a very entertaining and quaint person, but the man of the future, if we only had the facts, would appeal to us more strongly. Yet where are the books? As Ruskin has said somewhere, apropos of Darwin, it is not what man has been, but what he will be, that should interest us.

The contemplative man in his easy chair, pondering this saying, suddenly beholds in the fire, through the blue haze of his pipe, one of these great unwritten volumes. It is large in size, heavy in lettering, seemingly by one Professor Holzkopf, presumably Professor at Weissnichtwo. 'The Necessary Characters of the Man of the Remote Future deduced from the Existing Stream of Tendency' is the title. The worthy Professor is severely scientific in his method, and deliberate and cautious in his deductions, the contemplative man discovers as he pursues his theme, and yet the conclusions are, to say the least, remarkable.

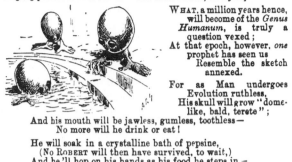

1,000,000 A.D.

["The descendants of man will nourish themselves by immersion in nutritive fluid. They will have enormous brains, liquid, soulful eyes, and large hands, on which they will hop. No craggy nose will they have, no vestigial ears; their mouths will be a small, perfectly round aperture, unanimal, like the evening star. Their whole muscular system will be shrivelled to nothing, a dangling pendant to their minds."—*Pall Mall Gazette, abridged.*]

WHAT, a million years hence,
    will become of the *Genus Humanum*, is truly a
        question vexed ;
At that epoch, however, *one*
    prophet has seen us
        Resemble the sketch
            annexed.

For as Man undergoes
    Evolution ruthless,
        His skull will grow "dome-
            like, bald, terete " ;

And his mouth will be jawless, gumless, toothless—
    No more will he drink or eat !

He will soak in a crystalline bath of pepsine,
    (No ROBERT will then have survived, to wait,)
And he 'll hop on his hands as his food he steps in –
    A quasi-cherubic gait !

No longer the land or the sea he 'll furrow ;
    The world will be withered, ice-cold, dead
As the chill of Eternity grows, he 'll burrow
    Far down underground instead.

If the *Pall Mall Gazette* has thus been giving
    A forecast correct of this change immense,
Our stars we may thank, then, that *we* shan't be living
    A million years from hence !

Above: The 'Punch' parody of Wells' 'The Man of the Year Million' from the issue of 25 November 1893.

Right: H. G. Wells' own sketch of what he believed a Martian looked like.

We must figure the excellent Professor expanding the matter at great length, voluminously technical, but the contemplative man – since he has access to the only copy – is clearly at liberty to make such extracts and abstracts as he chooses for the unscientific reader. Here, for instance, is something of practicable lucidity that he considers admits of quotation.

'The theory of evolution,' writes the Professor, 'is now universally accepted by zoologists and botanists, and it is applied unreservedly to man. Some question, indeed, whether it fits his soul, but all agree it accounts for his body. Man, we are assured, is descended from ape-like ancestors, moulded by circumstances into men, and these apes again were derived from ancestral forms of a lower order, and so up from the primordial protoplasmic jelly. Clearly then, man, unless the order of the universe has come to an end, will undergo further modification in the future, and at last cease to be man, giving rise to some other type of animated being. At once the fascinating question arises, What will this being be? Let us consider for a little the plastic influences at work upon our species.

'Just as the bird is the creature of the wing, and is all moulded and modified to flying, and just as the fish is the creature that swims, and has had to meet the inflexible conditions of a problem in hydrodynamics, so man is the creature of the brain; he will live by intelligence, and not by physical strength, if he live at all. So that much that is purely "animal" about him is being, and must be, beyond all question', suppressed in his ultimate development. Evolution is no mechanical tendency making for perfection, according to the ideas current in the year of grace 1897; it is simply the continual adaptation of plastic life, for good or evil, to the circumstances that surround it. . . . We notice this decay of the animal part around us now, in the loss of teeth and hair, in the dwindling hands and feet of men, in their smaller jaws, and slighter mouths and ears. Man now does by wit and machinery and verbal agreement what he once did by bodily toil; for once he had to catch his dinner, capture his wife, run away from his enemies, and continually exercise himself, for love of himself, to perform these duties well. But now all this is changed. Cabs, trains, trams, render speed unnecessary, the pursuit of food becomes easier; his wife is no longer hunted, but rather, in view of the crowded matrimonial market, seeks him out. One needs wits now to live, and physical activity is a drug, a snare even; it seeks artificial outlets, and overflows in games. Athleticism takes up time and cripples a man in his competitive examination, and in business. So is your fleshy man handicapped against his subtler brother. He is unsuccessful in life, does not marry. The better adapted survive.'

Above: A Martian from an early American edition of 'The War of the Worlds'.

Above right: Inhabitants of the moon – a picture from the 'Strand' serialisation of 'The First Men in the Moon'.

The coming man, then, will clearly have a larger brain, and a slighter body than the present. But the Professor makes one exception to this. 'The human hand, since it is the teacher and interpreter of the brain, will become constantly more powerful and subtle as the rest of the musculature dwindles.'

Then in the physiology of these children of men, with their expanding brains, their great sensitive hands and diminishing bodies, great changes were necessarily worked. 'We see now,' says the Professor, 'in the more intellectual sections of humanity an increasing sensitiveness to stimulants, a growing inability to grapple with such a matter as alcohol, for instance. No longer can men drink a bottleful of port; some cannot drink tea; it is too exciting for their highly-wrought nervous systems. The process will go on, and the Sir Wilfrid Lawson of some near generation may find it his duty and pleasure to make the silvery spray of his wisdom tintinnabulate against the

tea-tray. These facts lead naturally to the comprehension of others. Fresh raw meat was once a dish for a king. Now refined persons scarcely touch meat unless it is cunningly disguised. Again, consider the case of turnips; the raw root is now a thing almost uneatable, but once upon a time a turnip must have been a rare and fortunate find, to be torn up with delirious eagerness and devoured in ecstasy. The time will come when the change will affect all the other fruits of the earth. Even now, only the young of mankind eat apples raw – the young always preserving ancestral characteristics after their disappearance in the adult. Some day even boys will regard apples without emotion. The boy of the future, one must believe, will gaze on an apple with the same unspeculative languor with which he now regards a flint' – in the absence of a cat.

'Furthermore, fresh chemical discoveries came into action as modifying influences upon men. In the prehistoric period even, man's mouth had ceased to be an instrument for grasping food; it is still growing continually less prehensile, his front teeth are smaller, his lips thinner and less muscular; he has a new organ, a mandible not of irreparable tissue, but of bone and steel – a knife and fork. There is no reason why things should stop at partial artificial division thus afforded; there is every reason, on the contrary, to believe my statement that some cunning exterior mechanism will presently masticate and insalivate his dinner, relieve his diminishing salivary glands and teeth, and at last altogether abolish them.'

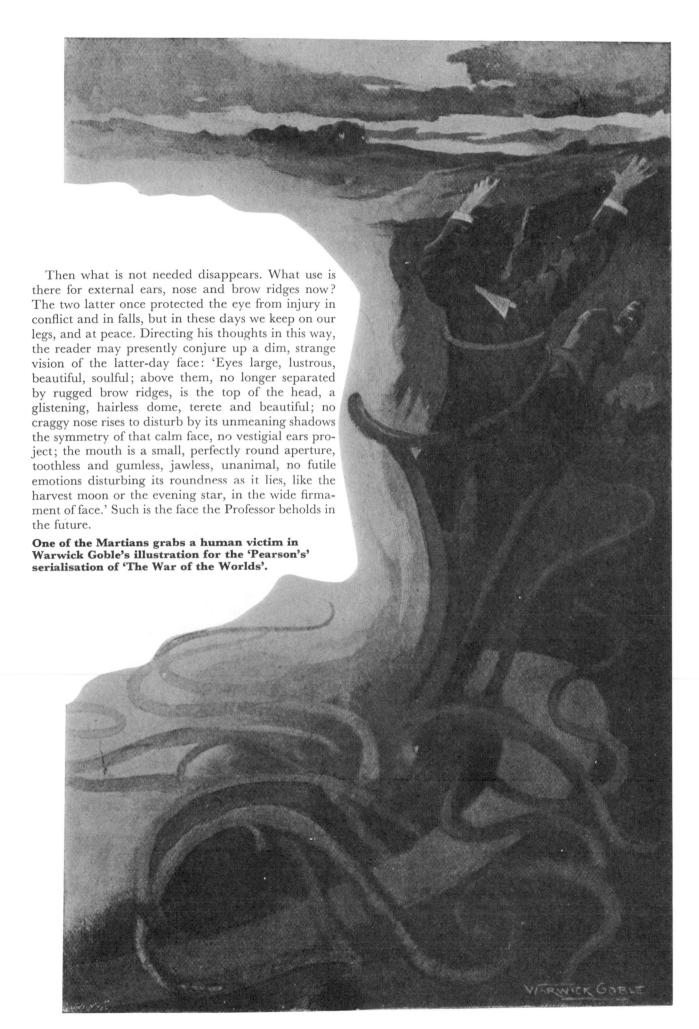

Then what is not needed disappears. What use is there for external ears, nose and brow ridges now? The two latter once protected the eye from injury in conflict and in falls, but in these days we keep on our legs, and at peace. Directing his thoughts in this way, the reader may presently conjure up a dim, strange vision of the latter-day face: 'Eyes large, lustrous, beautiful, soulful; above them, no longer separated by rugged brow ridges, is the top of the head, a glistening, hairless dome, terete and beautiful; no craggy nose rises to disturb by its unmeaning shadows the symmetry of that calm face, no vestigial ears project; the mouth is a small, perfectly round aperture, toothless and gumless, jawless, unanimal, no futile emotions disturbing its roundness as it lies, like the harvest moon or the evening star, in the wide firmament of face.' Such is the face the Professor beholds in the future.

One of the Martians grabs a human victim in Warwick Goble's illustration for the 'Pearson's' serialisation of 'The War of the Worlds'.

Of course parallel modifications will also affect the body and limbs. 'Every day so many hours and so much energy are required for digestion; a gross torpidity, a carnal lethargy, seizes on mortal men after dinner. This may and can be avoided. Man's knowledge of organic chemistry widens daily. Already he can supplement the gastric glands by artificial devices. Every doctor who administers physic implies that the bodily functions may be artificially superseded. We have pepsine, pancreatine, artificial gastric acid – I know not what like mixtures. Why, then, should not the stomach be ultimately superannuated

form a useless solid cord: the animal is nourished – it is a parasite – by absorption of the nutritive fluid in which it swims. Is there any absolute impossibility in supposing man to be destined for a similar change; to imagine him no longer dining, with unwieldy paraphernalia of servants and plates, upon food queerly dyed and distorted, but nourishing himself in elegant simplicity by immersion in a tub of nutritive fluid?

'There grows upon the impatient imagination a building, a dome of crystal, across the translucent surface of which flushes of the most glorious and pure prismatic colours pass and fade and change. In the

Searching for life in the heavens – Percival Lowell's Observatory.

centre of this transparent chameleon-tinted dome is a circular white marble basin filled with some clear, mobile, amber liquid, and in this plunge and float strange beings. Are they birds?

'They are the descendants of man – at dinner. Watch them as they hop on their hands – a method of progression advocated already by Bjornsen – about the pure white marble floor. Great hands they have, enormous brains, soft, liquid, soulful eyes. Their whole muscular system, their legs, their abdomens, are shrivelled to nothing, a dangling, degraded pendant to their minds.'

The further visions of the Professor are less alluring.

'The animals and plants die away before men, except such as he preserves for his food or delight, or such as maintain a precarious footing about him as commensals and parasites. These vermin and pests must succumb sooner or later to his untiring inventiveness and incessantly growing discipline. When he learns (the chemists are doubtless getting towards the secret now) to do the work of chlorophyll without the plant, then his necessity for other animals and plants upon the earth will diappear. Sooner or later, where there is no power of resistance and no necessity, there

altogether? A man who could not only leave his dinner to be cooked, but also leave it to be masticated and digested, would have vast social advantages over his food-digesting fellow. This is, let me remind you here, the calmest, most passionless, and scientific working out of the future forms of things from the data of the present. At this stage the following facts may perhaps stimulate your imagination. There can be no doubt that many of the Arthropods, a division of animals more ancient and even more prevalent than the Vertebrata, have undergone more phylogenetic modification' – a beautiful phrase – 'than even the most modified of vertebrated animals. Simple forms like the lobsters display a primitive structure parallel with that of the fishes. However, in such a form as the degraded ''Chondracanthus'', the structure has diverged far more widely from its original type than in man. Among some of these most highly modified crustaceans the whole of the alimentary canal – that is, all the food-digesting and food-absorbing parts –

comes extinction. In the last days man will be alone on the earth, and his food will be won by the chemist from the dead rocks and the sunlight.

'And – one may learn the full reason in that explicit and painfully right book, the *Data of Ethics* – the irrational fellowship of man will give place to an intellectual co-operation, and emotion fall within the scheme of reason. Undoubtedly is it a long time yet, but a long time is nothing in the face of eternity, and every man who dares think of these things must look eternity in the face.'

Then the earth is ever radiating away heat into space, the Professor reminds us. And so at last comes a vision of earthly cherubim, hopping heads, great unemotional intelligences, and little hearts, fighting together perforce and fiercely against the cold that grips them tighter. For the world is cooling – slowly and inevitably it grows colder as the years roll by. 'We must imagine these creatures,' says the Professor, 'in galleries and laboratories deep down in the bowels of the earth. The whole world will be snow-covered and piled with ice; all animals, all vegetation vanished, except this last branch of the tree of life. The last men have gone ever deeper, following the diminishing heat of the planet, and vast metallic shafts and ventilators make way for the air they need.'

So with a glimpse of these human tadpoles, in their deep close gallery, with their boring machinery ringing away, and artificial lights glaring and casting black shadows, the Professor's horoscope concludes. Humanity in dismal retreat before the cold, changed beyond recognition. Yet the Professor is reasonable enough, his facts are current science, his methods orderly. The contemplative man shivers at the prospect, starts up to poke the fire, and the whole of this remarkable book that is not written vanishes straightway in the smoke of his pipe. This is the great advantage of this unwritten literature: there is no bother in changing the books. The contemplative man consoles himself for the destiny of the species with the lost portion of Kubla Khan.

The astronomer Ogilvy who spots the invading Martians in 'The War of the Worlds'. Another of Warwick Goble's illustrations for 'Pearson's Magazine'.

Canals on the Planet Mars

To the Editor, *The Times*,

I possess thirty or forty views of Mars presented to me 16 years ago by the Reverend Mr. Dawes ("Eagle-Eyed Dawes", as he was aptly termed), in which, though he used but an 8inch telescope, some of the long, narrow passages are shown.

I mention this because it may serve to corroborate what otherwise might seem improbable – the circumstance that Signor Schiaparelli should have seen with his comparatively small telescope what has escaped the attention of observers using such instruments as the Herschelian reflectors, the 3ft reflector made by Mr. Common, and the magnificent 26inch reflector at Washington. Albeit until observers with such instruments as these have distinctly seen what Signor Schiaparelli has mapped, we must not too hastily assume that these are real features of Mars. Mr. Nathaniel Green, whose fine lithographs adorn a recent volume of the "Memoirs of the Astronomical Society" considers that these narrow passages are due to an optical illusion (which he has himself experienced.)

Should it be proved that the network of dark streaks has a real existence, we should by no means be forced to believe that Mars is a planet unlike our

Is There Life on Mars?

The likelihood of life on other planets – particularly on the Moon and Mars – was a topic exercising the thoughts of scientists and laymen alike in the closing years of the nineteenth century. The letter here from The Times *by Richard Proctor was among the bundle of material that Wells drew on when writing* The War of the Worlds *(1898) and he was also well aware of the important work being carried out by the American astronomer, Percival Lowell, at his observatory in Flagstaff, Arizona, and reported in his book,* Mars, *published in 1896. The article 'The Truth About Mars' was written by the now-legendary fantasy fiction author, H. P. Lovecraft for an amateur magazine,* The Phoenician *in 1917, and is typical of attitudes at the time. The most interesting item, though, is 'Intelligence on Mars' which appeared anonymously in the* Saturday Review *of 4 April 1896. Its fascination and insight is heightened all the more by the revelation that it was almost certainly the work of . . . H. G. Wells.*

One of Percival Lowell's pictures of Mars based on studies made at his observatory (1896).

observer whose excellent telescope was situated in the clear air of Flagstaff, Arizona, developed an elaborate theory, averring that the canals which lead from the polar caps toward the center of the planet in absolutely straight lines were built by the inhabitants.

How baseless as most of these speculations may be, and probably are, it is nevertheless not impossible that LIVING BEINGS OF SOME SORT MAY DWELL UPON THE SURFACE OF MARS. It is, however, left to the imagination of the reader or of the ingenious novelist to portray their appearance, size, intelligence and habits.

In these days, when our planet is so convulsed with the absurd hostilities of its insignificant denizens, it is calming to turn to the vast ethereal blue and behold other worlds, each with its unique and picturesque phenomena, where no echo of terrestrial strife or woe can resound.

earth; but we might perhaps infer that engineering works on a much greater scale than any which exist on our globe have been carried on upon the surface of Mars. The smaller force of Martian gravity would suggest that such works could be much more easily conducted on Mars than on the earth. It would be rash, however, at present to speculate in this way.

Believe me faithfully yours,

RICHARD A. PROCTOR
April 13, 1882.

The Truth about Mars

H. P. LOVECRAFT

The faintest and least clearly defined features of Mars are the so-called "canals," extremely narrow dark streaks which cover the planet's surface like a network.

They were discovered in 1877 by Schiaparelli of Milan, and have since received attention in connection with the fantastic notion that they are gigantic ditches, constructed by the hands of intelligent inhabitants of Mars.

There is in truth something worthy of note in the almost mathematical rectitude of these lines, the dark circular spots called "oases" which mark their intersections, and their probable changes from season to season; but so faint and difficult to see are they, that their very existence was doubted until recently, when some of them were successfully photographed.

They change from time to time, perhaps with the seasons of the years of Mars. The immense scale, out of all proportion to the known works of mankind, on which are "constructed" the canals, is explained by the lesser force of gravity on Mars.

The true nature of the canals is a matter of great dispute, although the late Percival Lowell, a private

Intelligence on Mars

ANONYMOUS

Year after year, when politics cease from troubling, there recurs the question as to the existence of intelligent, sentient life on the planet Mars. The last out-

Mars as visualised in Camille de Flammarion's 'La Planete Mars' (1895).

crop of speculations grew from the discovery by M. Javelle of a luminous projection on the southern edge of the planet. The light was peculiar in several respects, and, among other interpretations, it was suggested that the inhabitants of Mars were flashing messages to the conjectured inhabitants of the sister-planet, Earth. No attempt at reply was made; indeed, supposing our Astronomer-Royal, with our best telescope, transported to Mars, a red riot of fire running athwart the whole of London would scarce be visible to him. The question remains unanswered, probably unanswerable. There is no doubt that Mars is very like the earth. Its days and nights, its summers and winters differ only in their relative lengths from ours. It has land and oceans, continents and islands, mountain ranges and inland seas. Its polar regions are covered with snows, and it has an atmosphere and clouds, warm sunshine and gentle rains. The spectroscope, that subtle analyst of the most distant stars, gives us reason to believe that the chemical elements familiar to us here exist on Mars. The planet, chemically and physically, is so like the earth that, as protoplasm, the only living material we know, came into existence on the earth, there is no great difficulty in supposing that it came into existence on Mars. If reason be able to guide us, we know that protoplasm, at first amorphous and unintegrated, has been guided on this earth by natural forces into that marvellous series of forms and integrations we call the animal and vegetable kingdoms. Why, under the similar guiding forces on Mars, should not protoplasm be the root of as fair a branching tree of living beings, and bear as fair a fruit of intelligent, sentient creatures?

Let us waive objections, and suppose that, beginning with a simple protoplasm, there has been an evolution of organic forms on the planet Mars, directed by natural selection and kindred agencies. Is it a necessary, or even a probable, conclusion that the evolution would have culminated in a set of creatures with sense-perception at all comparable to that of man? It will be seen at once that this raises a complicated, and as yet insoluble, problem – a problem in which, to use a mathematical phrase, there are many independent variables. The organs of sense are parts of the body, and, like bodies themselves and all their parts, present forms which are the result of an almost infinite series of variations, selections, and rejections. Geographical isolation, for instance, has been one of the great modifying agencies. Earth movements, the set of currents, and the nature of rocks acting together have repeatedly broken up land-masses into islands, and, quite independently of other modifying agencies, have broken up groups of creatures into isolated sets, with the result that these isolated sets have developed in diverging lines. He would be a bold zoologist who should say that existing animals and plants would have been as they are to-day had the distribution of land and water in the cretaceous age been different. Since the beginning of the chalk, all the great groups of mammals have separated from the common indifferent stock, and have become moulded into men and monkeys, cats and dogs, antelopes and deer, elephants and squirrels. It would be the wildest dream to suppose that the recurrent changes of sea and land, of continent and islands, that have occurred since the dawn of life on

the earth, had been at all similar on Mars. Geographical distribution is only one of a vast series of independently varying changes that has gone to the making of man. Granted that there has been an evolution of protoplasm upon Mars, there is every reason to think that the creatures on Mars would be different from the creatures of earth, in form and function, in structure and in habit, different beyond the most bizarre imaginings of nightmare.

If we pursue the problem of Martian sensation more closely, we shall find still greater reason for doubting the existence of sentient beings at all comparable with ourselves. In a metaphysical sense, it is true, there is no external world outside us; the whole universe from the furthest star to the tiniest chemical atom is a figment of our brain. But in a grosser sense, we distinguish between an external reality and the poor sides of it that our senses perceive. We think of a something not ourselves, at the nature of which we guess, so far as we smell, taste, touch, weigh, see, and hear. Are these senses of ours the only imaginable

Wells in his middle twenties in 1892.

probes into the nature of matter? Has the universe no facets other than those she turns to man? There are variations even in the range of our own senses. According to the rate of its vibrations, a sounding column of air may be shrilled up, or boomed down beyond all human hearing; but, for each individual, the highest and lowest audible notes differ. Were

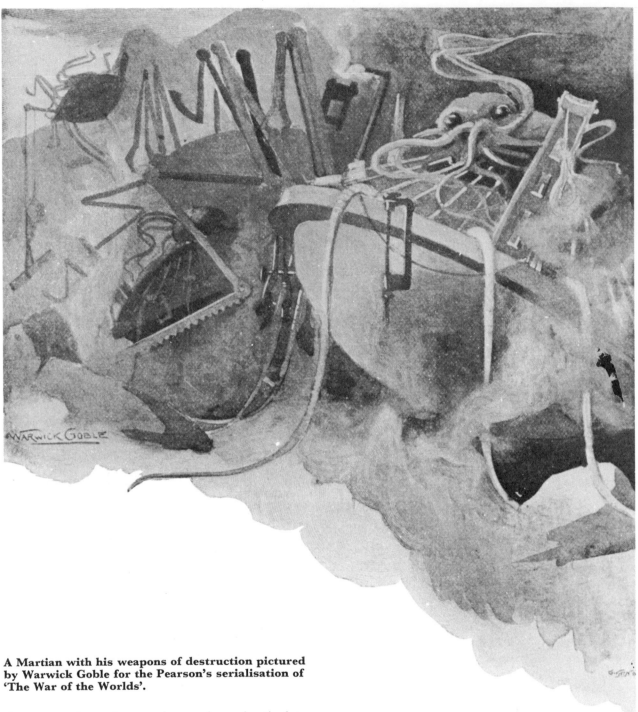

A Martian with his weapons of destruction pictured by Warwick Goble for the Pearson's serialisation of 'The War of the Worlds'.

there ears to hear, there are harmonies and articulate sounds above and below the range of man. The creatures of Mars, with the slightest anatomical differences in their organs, might hear, and yet be deaf to what we hear – speak, and yet be dumb to us. On either side the visible spectrum into which light is broken by a prism there stretch active rays, invisible to us. Eyes in structure very little different to ours might see, and yet be blind to what we see. So is it with all the senses; and, even granted that the unimaginable creatures of Mars had sense-organs directly comparable with ours, there might be no common measure of what they and we hear and see, taste, smell, and touch. Moreover it is an extreme supposition that similar organs and senses should have appeared. Even among the animals of this earth, we guess at the existence of senses not possessed by ourselves. Our conscious relations to the environment are only a

small part of the extent to which the environment affects us, and it would be easy to suggest possible senses different to ours. With creatures whose evolution had proceeded on different lines, resulting in shapes, structures and relations to environment impossible to imagine, it is sufficiently plain that appreciation of the environment might or must be in a fashion inscrutable to us. No phase of anthropomorphism is more naïve than the supposition of men on Mars. The place of such a conception in the world of thought is with the anthropomorphic cosmogonies and religions invented by the childish conceit of primitive man.

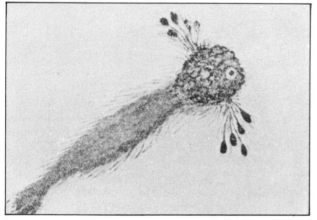

A series of pictures from a remarkable
contemporary book which claimed not only that
there was life on Mars, but that contact had been
made with the friendly and hospitable residents of
the planet. 'From India to the Planet Mars' by the
Swiss, Theodore Flournoy, was published in
America in 1901 and these pictures aroused a storm
of controversy, as they were said to have been
transmitted through a Medium on Earth. The top
illustration shows the Martian landscape and some
typical homes while (left) is an actual Martian
named Asané. The creature (above) is a household
pet, while the script is said to be an actual example
of Martian handwriting.

Ecstasy and Time Travel in Sevenoaks

The Genesis of Modern Science Fiction

BASIL COPPER

Not surprisingly, a restless spirit such as young Wells soon grew tired of the short-lived satisfaction he got from writing articles – and the customary small payments for which he often had to wait for months. So, in 1894, he decided to try his hand at writing a full-length novel – utilising as his basis the time travel story he had begun as a student, 'The Chronic Argonauts'. He knew the decision was an important one – and that only if he succeeded could he hope to make a career as a writer. In the following article, Basil Copper describes this turning point in Wells' life, and its effect on him personally and the world of literature in general. Appropriately, Mr Copper, who is one of the leading British writers in the fantasy genre, is himself a resident of Sevenoaks where Wells worked on his crucial project, and he writes with keen insight into both the man and the place.

H. G. Wells' first literary work of any importance and one that was to launch the former draper's assistant on a dazzling career was written incredibly quickly in 1894 in a then very rural Sevenoaks in a trim suburban villa in the town's Eardley Road, where he had rented rooms and, a married man, was living illicitly with the young and attractive Catherine Amy Robbins – who became his second wife, 'Jane'.

Their affair and the genesis of *The Time Machine* is only one of a series of astonishing literary incidents at Sevenoaks, a trim and beautiful country town a short distance from the bustle of Charing Cross, which has in its time housed talents as diverse as Jane Austen; Lindbergh; the tramp-poet W. H. Davies; Vita Sackville-West and Violet Trefusis; Virginia Woolf; the exotic Chinese film star Anna May Wong and even –

The young H. G. Wells and his wife 'Jane' just before the first World War.

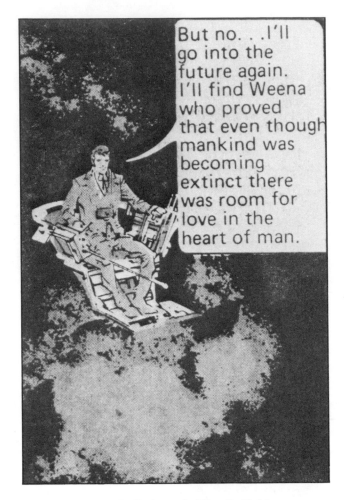

briefly – Gertrude Stein and Alice B. Toklas.

When Wells came to write it in a small, first-floor front room of the Eardley Road house, Tusculam Villa, he knew that he had to succeed. He had behind him in the literary field only a *Text Book of Biology*; a co-authored work, *Honours Physiography*; and *Select Conversations with an Uncle*. These works had appeared within the previous two years but now he was to attempt something entirely different.

The Sevenoaks-written novel was an astonishing debut on the scene of world literature and it and its immediate successors within the brief span of a further two years were to sweep him to the forefront of famous authors in a story sequence which began with *The Time Machine*; progressed through *The Wonderful Visit*; *The Stolen Bacillus and Other Stories*; *The Island of Doctor Moreau*; the delightful and Dickensian *The Wheels of Chance*, a homage to the then popular new sport of cycling, and culminated in *The Invisible Man*.

All this within the brief span of 1895-97; and all the works are still in print and widely read; many of them still the subject of film and television dramatisation. Wells himself said of *The Time Machine*, 'It's my trump card and if it does not come off very much I shall know my place for the rest of my career''.

It not only 'came off' but set the pattern for the new literary form of science-fiction. Despite the popularity of such writers as Jules Verne and the occasional forays into the field by pens as gifted as Edgar Allan Poe and Conan Doyle, such adventurous fantasies were not considered literature. With Wells the science-fiction story not only became immensely popular but rapidly established itself as literature in the generally accepted sense, the reason for a pre-eminence which continues to this day.

Wells, almost single-handed made science fiction respectable and he still stands almost alone in the field, despite the spate of novels from extremely distinguished writers which continues to pour out in both hardback and paperback.

Wells brought to fine art in *The Time Machine* his gift for the ordinary made extraordinary; incredible happenings described in bare matter-of-fact prose, usually seen through fairly prosaic protagonists. It was a method to be visually perfected by another Englishman in a different medium – Alfred Hitchcock.

Hitchcock, in his best films, those he made in England, notably in *Sabotage* and *The Man Who Knew Too Much* was a master of this shock technique of the ordinary made extraordinary – as when the little old lady produces the revolver from her handbag.

Oddly, Hitchcock himself was a frequent visitor to Sevenoaks in the 'fifties and the present writer spotted him outside the old Granada Cinema one evening after he had visited Lord Bernstein's picture palace to see his own film of Patrick Hamilton's *Rope*.

When he wrote *The Time Machine*, Wells was already married to his shy and passive cousin, Isabel Williams, the ceremony taking place in October 1891, but the marriage lasted only a bare three years. Poor Isabel with her limited outlook and contented mind was no match for the passionate and visionary young schoolteacher-scientist, whose damaged lungs had haemorrhaged on several occasions and led him to believe that a term had been set to his life.

Wells walked out on Isabel in January 1894, and Isabel, long-suffering and uncomplaining to the end, seems simply to have accepted the situation. For Wells had fallen deeply in love with one of his pupils, the frail-looking but steely-willed Catherine Amy Robbins of Putney, who was being coached by Wells for a London University Bachelor of Science degree.

In the hermetic, enclosed world of the laboratory the intimacy between teacher and pupil quickened apace and though both Miss Robbins's mother and his wife and her family were appalled at their decision, they decided to live together.

In January 1894, the young lovers set up house and in August of that year the pair, accompanied by Mrs Robbins! – surely an uneasy chaperone under the odd circumstances – caught the train at Charing Cross for Sevenoaks.

In the fortnight they spent on holiday in rented rooms in the semi-detached house at 23, Eardley Road – still unmarked in any way, though perhaps it deserves a commemorative plaque – Wells, aged only twenty-eight, wrote *The Time Machine* from some commissioned articles. This must be something of a literary record.

Though a fluent writer, Wells had written nothing remotely comparable so far; he was supposed to be convalescent and enjoying a holiday; he had Mrs

Below: Number 23, Eardley Road, Sevenoaks, where 'The Time Machine' was written in 1894. (Photo: Gerald McKee). Above facing page: A frame by Alex Nino from the Marvel Comics version of the story published in 1976.

AUG.

Famous
FANTASTIC
Mysteries

25¢

2 **INCOMPARABLE CLASSICS OF FANTASY**
THE TIME MACHINE
by **H. G. WELLS**

DONOVAN'S BRAIN
by **CURT SIODMAK**

Robbins and Catherine – better-known to history as Jane, his second wife – with him; and the book, closely textured, highly imaginative and a finished work of literature running to approximately 35,000 words, was obviously written in his 'spare time'.

As one who has passed the house hundreds of times, I find it strange to imagine Wells at that far-off period, Jane and her mother not far away, sitting at the window in the summer dusk, perhaps silhouetted against the lamp-light, writing industriously at a small wooden table the room would most likely have contained.

The commission had come about in the most casual manner possible but *The Time Machine* was to give Wells' career an impetus which carried him forward in a dazzling arc through a series of works which showed unflagging genius until the inevitable slackening of invention in the nineteen-thirties as he entered his seventh decade.

The Time Machine had its origin in a commission from the celebrated editor and literary personality, W. E. Henley, who had already published in a magazine, *The National Observer*, some articles by Wells on time travelling. The genesis of *The Time Machine* was involved and complex because the 'Time Traveller' articles themselves had evolved from other material, 'The Chronic Argonauts', which Wells had originally written for *The Science Schools Journal*.*

Now Henley, who was about to take over the editorship of the newly-founded publication *The New Review*, early in 1894, suggested to Wells that he should rework the material into a novel. Not only that but he offered the impoverished young man the then munificent fee of a hundred guineas for the serial rights and further undertook to get the book published. He was true to his word and Heinemann offered another fifty pounds advance on a contract for the novel.

Wells immediately saw the advantages in such arrangements and realised that books were obviously more profitable and prestigious than cursory articles. Once arrived at the rented rooms in Sevenoaks he set to work industriously, though there is no evidence that his labours on the book interfered with the social aspects of the holiday.

Facing page: Cover by Saunders for the August 1950 issue of 'Famous Fantastic Mysteries' which featured 'The Time Machine'.

Right: The voluptuous Weena seemingly unperturbed by the presence of Morlocks – one of Virgil Finlay's superb illustrations for 'Famous Fantastic Mysteries'.

His literary labours were interrupted – though not stemmed – by a series of amusing incidents brought about by his inquisitive landlady. This lady emerges like something out of a music-hall sketch and it is tempting to conjecture that Wells may have put something of her into the odious Morlocks of the novel, who prey on the gentle, sweet-natured Eloi.

For this good Sennockian, in the tradition of a certain type of landlady from time immemorial, could not contain her curiosity and when Wells and his two companions were out in the town, searched her lodgers' rooms. She found divorce papers from his wife's solicitors which had been served on Wells just before the party left London. Not only that, but she was scandalised to learn that Wells and Jane were unmarried.

Not wishing to risk a frontal assault on her target – perhaps with an eye to the rental from the rooms – she resorted to verbal innuendo in the form of slanderous complaints to her neighbours adjoining the house in Eardley Road. Her loud remarks, with whining comments on a sinful young couple who had taken advantage of her innocence, came floating up obtrusively to Wells on hot August nights as he sat at the open window of his room writing *The Time Machine* in longhand. Trying as this must have been, for the

---

*'The Chronic Argonauts' has recently been reprinted in *Strange Signposts* edited by Sam Moskowitz and Roger Elwood (New York, 1966) and *The Magic Valley Travellers* edited by Peter Haining (London & New York, 1974).

Above: Another Virgil Finlay illustration of the towering Sphinx which dominates the lives of the Eloi in 'The Time Machine'. From 'Famous Fantastic Mysteries'.

Right: The same scene from 'The Time Machine' but drawn half a century apart. The cover is from a 1920's edition of the book published by the Reader's Library, and the panel from the Marvel Comics picture strip version issued in 1976.

landlady did not mince her words and added comments on the couple's morals and their wicked imposition on her good nature, Jane also grew fretful, depressed and pale under this insidious barrage of abuse.

The tragi-comedy must have been exasperating indeed, for Mrs Robbins in her turn was scandalised and disapproving of the relationship between Wells and her daughter; she was obviously in the way and some evenings retired to her own room discomfited after suffering the joking high spirits of Wells, who remained unruffled and oblivious of everything except the importance of getting his first short novel finished.

Under these unpropitious circumstances one of the most brilliant essays in science fiction – and certainly the finest first novel of its kind – was born. Wells himself has described finishing off the last manuscript pages at white heat while moths dashed themselves against his lamp but even his imperturbable spirit must have quitted Sevenoaks with relief and the small party returned to London, Wells himself on the threshold of an enduring fame.

The story and plot of *The Time Machine* are almost too well-known at this distance to bear extended examination, but some neglected points deserve analysis and expansion. The Time Traveller, whose wonderful machine takes him on such astonishing adventures, remains optimistic, though his translation to the distant future – the year suggested is 802701 – is bleak indeed to the modern reader and must have seemed even more so in the comfortable expansive Victorian age in which the novel appeared.

The Eloi, the gentle but ineffective people who seem to have descended from ourselves, do no work and, like the overlords in Fritz Lang's silent film *Metropolis*, appear to spend most of their time in amorous dalliance and other pleasures of the flesh.

But there is a price for all this and they are preyed on by the Morlocks, a sinister and savage race dwelling underground, who seize members of the Eloi from time to time to work in their vast subterranean enterprises (another anticipation of Lang's vision).

The insipidity of the Eloi, with their Dresden-china prettiness, as Wells describes it, is in sharp contrast to the bleached, hair Morlocks with their 'pale, chinless faces and great, lidless, pinkish-grey eyes'. Wells calls them 'nauseatingly inhuman' and they are blind and helpless when the Time Traveller strikes matches in the darkness of their world of eternal night beneath the earth.

Nevertheless, these creatures are the masters of the beautiful-sinister world in which the Time Traveller finds himself and he realises that the Dark Nights of which the girl Weena had spoken – the period when the moon wanes – are a particular time of peril for the Eloi.

Everywhere in *The Time Machine*, Wells' mastery of his chosen medium is self-evident; the brilliant, clipped prose, assured and incisive with its insistence on the ordinary made extraordinary. There is a good example of this when the Time Traveller first arrives in the future. The beautiful but ineffectual Eloi, with their blond hair and finely chiselled features, crowd round his strange machine like children. In time he realises the danger as their hands reach for the gadgets; he unscrews the levers which operate the machine and puts them in his pocket for safety.

The incident is in no way stressed but the reader, by the very ordinariness of the description, is suddenly made aware of the appalling danger run by the Time Traveller; that he may be stranded in this strange world of the future, the machine itself travelling on without him, lost to him for ever. The sinister aspects of the novella, though muted, are always there.

The hero ponders that the Morlocks, emerging

from their underground lairs, have reintroduced Fear into this paradise. The Eloi were learning one old lesson anew. The Morlocks steal the Time Machine and take it underground; the Time Traveller has to descend, like Orpheus, and later escapes up a narrow ventilation shaft from the clutching hands of the Morlocks, at the risk of his life. The reader shares the hero's horror and repugnance and there is real shock in Wells' casual lines, 'And suddenly there came into my head the memory of the meat I had seen in the Underworld.''

The Morlocks, of course, use the gentle, fatalistic Eloi as their source of food; as 'mere, fatted cattle', Wells calls it. The hero is as much disgusted at the supine selfishness of the Eloi, content to dance away the golden days until their descent into the darkness to become unresisting victims, as he is of the Morlocks themselves.

Wells adds another dimension to the tale with the subtle, understated love story; the hero's almost unconscious affection for the girl Weena. It is this dimension as much as the science-fiction trappings, which enmesh the reader; Wells never forgot humanity – ideas were more important to him than gadgetry – and his little people caught in the trap of tremendous events here are the prototype of those in the immeasurably greater novels he was to produce in the next three decades.

The Time Traveller returns to the (nineteenth-century) present during the narrative to relate his adventures to his half-sceptical friends and, reluctantly, he is drawn back – or rather, forward – to the world of the Morlocks and the Eloi as much by his love for the girl as by his desire to see justice done. As in so many other things Wells was a great forerunner here; how often, in later years, was the hero to travel through time to find his love. From *Outward Bound* to *Brigadoon*; from Priestley to Frank Capra the theme was to be perennially popular; on the printed page; on the stage and, finally, on the screen.

Eventually, Fire, the great cleanser, comes to the hero's rescue; he burns and destroys the Morlocks but loses Weena in the process. And, inevitably, he is lost to the world of men as he travels through space and time once again. His friend enters the laboratory to see 'a ghostly, indistinct figure sitting in a whirling mass of black and brass for a moment – a figure so transparent that the bench behind with its sheets of drawings was absolutely distinct.'

In his final, bleak vision Wells had shown his protagonist a million years into the future, the earth dying, the only living creatures a debased form of giant crab. But even Wells had recoiled from this cheerless ending; it would be pleasant for the romantics to think that the Time Traveller had gone again to find his love. Wells, even at twenty-eight, was too great a realist to fall into that trap; we had left Weena dead, though it is true the hero might have chosen to return some time before her death.

But the Time Traveller must venture endlessly. Who knows in what age he is wandering or the wonders he will discover? His friend muses at the end of this enchanting book, 'But to me the future is still black and blank – is a vast ignorance, lit at a few casual places by the memory of his story.'

The Time Traveller had gone. So had Wells. Gone from Sevenoaks into a glittering future which made him a world-figure as novelist, prophet, science-fiction visionary, historian, scientist and social commentator. Now he has gone from this earth. But his legacy lives on; not only in the books, the films and the prophecies, but in modern science and the world of space travel which he envisaged so truly.

The small, narrow-fronted house in Sevenoaks was touched briefly by genius but nobody knew; few people in the town today know – or care. It does not matter, after all, in the long view. Wells himself, though a great egoist in some things, would not have minded. For he is still out there somewhere, riding the stars.

Two artists' idea of the Time Machine. (Below) A rather antiquated montage designed by Peter Edwards for the Everyman Paperback edition published in 1964 and (right) Alex Nino's cover for the Marvel Classics Comic version which appeared in 1976.

'The Man Who Discovered Wells', W. T. Stead, the editor and journalist, who first praised the young author's work.

A Man of Genius

*W*ells did not have to wait long to find out if his gamble with The Time Machine *had paid off – after the appearance of the very first episode it was being hailed by the public and, more particularly, the great crusading editor and journalist, W. T. Stead (1849-1912). With each instalment, Stead's enthusiasm for the story and its young writer grew and his excited comments in his important magazine,* Review of Reviews, *must surely accord him the honour of having 'discovered' Wells. For his part, the young writer was seeing his name in print in a critique for the first time and it undoubtedly gave him great heart. Certainly, anyone who is hailed as a genius with his first novel has reason to believe he can become a writer! Below is the first of Stead's notices from the March 1895 issue of the* Review *which not only encouraged Wells to get the story in book form, but begin planning further works in the same vein . . . .*

H. G. Wells who is writing the serial in the *New Review*, is a man of genius. His invention of the Time Machine was good, but his description of the ultimate evolution of society into the aristocrats and the capitalists who live on the surface of the earth in the sunshine, and the toilers who are doomed to live in the bowels of the earth in black darkness, in which they learn to see by the evolution of huge owl-like eyes, is gruesome and horrible to the last point. The story is not yet finished, but he has written enough to show that he has an imagination as gruesome as that of Edgar Allan Poe.

A Man Who Built a Real Time Machine

P. H. ALEXANDER

One surprising result of the success of H. G. Wells's *The Time Machine* was the attempt by a London inventor to devise a time machine for use in public entertainment! Though virtually forgotten today, the story attracted considerable attention in 1895 when the scheme to transport audiences 'through a wonderland of times and places while stationary in their seats' was first proposed by a Mr Robert W. Paul.

Mr Paul was a scientific instrument maker by profession, but also deeply involved in the pioneer film industry which was then just getting under way. Although Edison had already devised his peep-show machines, the Kinetoscopes, in 1895 Paul achieved the first successful projection of pictures on to a screen. Naturally enough, he was soon looking for ways to expand his invention, and at that very moment chanced upon Wells's *The Time Machine*.

He was captivated by the story – and also quickly realised how it might be applied to his own work. He

Frank Paul illustration for the 'Amazing Stories' serialisation of 'The Time Machine' in 1927.

would devise an entertainment combining film screens with rocking platforms to give an audience the sensation of 'travelling' while they watched suitable scenes pass by.

Mr Paul knew he required the approval of Wells and therefore proposed a meeting. Describing his encounter with the young author, he wrote later:

'Having read *The Time Machine*, I thought it a suitable basis for a proposed entertainment and, therefore, asked Mr Wells to discuss the idea. He called at my suggestion, at my old office at 44, Hatton Garden – probably at the end of 1895 – and I clearly recall the incident. I had already taken steps to develop the Kinetoscope into a projecting apparatus, which I then named the Theatrograph.

'Mr Wells was evidently interested and helped by suggesting various books, including *Extinct Monsters* by Hutchinson, which I still have. The optical devices and means for carrying out the idea were, so far as I recollect, not discussed in detail; the specifications had already been lodged in the Patent Office. I do not think Mr Wells showed any interest, or knowledge of the working details, in respect of motion pictures; very few people knew of such, or of their possibilities.

'He did not pursue the matter, and it was not feasible for me to carry it out to its realisation, on the score of expense, and in the face of the opinion of those who, like Sir Augustus Harris, firmly believed that the motion picture would be "dead" in a few months' anyhow.'

Despite this, there can be little disputing that Mr Paul's project did anticipate several successful and now well-known film techniques by more than three decades. For the machine not only incorporated the cut-back and close up, but also fade-ins and fade-outs, the overlapping and dissolving of scenes one into another, and the supplemental tonal effects of sunshine, rain, fog, moonlight and so on. Such techniques, if exploited and developed then, might well have changed the later history of film making. (The full details of Mr Paul's project can be found in the British Patents Office where the scheme is lodged

under application number 19984: but for that extra 9 a most appropriate number!)

This story is also mentioned in Terry Ramsaye's history of film making, *A Million and One Nights*, and the writer makes the interesting claim that Wells was probably the first author of note to be brought into contact with the then embryo-motion picture business through this scheme – although, of course, he had nothing to do with the patent specification.

Mr Ramsaye also makes the ingenious suggestion that Robert Paul's idea might have actually inspired Wells's story in the first place – rather than the other way around!

'The operation of the Time Traveller' he says, 'was very like the starting of the peep-show Kinetoscope, and the optical effect experienced by the fictional adventurer was identical with that experienced in viewing a speeding film.'

However, as the first Kinetoscopes arrived in London only towards the autumn of 1894, and the story was already virtually in finished shape – including many of the significant incidents – in 1893, there is no likelihood of such a suggestion being true!

Below: A cartoon from 'The Times,' 14 June 1977, showing how evergreen is the appeal of Wells' story.

Right: A picture of Pterodactyls from Hutchinson's 'Extinct Monsters' which was to be used in the creation of Robert W. Paul's 'real' Time Machine.

The Island of Dr Moreau

H.G. Wells' next major work, The Island of Dr Moreau *was in for a very different kind of treatment at the hands of the press – although the public by and large enjoyed it and made it another success. The* Times (*which, incidentally, had referred to Wells as 'H. S. Wells' in a critique of his intervening book,* The Wonderful Visit *and taken him to task over his spelling!) led the cries of outrage which greeted the publication of the book, while the* Saturday Review, *which had frequently published the young author,* recruited Sir Peter Chalmers Mitchell, the famous zoologist and Secretary of the Zoological Society of London, to pass a scientific but nonetheless damning opinion in its issue of 11 April 1896. Mitchell's criticisms, however, only served to promote the book hugely among the curious – although Wells was hurt and upset by them, particularly when as a direct result other newspapers began referring to him as 'a professor of the gruesome' and 'a past master in the art of producing creepy sensations'. However, in the November of that same year the young author read the news of some scientific experimentation with animals which seemed to substantiate the thesis of his book, and he quickly penned a reply to Chalmers Mitchell, the Saturday Review and all the others who had attacked him. This letter is reproduced here, too.

A Loathsome and Repulsive Book

We hesitate as to whether we ought to notice *The Island of Dr Moreau* by H. G. Wells at all. We know that sending a book to the *Index Expurgatorius* is a sure means of giving it a certain advertisement. Yet we feel bound to expostulate against a new departure which may lead we know not wither, and to give a word of warning to the unsuspecting who would shrink from the loathsome and repulsive.

This novel is the strongest example we have met in the perverse quest after anything in any shape that is freshly sensational. Suffice it to say that the most cold-blooded of vivisectors, who years before, as he confesses, has lost all sense of sympathetic pain, makes a torture hell of one of the loveliest isles in the Pacific. His vile experiments are doubly diabolical in as much as he imparts to his mangled victims so much of humanity as gives them the fullest sense of their sufferings and degradation.

The ghastly fancies are likely to haunt and cling, and so the book should be kept out of the way of young people and avoided by all who have good taste, good feeling, or feeble nerves. It is simple sacrilege to steep fair nature in the blood and antiseptics of the vivisecting anatomical theatre.

The Times
17 June 1896.

Two versions of 'The Island of Dr Moreau'. Bottom, left: Frank Paul illustrating the story for 'Amazing Stories' in October 1926, and below: Charles Raymond's cover for the Penguin edition of the book published in 1962.

Cheap Horrors

CHALMERS MITCHELL

Those who have delighted in the singular talent of Mr. Wells will read *The Island of Doctor Moreau* with dismay. We have all been saying that here is an author with the motions of an artist and the intellectual imagination of a scientific investigator. He has given us in *The Time Machine* a diorama of prophetic visions of the dying earth, imagined with a pitiless logic, and yet filled with a rare beauty, sometimes sombre and majestic, sometimes shining with fantastic grace. He has brought down among us the angel of our dreams, and, while using the faculties a naturalist would employ in studying the new habitat of a species, he has made us laugh and weep, flush with an unsuspected shame, hug a discovered virtue [in his book *The Wonderful Visit*, 1895]. Behind these high gifts, behind the simple delight of his story-telling, there has seemed to lie a reasoned attitude to life, a fine seriousness that one at least conjectures to be the background of the greater novelists. When the prenatal whispers of *The Island of Doctor Moreau* reached me, I rejoiced at the promise of another novel with a scientific basis, and I accepted gladly the opportunity given me to say something of it, from the scientific point of view, as well as from that of a devoted novel-reader. But, instead of being able to lay my little wreath at the feet of Mr. Wells, I have to confess the frankest dismay.

For Mr. Wells has put out his talent to the most flagitious usury. His central idea is a modelling of the human frame and endowment of it with some semblance of humanity, by plastic operations upon living animals. The possibilities of grafting and moulding, of shaping the limbs and larynx and brain, of transfusing blood, of changing physiological rhythm, and vague suggestions of hypnotizing dawning intelligence with the elemental rules of human society – these would seem to offer a rich vein to be worked by Mr. Wells's logical fancy. They are, indeed, finely imagined, and the story of the hero, suddenly brought into an island peopled with such nightmare creatures, is vivid and exciting to the last degree. To realize them, you must read of the bewilderment and horror of the hero, while he thinks the creatures are men outraged and distorted: of his fear for his own fate at the hands of the artificer of the unnatural: of his gradual acquaintance with the real nature of the monsters: of his new horror at the travesties of human form and mind: of the perils that begin when the 'stubborn beast-flesh' has overcome the engrafted humanity, and the population has risen in rebellion against its creator. All this is excellent; but the author, during the inception of his story, like his own creatures, has tasted blood. The usurious interest began when the author, not content with the horror inevitable in his idea, and yet congruous with the fine work he has

Wells' story of an Angel who comes to Earth, 'The Wonderful Visit' (1896).

One of the beast men in 'Gulliver's Travels' who are said to have inspired Wells' 'The Island of Dr Moreau'. This illustration from the 1876 edition is by T. Morten.

given us hitherto, sought out revolting details with the zeal of a sanitary inspector probing a crowded graveyard.

You begin with a chromolithographic shipwreck, and three starving survivors playing odd-man-out for a cannibal feast. The odd man breaks faith, and, in the resulting struggle, the hero is left alone in a blood-bespattered boat. When he is rescued, a drunken doctor, no doubt disinclined to change the supposed diet, restores him with a draught of iced blood. When the island is reached he is not allowed by Mr. Wells to land until, refused hospitality by Dr. Moreau and cast adrift by the drunken captain, he has again meditated upon starvation, this time without any mates for whose blood he may pass halfpence. Dr. Moreau himself is a *cliché* from the pages of an anti-vivisection pamphlet. He has been hounded out of London because a flayed dog (you hear the shuddering ladies handing over their guineas) has been liberated from his laboratory by a spying reporter. It is the blood that Mr. Wells insists upon forcing on us; blood in the sink 'brown and red,' on the floor, on the hands of the operators, on the bandages that swathe the creatures or that they have left hanging on the bushes – physically disgusting details inevitable in the most conservative surgery; but still more unworthy of restrained art, and, in this case, of scientific *vraisemblance*, is the insistence upon the terror and pains of the animals, on their screams under the knife, and on Dr. Moreau's indifference to the 'bath of pain' in which his victims were moulded and recast. Mr. Wells

OCT.

Famous

FANTASTIC

Mysteries

25¢

THIRD PERSON SINGULAR
by CLEMENCE DANE

THE ISLAND OF DR. MOREAU
A NOVEL OF SPECTRAL TERROR
by H.G. WELLS

must know that the delicate, prolonged operations of modern surgery became possible only after the introduction of anaesthetics. Equally wrong is the semi-psychological suggestion that pain could be a humanizing agency. It may be that the conscious subjection to pain for a purpose has a desirable mental effect; pain in itself, and above all continuous pain inflicted on a struggling, protesting creature, would produce only madness and death. Mr. Wells will not even get his hero out of the island decently. When Dr. Moreau has been killed by his latest victim – a puma become in the laboratory 'not human, not animal, not hellish, brown, seamed with red branching scars, red drops starting out upon it' – Mr. Wells must needs bring in an alien horror. The 'boat from the machine' drifts ashore with two dead men in it – men 'dead so long that they fell in pieces' when the hero dumped them out for the last of the island monsters to snarl over.

It may be that a constant familiarity with the ways and work of laboratories has dulled my sense of the aesthetic possibilities of blood – anatomists, for the most part, wash their hands before they leave their work – and that a public attuned to Mr. Rider Haggard's view of the romantic may demand the insertion of details physically unpleasant; but, for my own part, I feel that Mr. Wells has spoiled a fine conception by greed of cheap horrors. I beg of him, in the name of many, a return to his sane transmutations of the dull conceptions of science into the living and magical beauty he has already given us. We that have read his earlier stories will read all he chooses to write; but must he choose the spell of Circe?

There remains to be said a word about the scientific conceptions underlying Dr. Moreau's experiments. I quite agree that there is scientific basis enough to form the plot of a story. But in an appended note, Mr. Wells is scaring the public unduly. He declares:— 'There can be no denying that whatever amount of scientific credibility attaches to the detail of this story, the manufacture of monsters – and perhaps even of *quasi*-human monsters – is within the possibilities of vivisection.' The most recent discussion of grafting and transfusion experiments is to be found in a treatise by Oscar Hertwig, a translation of which Mr. Heinemann announces. Later investigators have failed to repeat the grafting experiments of Hunter, and a multitude of experiments on skin and bone grafting and on transfusion of blood shows that animal-hybrids cannot be produced in these fashions. You can transfuse blood or graft skin from one man to another; but attempts to combine living material from different creatures fail.

Scientific Justification for The Island of Dr Moreau?

To The Editor, *The Saturday Review*,
Sir,

In a special article in *The Saturday Review* of 11 April 1896 reviewing my "Island of Dr. Moreau", Mr. Chalmers Mitchell, in addition to certain literary criticisms, which rest upon their merits, gave the lie

Facing page: **Stephen Lawrence's front cover for the 'Famous Fantastic Mysteries' publication of 'The Island of Dr Moreau', October 1946.**

Above: **Dreams of the Beast Men – one of Stephen Lawrence's striking illustrations for 'The Island of Dr Moreau'.**

direct to a statement of mine that the grafting of tissues between animals of different species is possible. This was repeated more elaborately in *Natural Science*, and from these centres of distribution it passed into the provincial press, where it was amplified to my discredit in various, animated, but to me, invariably painful phrasing. And the contradiction, with the implication of headlong ignorance it conveys, is now traversing the Continent of America (where phrasing is often very vivid indeed) in the wake of the review copies Mr. Stone is distributing.

I was aware at the time that Mr. Chalmers Mitchell was mistaken in relying on Oscar Hertwig as the final authority on this business, but he was making the rash assertion and not I; but for a while I was unable to replace the stigma of ignorance he had given me, for the simple reason that I knew of no published results of the kind I needed. But the *British Medical Journal* for 31 October 1896 contains the report of a successful graft, by Mr. Mayo Robson, not merely of connective but of nervous tissues between rabbit and man. I trust, therefore, that *Natural Science* will now modify its statements concerning my book, and that the gentlemen of the provincial press who waxed scornful, and even abusive, on Mr. Chalmers Mitchell's

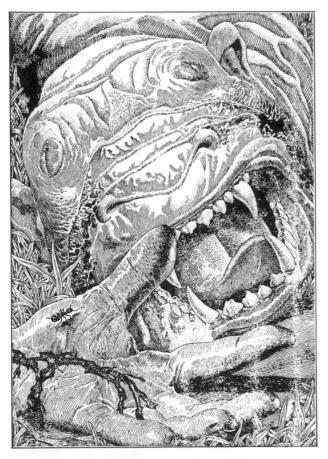

Above: 'It was a limbless thing with a horrible face, that writhed along the ground in serpentine fashion'. Another of Stephen Lawrence's illustrations like that below of Pendrick's confrontation with one of the brutes on 'The Island of Dr Moreau'.

authority, will now wax apologetic. There is quite enough to misunderstand and abuse in the story without any further application of this little mistake of Mr. Chalmers Mitchell.

Yours very truly,

H. G. WELLS
7 November 1896.

During July, August and September 1977, a series of intriguing small advertisements appeared in the world famous 'Agony' or Personal Column of The Times. *Only those who knew the work of H. G. Wells and appreciated the significance of the references to Dr Moreau realised it was part of a publicity campaign to herald the arrival of the latest film based on* The Island of Dr Moreau *made by American International and starring Burt Lancaster and Michael York. Here is a selection of some of the advertisements.*

DR. MOREAU requires lab. assistant. Experience not necessary. Strong stomach.

Wednesday, 20 July

DR. MOREAU does brain transplants while you wait.

Thursday, 21 July

HEART OF BABOON, eye of newt and other spare parts required by Dr. Moreau.

Saturday, 23 July

QUESTION for Dr. Moreau: What do you do with the leftovers?

Monday, 1 August

DON'T MAKE a pig of yourself without consulting Dr. Moreau.

Wednesday, 3 August

WERE YOU cut out to be a patient of Dr. Moreau?

Saturday, 6 August

DR. MOREAU will have you in stitches.

Monday, 8 August

DR. MOREAU goes in one ear and out the other.

Tuesday, 9 August

I'M JUST WILD about Dr. Moreau. He has so much animal magnetism.

Wednesday, 10 August

IF YOU WANT TO GET AHEAD see Dr. Moreau.

Friday, 12 August

OVERWEIGHT? Dr. Moreau will cut you down to size.

Saturday, 13 August

ARE YOU A MAN – or a mouse? Get an expert opinion from Dr. Moreau.

Monday, 15 August

DR. MOREAU made a monkey out of me. See what he can do for you.

Tuesday, 16 August

DR. MOREAU seeks Harley St. offices. Sound-proofing essential.

Thursday, 18 August

LEND a hand to Dr. Moreau and you'll never get it back.

Friday, 19 August

UNFORTUNATELY Dr. Moreau's services are not available on the National Health.

Friday, 2 September

DR. MOREAU is coming soon. Can't you feel it in your bones?

Saturday, 3 September

Edgar Rice Burroughs' 'The Monster Men' was inspired by 'The Island of Dr Moreau'. This cover by Mahlon Blaine was for the 1962 Canaveral Press edition.

The Island of Professor Menu

JAMES F. SULLIVAN

The controversial nature of The Island of Dr Moreau *made it a natural target not only for journalists and critics, but parodists as well. One of the most widely read humourists of the time was James F. Sullivan, who contributed to numerous magazines and publications, and was also a leading light on* Punch. *He found the Wells novel and the fuss surrounding it absolutely irresistible, and as a result wrote* The Island of Professor Menu *which appeared in the autumn of 1896. Mr Sullivan also drew the delightful*

and amusing sketches which are reproduced with the story here.

[*When I had finished writing the following story, I was seized with an impression of having read something like it before – possibly during a previous existence. It seemed as though I had in some mysterious way drawn up the incidents from the* WELLS *of Memory.* – AUTHOR.]

I

It was on a voyage from Victoria to the Sandwich Islands that the good ship *Victoria Sandwich* (so named from the places she plied between) had foundered.

Seven of us had drifted for about three years on a lee-scupper, the only object on which we could save ourselves, all the boats being smashed. We had suffered so much from hunger that we had been forced to eat one another, turn and turn about; and my last recollection is of the Friday when my weekly turn came round again to eat the other six.

Then I fainted from repletion; and when I next became conscious, I was lying, still ill with acute indigestion, in a bunk on board the schooner *Gum Drop*.

A doctor sat by my side holding my wrist. There was an indescribable peculiarity about this man which made me detest him.

This illustration and those on the following pages are all by James F. Sullivan and accompanied the original publication of 'The Island of Dr Menu' in 1896.

He said, "The Captain of this vessel objects to queer combinations." I was too weak to inquire what queer combinations were.

As soon as my indigestion had lessened a little, I went on deck. Standing on the companion was a man with an indescribable peculiarity about him which made me detest him.

"What are you doing here?" said the doctor. "Your place is in the kitchen garden – you know that."

"They won't have me in the kitchen garden – they

say I'm running to seed," replied the man, with a cowed look.

"If you don't go, I'll have you boiled!" said the doctor threateningly.

Chained to the mast were a flock of sheep; and I noticed that when the man put his head above the top of the companion-ladder they all stretched their necks at him, baaing eagerly.

Presently there was a great outcry; and the strange man ran up the ladder, followed by the Captain, who was roaring angrily. The Captain's language was dreadful – he hardly said a single sentence without a whole string of expressions such as "Dear me!" "Bless my whiskers!" "Lork-a-mussy!" and similar dreadful phrases. He tore off great pieces of the strange man's clothing, and rolled them up tightly into a ball, which he put in his mouth and chewed. In the scuffle, the strange-looking man fell among the sheep, which instantly began to browse his hair off, while he screamed loudly.

"Captain!" said the doctor angrily, "it is bad taste to eat your passengers."

The Captain turned savagely upon him, and rolled off a long list of fearful expressions, of which "My Aunt!" and "Golly!" were among the mildest.

There was an indescribable peculiarity about the

Captain which caused me to detest him.

The Captain came back, still in a rage. "Passenger you call him!" he said; "I call him a vegetable – a lunatic vegetable! I can't stand him – my men can't stand him. He gets his roots all round the tackle so that they can't work it! Yesterday they turned round the screw, and stopped the ship. I won't have it, I tell you! He scatters seeds all over the deck. It was a clean deck before he came aboard – look at it now! My Aunt!"

I looked forward at the forecastle: the whole deck was hidden by a luxuriant crop of mingled wheat, potatoes, dandelions, poppies, and other plants. Wall-flowers were growing in all the tackle blocks and the holes of the dead-eyes; there were nasturtiums trailing up the mast; thistles waved in the tops; the bulwarks were covered with stonecrop and London-pride.

"Horried!" said the Captain. "Catch me taking aboard a cargo of maniac vegetables and seed-scatterers again! I suppose you took this ship for a seed-vessel!" And with this parting shot he flew to the ginger-beer bottle for solace. I found that he was always in a state of ginger-beer.

On looking about me, I perceived the meaning of his last allusion: the deck was piled up to the tops with threepenny packets of seeds.

The doctor (whose name was Merioneth) and I stood leaning over the bulwarks in the moonlight.

"You appear to be a bit of a gabbler," he said suddenly; "so I feel inclined to tell you the secret of my life."

I looked round, and perceived the strange man eyeing me furtively; and a sensation of horror crept over me as I seemed to detect in his eyes a resemblance to those of a potato. He averted his glance quickly, and planted his eyes in the furrows of the sea.

There was a faint perfume of mingled cookery in the air – that perfume which makes one long to creep down into the kitchen when cook is not looking, and dip a great slice of bread into the dripping-pan. Have you ever done this? If you have not, try it! But mind the grease does not drip on your new clothes, or cook will find it all out – and then!

This perfume of cookery grew stronger as the schooner progressed on her way. It filled the whole air from horizon to horizon. Among the scents, I could clearly distinguish those of fried onions, hot cake, Irish stew, herrings, pork chops, raspberry jam, and sausages. I was beginning to get hungry; but since my indigestion consequent upon eating six castaways, I had not dared to eat anything.

In the course of a few days we sighted an island with a volcano in the middle. From this volcano or burning mountain came a long thin line of smoke; and it was this smoke which distributed the savoury perfumes I have mentioned.

This smell of general cookery from the volcano had become overpowering. Just think of it! Suppose the doctor had forbidden you to eat anything for a weak, and your cook were preparing for a great dinner-party, and all these perfumes came to you from the kitchen! What would you do? Exactly. That's what I did. I sat down and cried.

When we neared the volcanic island, the Captain, assisted by his men, hastily enclosed Merioneth, the flock of sheep, the packets of seeds, the strange man, a large pig, a pine-apple, and all the other properties which Merioneth had with him, in a great net, which was promptly hauled up to the yard-arm. Then, as the vessel rapidly passed the island, the net was cast loose, and fell with a thump on the shore.

"Hullo! *You* still here? Three blind mice!" said the Captain to me. "Overboard you go!"

The Captain's hair and beard were ginger-coloured in consequence of his addiction to ginger-beer.

He lowered me into the lee-scupper, which was still towing astern In my despair I screamed madly for the waiter – the chamber-maid – nurse – anything.

Then I saw that Merioneth had taken pity on me, and was putting out from the island in a packet – one of the threepenny packets I had seen on deck.

II
THE DOCK-LABOURERS

The packet was propelled by three boatmen. There was an indescribable peculiarity about them which caused me to detest them. I noticed that they had large green hands which they held in the air, varying the position from time to time. I had never seen men so wrapped up before; they were entirely swathed in bass-matting bound round with raffia-grass.

I noticed that each of them had a label tied to him, and that the flock of sheep in the stern kept trying to get at them. In the stern sat a man whom I had not seen before: he had a large, flat, white linen cap, and sleeves and apron of the same material. In one hand he held a ladle. His hair struck me – it was bright green.

We landed; and I could not help noticing the gait of the three boatmen. They walked very stiffly, stopping to pull away their legs from the ground from time to time, as though the legs were beginning to take root.

These men drove the sheep, and carried the packets of seeds and other articles, up to a door in the wall of the crater of the volcano. There appeared to be some secret about this crater; for no one was permitted to enter.

I still had not partaken of food since the consumption of the six castaways, and was faint with hunger. Under these circumstances I was maddened by the

THE
DOCK-LABOURER.

appetising perfume of cooking which proceeded from the vicinity of the crater and pervaded the island.

Merioneth noticed my condition, and hastily breaking a few fingers and toes off the strange man, threw them to me.

"It's all right, Peppermint," he said (my name is Peppermint). "They'll grow again in no time. He doesn't mind."

The fingers were crimson, the toes white. They ate short and crisp. The strange man did not appear to mind.

While I was devouring them, the green-haired man in white linen came down to where I sat on the beach.

"Thanks for calling," he said; "but I suppose you know you're not welcome here? Of course I know well enough who sent you – the School of Cookery. You've come to find out what you can: but you won't find out much, I can tell you. What are we to do with the beast? he said to Merioneth.

"There's my room," said Merioneth.

They conducted me to a door in the wall of the crater; this door led into a room which had another door leading into the crater. This second door they hastily shut.

III
THE FRYING IN THE FUMAROLE

The perfume of cooking was maddening here. All the most deliriously appetising odours I have ever come across in all the restaurants I have ever known would have been but a drop in the ocean to this. There was a vast sound of frying in the air; it evidently proceeded from the interior of the crater.

Merioneth said he would lunch with me, but that Menu was too preoccupied with some work to come.

"Menu!" said I; "I know that name."

"Do you?" said he. "What a donkey I was to mention it to you."

"Merioneth," said I suddenly, "why has the strange man green hair – something like your friend's, and eyes like those of potatoes?"

"Eh?" he said. "Never noticed it!" Then he went out, and I heard him call "Menu!"

Where had I heard the name of Menu before? What were the words I had read in the newspaper years ago? "The Menu Puddles," was it? "The Menu Muddles!"

Then it came back to me. Menu, the celebrated experimental cook, who had been driven from London because of the effect of his awful experiments on the digestions of the customers at his restaurant! He had had to leave England.

What could it mean? A locked crater on a lonely island, a notorious experimental chef, and this fearful perfume of cookery!

IV
THE THINGUMMY IN THE PLANTATION

I fled from the maddening odour into the woods. There was an indescribable peculiarity about the trees which caused me to detest, and want to eat, them.

I became aware of a strange grotesque form peering

at me from among the foliage. It had one glass eye, set in a cylinder of brass; the fore-part of its body appeared to be square and of the colour of mahogany; while the hinder part, as far as I could make out, bore some strange resemblance to a tortoise; and it appeared to have fins and a tail, somewhat like those of a skate.

I fled, shrieking; it was growing dark. I was conscious of a pattering of feet following me.

Screaming for the police, I leapt from a high cliff on to the beach; the Thingummy followed. Then I picked up a stone, and, facing round, hurled it. It broke the Thingummy's one glass eye into bright splinters; and the Thingummy put up for repairs.

V
THE FRYING OF THE HAM

I returned to my room. The perfume of varied cookery had now concentrated itself into the most maddening odour I had ever been tortured by – it was as though all the ham in the world were being fried inside there. This time it was no mere soles, nor potatoes, nor even sausages – it was ham!

As I realised this I rose, seized the handle of the door into the crater, and flung it open before me. There was brown gravy in the dripping-pan. I saw *something* upon a vast silver grill; and then blotting this out appeared the face of old Menu, crimson with heat.

In a moment he had gripped me by the shoulder with a hand smeared with gravy, had twisted me off my feet, and flung me headlong back into my own room.

"Ruin the work of a lifetime!" I heard Menu say. "But I'll roast his ribs!"

I picked myself up and stood trembling, my mind a chaos of the most dreadful misgivings. Could it be possible? Would he really cook me? Did he propose to serve me up whole, with a lemon in my mouth; or would he make an Irish stew of me? Hungry as I was, I did not like this idea.

I fled again into the plantation round the corner.

I wandered until I came to a strange kitchen garden containing a row of hothouses on one side, and a row of cages and aquaria on the other. In the middle were neat beds.

Out of one of the cages came a strange creature – at least it began to come out, though it appeared as if it would never finish. It had the head and body of a sheep, save that the body was many yards in length. Arranged quite closely together beneath its body were one hundred legs – those on its right side being roast, and those on its left boiled; along the middle of its back grew a long line of turnips, boiled to a turn.

As I was observing it, an extraordinary bird hopped down from a perch in another cage; it had not feathers or down on its body, which was of the colour of putty. It commenced to knead itself with its feet, lying on its back to do so.

Suddenly it perceived me. "Hullo!" it called out, "here's another New Combination! Tell him the law. You'll have to obey the law, you know – none escape!"

"None escape!" cried a host of Combinations suddenly appearing from the cages and hothouses. Then the sheep began to recite a strange code, the others joining in:—

THE DOUGH-DO.

to be furnished with vegetable marrow in place of the ordinary kind; and by sprinkling a little turnip-seed along his back I succeeded in obtaining this row of turnips. I had now completed my sheep; but what I desired was an animal always ready for the table.

"By planting the legs in a hot-bed (in the case of the boiled legs it was, of course, a hot-water bed), and keeping them in this situation for a considerable time, I obtained a gentle but prolonged heat which gradually and by quite natural means cooked the legs to a turn; and this heat, spreading genially over the whole body, also cooked the turnips. In the case of lambs I have a line of green peas and mint along the back. When I require more sheep, I just sow some seed from the turnips on this one's back.

"That bird you see kneading itself is the dough-do. It is now sufficiently kneaded; and you perceive another bird, with a tail like a paste-roller, advancing? That is the rolling-pin-tail; and I invented it to roll the dough-do.

"That bird over there whose tail branches naturally into pea-sticks covered with peas is the green-peacock. He also has vegetable marrow in his bones; in fact vegetable marrow – one of my greatest discoveries – is the chief connecting link between animal and vegetable life.

"Now look in this fishpond. There is the currant-jelly-fish. There is the cow-eel, from which excellent soup, combining the qualities of beef-tea and turtle-soup, may be obtained.

"Not to be under – or overdone; *that* is the law.
Are we not Combys?
"Not to be tough or stringy; *that* is the law.
Are we not Combys?
"Not to go to table without a dish; *that* is the law.
Are we not Combys?"

"Evil are the punishments of those who break the law. Back to the kitchen they shall go to be réchauffés!"

At that moment Menu and Merioneth appeared. "Hullo!" said Menu, "I thought we should find you here, though I suspect you haven't paid for admission. As you *are* here, let me take you round and show you the exhibits. All my own invention – all done by kindness, and in the interests of cookery. I found that cooks do not really understand cooking, and I took this island in order to improve the art. They would not have me any longer in London, because I gave people indigestion. But one must practise on somebody, you know. Merioneth here tries all my new Combination dishes now; that's why he looks so ill. I've invented the most wonderful Combinations in cookery – here's my list of patent dishes. Please take one; also a copy of my latest Combination-Cookery Book, price one shilling – thanks. That long creature is my patent centipede sheep – you see we get a hundred legs to one body; and the saving of space and fodder is great."

VI
ALL ABOUT THE COMBYS

"But," I said, "the process of putting him together must be very unpleasant for the sheep!"

"Not a bit," said Professor Menu. "All done by seeds – I've discovered that everything can be grown from seed, you know. First of all I bought a five-legged lamb from a travelling show, and layered his tail as one treats carnations – just like the old lady treated her cow in the 'Lost Idea' – I taught her, you know. The lambs which sprang from the tip of the tail varied in the number of legs they possessed; and I selected those with the greatest number, repeated the layering process, and very soon obtained a centipede lamb. By grafting his tail on a plant I caused his spine

THE CURRANT-JELLY-FISH.

Those creatures somewhat like lobsters are pie-crustaceans; and here is the crab-apple. By a mixture of the two, we obtain natural apple-dumplings. That large fish with a tough shell, growing on the aquatic plant, is the halibutternut; it provides a dish which is a combination of the fish course and the dessert. The pond is brilliantly lighted at night by a combination of the lamprey and the ray species, from which we obtain the lamp-ray. It beats the incandescent light hollow."

"And what," I asked, still shuddering, "was the thingummy which hunted me the other evening?"

"Oh, that must have been the snap-shotting-turtle –

55

produced by grafting an ordinary photographic camera on a snapping turtle. I subsequently improved the creature by a fusion of the X ray or Röntgen ray – a development of the common ray found in these waters. These submarine rays are indispensable for torpedo-boat catchers."

I now perceived a cockatoo with an unusually fine crest on his head.

"Ah yes," said Menu, "the celery-cockatoo. Having been struck by the uselessness of the sham heads of celery forming the crest of the bird, I conceived the notion of producing real celery in its place. This bird yields one good dish per week. Result of vegetable marrow again.

"Here is a plantation of vegetable marrow-bones – all growing ready cooked for table. The white napkin round each is the natural foliage."

At this point I was startled by a huge fly settling on my head. With a shriek, I flicked it off.

"Do not injure it," exclaimed the Professor. "That is a combination of which I am particularly proud – the lamb's sweetbread-and-butter-fly. It is a most valuable addition to the table. Try some of the fruit of this plant."

He pointed to a most curious plant, whose branches bore great tufts of various sweetmeats – fondants, burnt almonds, assorted creams, and so on in infinite variety.

I tasted some – having still eaten nothing (except those little pieces of the strange man) since my lunch on the six castaways. The sweets were delicious.

"That," said Professor Menu, "is the sweetstuff-briar. Those tufts upon it are, of course, candy-tufts. But let us get home to the crater, for I am wasting valuable time."

So saying, he hailed an enormous bird which was passing. Its back was covered with rows of seats like those on a road-car; only these seats were natural to the bird, and formed of quills luxuriously covered with downy feathers. We climbed up and took seats; and the bird started at a great pace toward the crater, stopping at corners to look out passengers.

"This great bird is the omnibustard," said the Professor; "I am going to fit him with a lightning-conductor to quick his pace."

We were now passing under a beautiful grove of trees; and I was charmed with the sounds of a magnificent string-band which was performing the overture to Tannhäuser.

"Ah – it's only my violinnets,' said Menu; "a combination of the common linnet and the violin. You will distinguish the deep notes of the bass violinnet – a combination of the two former ingredients with the common bass, very plentiful in the sea about here. That motif you hear now is being performed by the guitarmigans."

"Professor Menu," I said, "there is an indescribable peculiarity about you which causes me to detest you!

I don't like that affair about London and the digestions of the customers."

"Come in here," said Menu, pushing me into my room. "Look here – I'll try to convince you of my innocence and virtue. After all, indigestion is such a little thing! It is possible that, outside this little tiny atom of a world, indigestion is unknown. Do you suppose the moon suffers from indigestion?" said Professor Menu.

"I don't know," I replied, pondering; "she looks very yellow at times. You may have been giving the moon some of your Combination dishes."

"I assure you I haven't; it must be the green cheese; besides, what is a little indigestion when weighed against the scientific advantages of my Combinations?" There was an indescribable peculiarity about his reasoning which caused me to detest it.

"Look here!" said I, "how about that smell of frying ham?"

"It is not ham," he said earnestly. "It is the porcupineapple. It is my latest and grandest Combination – a magnificent dish with boundless possibilities. You saw the pig and the pineapple which Merioneth brought me from Victoria? This is a combination of the two, with many additions. Don't you see that this compilation of mine will combine the delights of roast pork and apple sauce walking about in the fields all ready for table."

"Hum!" I said, mad with hunger. "And who is the strange man who came with us in the ship?"

"He is the vegetarian," said Menu. "He is entirely vegetable—"

"But the peculiarity of his gait?" I interrupted suspiciously.

56

"Merely a kitchen-garden gait," explained Menu. "I have a great trouble in keeping the sheep from eating him, because his hair is composed of grass and spring-onions. His head is a very large potato, and has most expressive eyes; his legs are composed of giant rhubarb stalks; his fingers are radishes – you ate some, I recollect. He again has vegetable marrow in his bones, of course."

"And those strange men in the boat?"

"They are dock-labourers – merely a skilful use of the ordinary dock-plant grown in the London docks.

"First I made a mixture of the dock and the Swede – Swedes being the best sailors. You observed that their hands consisted of palms only – that is palm-fronds.

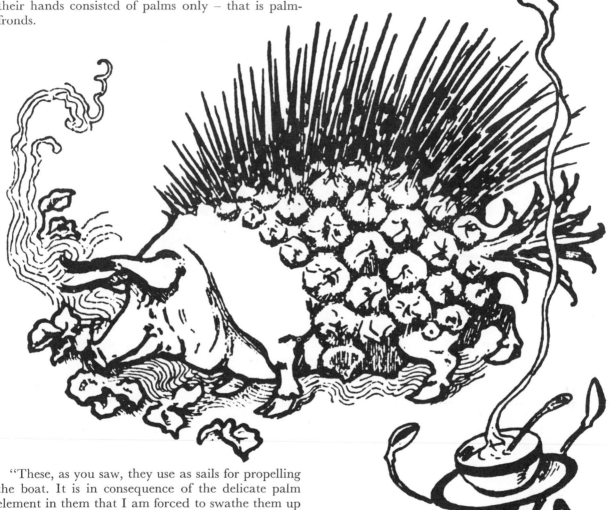

"These, as you saw, they use as sails for propelling the boat. It is in consequence of the delicate palm element in them that I am forced to swathe them up in bass-matting. Their great trouble is that when they are on land their sea-kail legs are always trying to take root. This gives a good deal of inconvenience. They can't keep their sea legs."

I jumped from my chair in terror as a loud report reached my ears.

"It's all right, Peppermint," said Merioneth. "It's only the ginger-poppies going off all at once."

"Come in," said Professor Menu, flinging open the door which led to the crater. I entered. Stretching across a great part of the main crater was a vast silver grill, on which were placed various recently invented sorts of meat, all frizzling and popping merrily. My hunger was dreadful. I sniffed round feebly, and burst into tears.

On various little fiery holes round the crater were stewpans, frying-pans, saucepans, and so on. A stream of boiling water issued from the crater and formed a convenient pool in which fowls, fish, and vegetables were boiling. The stream also heated receptacles for keeping the plates hot. In front of a wall of hot lava turned a gigantic spit, and beneath it stood a very curious beast, catching the gravy. That was the dripping-panther. There were a number of other curious beasts holding the washed plates – these were plate-raccoons. A strange bird was fussing about all over the place, tasting the various dishes, adding

57

a little salt here, a little pepper there, a little sauce in another place.

"That bird – a Combination of which I am very proud – is my apprentice, the professed cuckoo," explained Menu. "You see that other bird – that very fat three-cornered bird. He is filled with jam, and is the jam-puffin."

"And those things like rabbits, with dark brown dots all over them, and glaze on their backs?" I asked.

"Merely my currant-bunnies," explained the Professor. "Those irritable ones that are quarrelling together near the fire are hot-cross-bunnies."

"And those strangely affectionate oysters which would insist on coming to me to be patted, on the sea-shore?"

"Ah yes – friendly natives," said the professor.

VII
HOW THE COMBYS TASTED

At this moment the perfume of cookery became intolerable and frenzying, and I rushed out and sat down to have a good cry. There was a sound of scuffling inside the crater. The inner door of my room, which I had hastily shut in going out, burst open with a crash; and out rushed a THING.

It was neither animal nor vegetable – it was edible. It was the porcupineapple escaping from the spit, half done. In its mouth was a lemon.

My hunger maddened me: I fell upon it, half done as it was, and ate the whole of it. My appetite grew stronger with this relish.

"I mean to eat the whole of 'em," I screamed, "all curious Combinations – every man Jack of 'em. I'm going to have a regular bank-holiday, because I have my wits untied!"

"Don't, Peppermint, for goodness' sake!" cried Merioneth.

I was not to be restrained; five weeks' fast had made me ravenous. I attacked and devoured all I

THE LEAP INTO THE CRATER! HA!!

met: first the Vegetarian, beginning with his grass-and-spring-onion hair and finishing with his radish toes; then the three dock-labourers; then the centipede sheep, turnips and all – accompanied by the currant-jelly-fish; then the lamb's-sweetbread-and-butterfly – all of them, finishing up with dessert and sweets – the crab-apple-pie-crustacean, the candy-tufts of the sweet-stuff-briar.

Then I turned hungrily towards Menu and Merioneth; and they plunged precipitately down the crater, and were lost to me. I remember nothing more; but believe I was picked up by a passing vessel, or a policeman, or something, in Hammersmith Broadway.

Whatever opinions were being ventured about the value or otherwise of H. G. Wells' work, there was no denying that the publicity had made him famous. It was also gradually being accepted that although his work might on the surface seem sensational, a number of the things he was projecting in his stories were proving uncannily prophetic. This talent was highlighted for the first time in the summer of 1897 following the publication of The Plattner Story and Others. *The* Academy, *an influential magazine of the arts, praised the collection highly, its critic declaring in the 29 May issue, 'no more interesting volume of short stories has appeared for a long time, and none which is so likely to give equal pleasure to the simplest reader and the most fastidious critic.' Just over a month later, on 10 July, the magazine was reporting in its 'Notes & News' column that two of the stories in the book had turned from fiction into fact . . .*

The Prophetic Powers of Mr Wells

Mr. H. G. Wells prides himself that while some of his fantastic creations may appear improbable none of them are impossible. He should therefore be glad to know that in two of the short stories in his latest book he anticipated events in almost every particular.

One of the stories, "In The Abyss' relates the experiences of a naval officer who designed a hollow steel ball, which would take him to the bottom of the sea, and in which he could live for a few hours before returning to the surface. By a remarkable coincidence, a submarine balloon of precisely the same character as that which Mr. Wells' insight enabled him to describe has just been completed by a naval constructor at Vitry-sur-Seine, and will shortly be used for bringing up ships and cargoes lying in depths too great for ordinary diving work.

The globe is about eleven feet in diameter, and will accommodate three persons. It will be let down from a ship, and grappling irons manipulated from the inside will be used for making connections with things to be hauled to the surface. Count Piatti dal Pozzo, the inventor of this submarine workman, has already descended to a depth of ninety fathoms in it, and he proposes to go as deep as three hundred fathoms.

Another instance of Mr. Wells' prophetic power is afforded by the regrettable accident to Dr. Wolfert and a companion while testing a navigable balloon at Tempelhof a few days ago.

Mr. Wells described a very similar machine in the "Argonauts of the Air"; he manned it with two persons; he propelled it, like Wolfert, with a benzine motor, and he brought it to just the same kind of end. The incidents of the Tempelhof catastrophe are, indeed, almost identical with those given in the story.

Below left: Looking the part – H. G. Wells, successful author, 1901.

Above: A crashed airship from Wells' 'The War in the Air' illustrated by A. C. Michael (1908).

The Invisible Man

In September 1897 appeared the next example of young Wells' extraordinary talent, The Invisible Man. *This, though, was not such a unique idea as his earlier books, because he made no bones about the fact that he had got the idea from a piece of verse entitled 'The Perils of Invisibility' published under the name of 'Bab' in* Fun *magazine. 'Bab' was in fact the pen-name of W. S. Gilbert (1836-1911), the parodist and librettist, who became world-famous when he wrote a string of still immensely popular light operas in partnership with Arthur Sullivan. The Bab Ballads, as they became known, were later collected together and published in a single volume in 1869 with illustrations by Gilbert himself. 'The Perils of Invisibility' is the story of Old Peter, a fat man who is beset by a nagging wife, but is suddenly offered escape by being granted three wishes. Having plumped for health and riches, Old Peter finally requests invisibility*

so that he can avoid his troublesome spouse. However, the old woman overhears this and, although she cannot prevent the wish being granted, handicaps Peter to the extent that while he may go invisible, he still feels the cold and therefore must wear clothes. So the unfortunate man is left to tramp the countryside putting the people into a state of fear at the sight of his apparently unoccupied clothes out walking! The poem ends:

> *At night, when all around is still,*
> *You'll find him pounding up a hill;*
> *And shrieking peasants whom he meets,*
> *Fall down in terror on the peats!*
>
> *Old Peter walks through wind and rain,*
> *Resolved to train, and train, and train,*
> *Until he weighs twelve stone or so –*
> *And when he does, I'll let you know.*

The following review of the book is taken from The Spectator *of 25 September 1897.*

The central notion of Mr. H. G. Wells's grotesque romance, as he has frankly admitted, has been utilised by Mr. Gilbert in one of the *Bab Ballads*, being that of a man endowed with invisibility but susceptible to heat and cold, and therefore obliged to wear clothes. But while Mr. Gilbert treated the theme in a spirit of fantastic farce, Mr. Wells has worked it out with that sombre humour and remorseless logic which stamp him as a disciple, conscious or unconscious, of the author of *Gulliver*. Swift, however, excelled in the logical conduct to its extreme consequences of some absurd proposition; Mr. Wells's method is in its essentials much more realistic. He does not posit his invisible man; he tells us how he became invisible as the result of a discovery in physiology based upon actual scientific data, for Mr. Wells is no dabbler but deeply versed in these studies. It is characteristic, again, of his method that his invisible man should be neither a buffoon nor a humourist, but a moody, irritable egotist, with a violent and vindictive temper. Griffin, in short, is really a tragic figure. His dreams of unlimited power are rudely dispelled by experience of the terrible practical drawbacks of his position, his desperate efforts to live in rustic seclusion are baffled by the curiosity of the villagers, and the exigencies of his position gradually accentuate his natural unkindliness until it develops into sheer inhumanity. Theft is followed by murder, the whole countryside is raised against him, and after he has found an asylum for a while in the house of a doctor, a fellow-student, to whom he confides the whole story of his discovery and its futility, the doctor's suspicions are aroused, information is given to the authorities, and the invisible man takes flight, with the sole desire of revenging himself on his friend. The last scenes of all, in which the invisible man, now inflamed with homicidal

Top left: 'The Invisible Man' – an illustration by Earnest Wallcousins (1934).

Left: An intriguing little sketch made by Wells on the day 'The Invisible Man' was published, 8 September 1897.

Right: The little motif which appeared on the binding of the first edition of 'The Invisible Man'.

Below: Two illustrations from 'The Perils of Invisibility' the poem by W. S. Gilbert which gave Wells the idea for 'The Invisible Man'.

Bottom: The moment of truth for 'The Invisible Man' when he reveals what has happened to himself: three panels from the Marvel Comics version of the story, 1977.

mania, besieges the doctor's house, and is finally hunted down and battered to death by the mob, are as vivid and gruesome as anything that Mr. Wells has done. As, however, he is so strong in realistic detail, we may be allowed to ask whether it is not the case that his invisible man, as an albino, would have been handicapped by short sight. To sum up, *The Invisible Man* is an amazingly clever performance, of engrossing interest throughout; we should call it fascinating were it not that the element of geniality, which lent unexpected charm to *The Wheels of Chance*, is here conspicuously absent.

The War of the Worlds

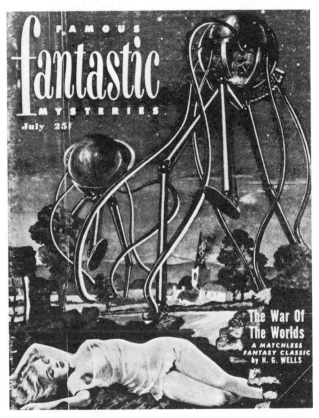

Above: Will this scantily-clad beauty halt the Martians? Stephen Lawrence drew this cover for 'Famous Fantastic Mysteries' publication of 'The War of the Worlds' in July, 1951. Actually, nothing like this happened in the story at all!

Facing page: A unique document with Pearson's comment on 'The War of the Worlds'. The scribbled note surrounded by Wells' little sketches, reads: 'Very nice tale so far. But do you mind taking the end out of the ink pot before I decide.'

The War of the Worlds remains to this day the most famous and widely read book H. G. Wells wrote. On its publication in 1898 it was greeted with laudatory reviews in both Britain and America (the items selected here are from The Academy *of 29 January 1898, and the American literary monthly,* The Bookman *of May 1898) and in no time it had assured his reputation for all time. The book can rightly be considered the forerunner of much that has subsequently been written in science fiction, and its influence is everywhere evident. In hindsight, its impact on the genre has been as great, if not greater, than any other work in the field.*

It has, of course, subsequently been imitated and parodied, serialised, filmed and broadcast (in America with the most extraordinary effect as we shall see later in the book) and even prompted sequels. Yet this groundbreaking masterpiece was born in the most prosaic way as Wells himself described in a Strand *magazine article in February 1920.*

The book was begotten by a remark of my brother Frank. We were walking together through some particularly peaceful Surrey scenery. 'Suppose some beings from another planet were to drop out of the sky suddenly,' said he, 'and begin laying about them here!' Perhaps we had been talking of the discovery of Tasmania by the Europeans – a very frightful disaster for the native Tasmanians! I forget. But that was the point of departure.

In those days I was writing short stories, and the particular sort of short story that amused me most to do was the vivid realization of some disregarded possibility in such a way as to comment on the false securities and fatuous self-satisfaction of the everyday life – as we knew it then. Because in those days the conviction that history had settled down to a sort of jog-trot comedy was very widespread indeed. Tragedy, people thought, had gone out of human life for ever. A few of us were trying to point out the obvious possibility in such a way as to comment on the false securities and fatuous self-satisfaction of the everyday some sort of world peace was not assured, but the books we wrote were regarded as the silliest of imaginative gymnastics. Well, the world knows better now.

The technical interest of a story like *The War of the Worlds* lies in the attempt to keep everything within the bounds of possibility. And the value of the story to me lies in this, that from first to last there is nothing in it that is impossible.

The Academy Review

Earth Invaded by Martians!

H. G. Wells's new book,
The War of the Worlds

I. – THE STORY.

Mr. Wells has done good work before, but nothing quite so fine as this. He has two distinct gifts – of scientific imagination and of mundane observation – and he has succeeded in bringing them together and harmoniously into play. Upon the scientific imagination depends the structure, the plot, of the whole thing. The worlds are Mars and the Earth. The Martians, whose planet, older and further from the sun than ours, was becoming uncomfortably cool, planned a descent upon a new abiding-place. Their extraordinary mechanical development enabled them to accomplish this. Projected with stupendous velocity in cylinders they alighted upon Woking Common. Here is Mr. Wells's description of one of them:

"A big greyish, rounded bulk, the size, perhaps, of a bear, was rising slowly and painfully out of the cylinder. As it bulged up and caught the light, it

The Authors' Syndicate.

Bankers:
THE UNION BANK,
CHANCERY LANE

Solicitors:
MESSRS FIELD, ROSCOE & CO
LINCOLN'S INN FIELDS

Auditors:
MESSRS OSCAR BERRY & CARR

TELEGRAPHIC ADDRESS.
BROTHER, LONDON

4 PORTUGAL STREET, LINCOLN'S INN FIELDS, W.C.

14th March 1896

Dear Mr. Wells,

Mr. Pearson is anxious to see the remainder of your story "The War of the Worlds" as soon as possible. As far as he has read he likes it very much, but says that a great deal depends on the finish of the story. I shall be glad if you will let me know when you think you can send me the remainder.

Faithfully yours,

W. Morris Colles

He was *scrambling* up the slope of the pit towards our *window* (for a moment, I thought he'd *seen* it -- and *me!*)...

...*stark terror* on his face, the Martians *cheering* him on with *gleeful hooting.*

Then, the Martians evidently decided that they'd had *enough* of this toy -- or, perhaps, they'd simply gotten *hungry.*

NNOOOOOGGG!

Whatever the reason, the man's time was up.

Their *next* victim was a *young boy.*

I actually saw the Martians *feeding* off his *just-butchered corpse,* and I wondered if this was to be *my* fate, the fate of *all mankind*...to be no more than *cattle* bound for an alien *slaughterhouse.*

Was 'The War of the Worlds' inspired in any way by Bram Stoker's vampire novel, 'Dracula'? This suggestion has been made by Gordon S. Haight of Yale University in a letter to 'Nineteenth Century Fiction' (March, 1958) in which he writes that as the Martians 'feed themselves by direct injection of human blood into the arteries' this could be 'a horror possibly suggested by the publication of Stoker's "Dracula" in 1897.' The pictures facing top left and above are from the Marvel Comics picture strip version of the story (1976) while the poster is for the 1931 film made by Universal Pictures with Bela Lugosi.

glistened like wet leather. Two large dark-coloured eyes were regarding me steadfastly. It was rounded, and had, one might say, a face. There was a mouth under the eyes, the lipless brim of which quivered and panted and dropped saliva. The body heaved and pulsed convulsively. A lank, tentacular appendage gripped the edge of the cylinder, another swayed in the air. . . . There was something fungoid in the oily brown skin, something in the clumsy deliberation of the tedious movements unspeakably terrible. Even at this first encounter, this first glimpse, I was overcome with disgust and dread. Suddenly the monster vanished. It had toppled over the brim of the cylinder and fallen into the pit, with a thud like the fall of a great mass of leather. I heard it give a peculiar thick cry, and forthwith another of these creatures appeared darkly in the deep shadow of the aperture.''

The narrator is a student of moral philosophy living at Maybury Hill, and he becomes an eye-witness of many of the strange events that follow: of the construc-

From Marvel Comics version of 'The War of the Worlds', 1976.

tion by the Martians of their fighting-machines, of their advance upon London, of the rout of the military and flight of the populace, and of the ultimate and remarkable collapse by which the world is freed from the invaders. The course of evolution on Mars has been very different to ours: the Martians have all

gone to brain. Here they move heavily because the gravitational force of the Earth is greater than they are accustomed to. But their mechanical appliances are irresistible. They mount themselves upon vast walking tripods.

"Seen nearer the thing was incredibly strange, for it was no mere insensate machine driving on its way. Machine it was, with a ringing metallic pace, and long flexible glittering tentacles (one of which gripped a young pine tree) swinging and rattling about its strange body. It picked its road as it went striding along, and the brazen hood that surmounted it moved to and fro with the inevitable suggestion of a head looking about it. Behind the main body was a huge thing of white metal like a gigantic fisherman's basket, and puffs of green smoke squirted out from the joints of the limbs as the monster swept by me. And in an instant it was gone."

With the accuracy of Mr. Wells's speculative science we deal elsewhere. It is extraordinarily detailed, and the probable departures from possibility are, at least, so contrived as not to offend the reader who has but a small smattering of exact knowledge. The consistency and definiteness of the descriptions create an adroit illusion. And, in any case, given the scientific hypotheses, the story as a whole is remarkably plausible. You feel it, not as romance, but as realism. Mr. Wells's art lies, we fancy, in the fact that, while his monsters are sufficiently like mankind to be terrible, his human beings are throughout so completely human. The inhabitants of Chertsey and Woking behave, in presence of the Martians, precisely as a Surrey suburban population would. Mr. Wells never relaxes his hold on the commonplace, everyday life, against which his marvels stand out so luridly. A thousand deft and detailed touches create an atmosphere of actuality, bring the marvels into the realistic plane. The moral philosopher himself is thoroughly natural from beginning to end. So is the drunken artilleryman, who devises a brilliant scheme for living the life of a rat in London subject to the invaders. He is not sure that it will not be better than civilisation. On the other hand, the imbecile and greedy curate with whom the narrator foregathers, and whom he is reluctantly compelled to slay, seems to us to introduce a needlessly farcical element. Mr. Wells must have suffered from curates lately, we should think.

As a crowning merit of the book, beyond its imaginative vigour and its fidelity to life, it suggests rather than obtrudes moral ideas. The artilleryman with his scorn of the "damn little clerks" who would willingly be fattened for Martian dietary, and might even be trained to hunt their wilder fellows, has some truth on his side. In the light of the imagined cataclysm certain follies and meannesses of our civilisation stand out. Our smallness, after all, in the universe receives its illustration. It is a thoughtful as well as an unusually vivid and effective bit of workmanship.

II. – MR. WELLS'S SCIENCE
Mr. H. G. Wells has probably a greater proportion of admirers among people actively engaged in scientific work than among any other section of the reading

public. It is not difficult to understand the reason of this. Nothing irritates a man of science more than incorrect assertions with reference to natural facts and phenomena; and the writer who essays to use such material must obtain information from Nature herself, or he will provoke the derision of better informed readers. Mr. Wells has a practical familiarity with the facts of science, and this knowledge, combined with his imaginative mind, enables him to command the attention of readers who are not usually interested in romance.

The fact that Mr. Wells has been able to present the planet Mars in a new light is in itself a testimony to originality. The planet has been brought within the world of fiction by several writers, but in *The War of the Worlds* an aspect of it is dealt with altogether different from what has gone before. We have had a number of stories of journeys to Mars, but hitherto, so far as we remember, the idea of an invasion by inhabitants of Mars has not been exploited. Astronomers can make out just enough of the planet's surface to justify the conclusion that water and ice or snow exist there, and that the land areas are at times traversed by a network of canals or channels more or less enigmatical in origin. According to Mr. Percival Lowell, who made an exhaustive study of Mars in 1894, these canals are really belts of fertilised land, and are the only habitable tracts on Mars, the remainder of the land surface being desert. The view that the Martians – it is less unreasonable to think that Mars is inhabited than that it is not – would look towards our Earth with longing eyes is thus quite within the bounds of legitimate speculation; and the fact that Mr. Wells put it forward before Mr. Lowell had brought before the attention of British astronomers the reasons for thinking that Mars at the present time is mostly a dreary waste from which all organic life has been driven, is a high testimony to his perceptive faculties. In other words, the reasons given for the invasion of the Earth by Mars are perfectly valid from a scientific point of view, and are supported by the latest observations of the nature of the planet's surface.

Then, as to the intellectual status of whatever inhabitants there may be on Mars, there is every reason for thinking that it would be higher than that of man. On this matter the following words, written by a distinguished observer of Mars – M. E. M. Antoniadi – in July last, give evidence to the view of the Martians presented by Mr. Wells. Referring to the origin of the canal systems, M. Antoniadi wrote:

"Perhaps the least improbable – not to say the most plausible – clue to the mystery still attaches to the overbold and almost absurd assumption that what we are witnessing on Mars is the work of rational beings immeasurably superior to man, and capable of dealing with thousands and thousands of square miles of grey and yellow material with more ease than we can cultivate or destroy vegetation in a garden one acre in extent."

Naturally, the view that beings immeasurably superior to man exist upon Mars is repugnant, but we see by the words quoted that astronomers are being forced to accept it as the easiest method of

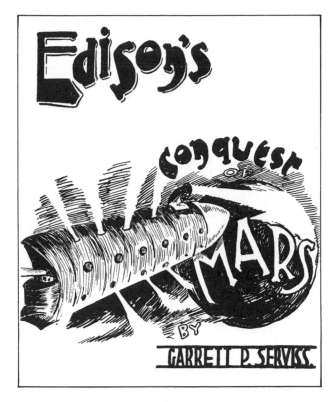

Wells' 'The War of the Worlds' was such a success when it was serialised in America in 'Cosmopolitan' magazine in 1897, that it is not surprising that it inspired a sequel, 'Edison's Conquest of Mars' in which a party of Earthmen set out to redress some of the havoc caused by the marauding Martians. The story was written by the journalist and amateur astronomer, Garrett P. Serviss, and appeared in the long-defunct 'New York Evening Journal' in the spring of 1898.

explaining the phenomena observed. Mr. Wells's idea of the invasion of the Earth by emigrants of a race possessing more effective fighting machinery than we have is thus not at all impossible; and the verisimilitude of the narrative appeals more strongly, perhaps, to scientific readers than to others not so familiar with accepted opinion upon the points deftly introduced.

The most striking characteristic of the work is not, however, the description of the Martians, but the way they are disposed of after they had invaded the Earth. We venture to assert that scientific material has never been more cleverly woven into the web of fiction than it is in the epilogue of this story. The observations of Pasteur, Chaveau, Buchner, Metschnikoff, and many others, have made the germ theory of disease an established truth. In the struggle for existence man has acquired, to a certain extent, immunity against the attacks of harmful micro-organisms, and there is little doubt that any visitors from another planet would not be able to resist these insidious germs of disease. The Earth itself furnishes analogous instances: Englishmen who migrate to the West Coast of Africa, or the strip of forest land in India known as the Terai, succumb to malarial disease, and the Pacific Islander who comes to reside in London or another large British city, almost certainly perishes from tuberculosis. Mr. Wells expresses the doctrine of acquired immunity so neatly that not to quote his words would be to do him an injustice. He says:

"These germs of disease have taken toll of humanity since the beginning of things – taken toll of our pre-human ancestors since life began here. But by virtue of this natural selection of our kind we have developed resisting power; to no germs do we succumb without a struggle, and to many – those that cause putrefaction in dead matter, for instance – our living frames are altogether immune. But there are no bacteria in Mars, and directly these invaders arrived, directly they drank and fed, our microscopic allies began to work their overthrow. Already when I watched them they were irrevocably doomed, dying and rotting even as they went to and fro. It was inevitable. By the toll of a billion deaths, man has bought his birthright of the earth, and it is his against all comers; it would still be his were the Martians ten times as mighty as they are. For neither do men live nor die in vain."

The book contains many other paragraphs which happily express scientific views, but we must refrain from quoting them. Not for an instant, however, do we think that Mr. Wells owes his success to mere correctness of statement. Science possesses a plethora of facts and ideas, yet not once in a generation does a writer arise competent to make use of them for purposes of romance. Already Mr. Wells has his imitators, but their laboured productions, distinguished either by prolixity or inaccuracy, neither excite the admiration of scientific readers nor attract the attention of the world in general.

The Martians Defeated! An illustration from the last episode of Garrett P. Serviss's 'Edison's Conquest of Mars' from the 'New York Evening Journal' of 1898. It is interesting to note that Serviss made his Martians considerably more human-like than those of H. G. Wells.

"A gun which shoots electricity is the latest invention of an enterprising American, and Mr. John Hartman, the inventor of the automatic carbine socket, which has been used in the United States Army for sixteen years, and who himself served in the Civil War, is the inventor of this new device. It is said that he has discovered conditions by which the rays of a searchlight can be charged with electricity, the beam of light thus taking the place of an ordinary wire. The individual coming within the light rays completes the circuit and falls dead. Experiments have been tried on rabbits, and with a current from a lamp of only fifty voltage he succeeded in killing a rabbit at fifty feet. We shall certainly await the details of this remarkable invention with curiosity."

I cut the above from a copy of the *Westminster Gazette* the other day, when engaged in reading Mr. Wells's new story. It set me thinking that if the Martians did not war on the world some human enemy armed with those heat-rays might, and instead of killing rabbits might kill men, until London became the silent, empty city that Mr. Wells's imagination has pictured with so much force.

That is one of the most striking points about Mr. Wells's work, that he always kindles the imagination. The thief who behind every hedge sees a constable is in a better plight than the average reader of *The War of the Worlds*, who, in every thunderstorm or convulsion of nature, will, for long years to come, think of those grim and impressive creatures from another world. There is an enormous gulf between Mr. Wells's wild imaginings and the imaginings of the men who are by some described roughly as his predecessors. The travels of Baron Munchausen and the adventures which we owe to Jules Verne are on an entirely separate plane. With these writers we are simply in fairyland; it is no disparagement that our delight in their adventure stories does not in the least disturb our sense of the fitness of things in our daily humdrum life. But Mr. Wells has set our minds agog; I do not say he has done it with that perfection of sanity which so great a subject might have called forth. A war of the worlds, if it really came, would bring us face to face with noble aspects of heroism, with infinite depths of terror, with a mingling of exquisite pathos, and – in spite of the horrors afforded – of grim humour, of a kind which do not come into the ken of Mr. Wells. I do not even deny that in *The War of the Worlds* there are certain small numbers of pages over which many readers may be excused for yawning, whereas to thoroughly convince us of so dire a catastrophe of nature as is here presented an inferior writer, equipped with some of Mr. Wells's material, would have prevented our interest from waning for a moment.

Personally, I confess to being frankly sorry that here, as in other of Mr. Wells's books, he is so little of an optimist. It has been a dream of good men for countless ages that swords shall be beaten into ploughshares and spears into pruning-hooks, and although Tennyson in our own day has talked of "the canker of peace," and told us roundly that the

Warwick Goble's heading and general view of the Martian invaders for the 'Pearson's' serialisation of 'The War of the Worlds' in 1897.

wars of armies are not more deadly than the wars of capitalists, he also has filled two or three generations with an aspiration for the time "when the war-drum throbs no longer". And yet Mr. Wells, the first novelist to turn to account for purposes of fiction the great revival of science – the New Learning – which we owe to Darwin and Lyell, to Huxley and Tyndall, unlike his masters, who were all optimists, has painted, and continues to paint, developments where life is more full of pitfalls than in our own time, and where great convulsions of nature find us morally not one whit better prepared than the eruption of Vesuvius found the people of Pompeii nearly two thousand years ago. None the less do I count the work of Mr. Wells as one of the most distinctly individual achievements of our time, on a lower literary plane, it may be, but as distinctly an individual achievement as the work of Swift in the eighteenth century, with which it has much in common. I note in passing as an interesting fact, that Mr.

Wells, among the many interpolations that he has made since his book appeared in the pages of a popular magazine, has expressed his distaste for the impossible illustrations with which the magazine serial was adorned. "I recall particularly," he says, "the illustration of one of the first pamphlets to give a consecutive account of the war. The artist had evidently made a hasty study of one of the fighting machines, and there his knowledge ended. He presented them as tilted, stiff tripods, without either flexibility or subtlety, and with an altogether misleading monotony of effect. The pamphlet containing these renderings had a considerable vogue, and I mention them here simply to warn the reader against the impression they may have created. They were no more like the machines I saw in action than a Dutch

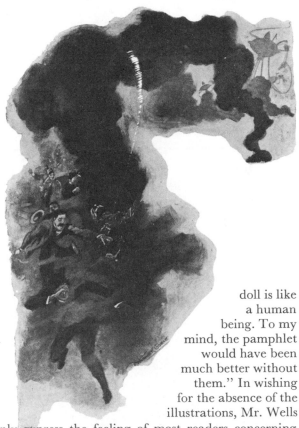

doll is like a human being. To my mind, the pamphlet would have been much better without them." In wishing for the absence of the illustrations, Mr. Wells only express the feeling of most readers concerning the illustrations to stories by their favourite authors. Who is there, since Fred Barnard illustrated Dickens's novels, and Mr. Tenniel *Alice in Wonderland*, that has entirely satisfied us in the illustration of our most approved authors? But all this is to digress from my point, which is to reiterate the conviction that among the younger writers of the day Mr. Wells is the most distinctly original, and the least indebted to predecessors. *The War of the Worlds* is a very strong and a very powerful book.

Above: More of Warwick Goble's marvellous illustrations for the 'Pearson's' serialisation of 'The War of the worlds' showing the creatures from another world running riot over the English countryside.

Facing page: Finally, simple germs bring about the downfall of the terrible invaders, but the memory of the horror they wrecked will never be forgotten . . .

The War of the Wenuses

Although in 1897, Wells was already thinking of extending his range of writing into other areas, he had an idea in his mind for 'another scientific romance of The Time Machine *and* The War of the Worlds *type'. The book was to be* When the Sleeper Wakes *which he wrote through that winter and the early part of the following year. It was not an entirely successful story – indeed Wells revised it in 1910 and republished it as* The Sleeper Awakes *– but it was another stage in his devlopment and showed how his mind was moving forward in the area of speculation about the future. The newspaper coverage of the book was surprisingly small, and perhaps the concensus of opinions was summed up by the anonymous reviewer of* The Athenaeum *in his article of 3 June 1899.*

In the Wake of the Martians

The world having survived the attack of the Martians, Mr. Wells carries on its history a stage further, and shows us what it will be two hundred years hence. The blasphemer will say, after reading Mr. Wells' prognostications, that it is a great pity that the Martians did not clear the whole place out, for a duller and more disreputable world than it becomes, always according to Mr. Wells, it would be difficult to conceive.

The chief innovation to be introduced is flying machines, which are of two kinds – aeropiles, a sort of flying private hansom, and aeroplanes, a volatile omnibus of huge capacity. For the rest, London and

As a result of its enormous impact on the public, The War of the Worlds *provided the inspiration for numerous parodies in all the media of entertainment. Perhaps the most successful was a story in verse, 'The War of the Wenuses' by two leading British humourists, Charles Graves and E. V. Lucas. The poem was dedicated, 'To H. G. Wells – this outrage on a fascinating and convincing romance,' and concerned the women of the planet Venus who had apparently grown tired of their own men because they were all invisible and consequently decided to visit Earth in the hope our men might be made of more substance. The women voyage to earth in a space ship made of crinoline, and their striking beauty soon bewitches every male who comes into contact with them. But they also quickly encounter resistence from the women of Earth and are sent packing whence they came. Nevertheless, even as they fly away they have not lost all hope of forming liasons with hen-pecked Earth-men as these closing lines describe:*

Do they think that the Wars of Wenus,
  Can be stopped by an epithet?
When the henpecked Earth-men pray us,
  To join them at afternoon tea,
Not rhyme nor reason can stay us,
  From flying to set them free.
When the men on that hapless planet,
  Handsome and kind and true,
Cry out, 'Hurry up!' O hang it!
  What else can a Wenus do?
I suppose it was rather bad form, girls,
  But really we didn't care,
For our planet was growing too warm, girls,
  And we wanted a change of air.

The man from the past rises to meet the future – a picture from 'When The Sleeper Wakes'.

other cities will be entirely roofed in, sweating will be a worse abuse than ever, and phonographs will take the place of books and newspapers. The Salvation Army will be interested to hear that its match factories are the germ of a vast system of slave labour, or something very like it; and as for the morals of our great-grand-daughters the less said about them the better.

The method by which Mr. Wells leads up to all this arid prophecy is by giving a man of this age a cataleptic trance for two hundred years, when he wakes up to find that his wealth, increasing at compound interest, has made him virtually master of the

Above: The remarkable 'Aeropile' which transports the men of the future through the air in 'When the Sleeper Wakes'.

Below: A panoramic view of the City of the Future – another illustration from 'When the Sleeper Wakes'.

world. At the end of the book he has an exciting fight from an aeropile; but on the whole he is a sorry, incoherent creature, who does not make the most of his opportunities. Mr. Wells cannot be congratulated on his latest effort; it is not very ingenious, and it is distinctly dull.

The Finding of Laura

JULES CASTIER

In 1899, Wells published another collection of the short stories he had been writing in between his novels – stories that were all much sought after by the leading magazines of the day such as Pearson's, Strand *and* The Idler *– and called the book,* Tales of Space and Time. *In greeting the collection,* The Academy *of 25 November called it an 'assemblage of examples of Mr. Wells' strange gifts' and singled one story, 'The Star' out for special praise. This tale, 'a masterpiece of dramatic progression' according to the* Academy, *described a runaway star on a collision course with the Earth and the effect it had on the people. There was no denying it was a considerable achievement to describe such an event in less than twenty pages, and the story soon became the subject of widespread public interest – it was almost as if, once again, Wells was describing something that* might *be imminent. In fact he had drawn on an earlier story,* La Fin du Monde (1893) *by the French author of cosmic romances, Camille de Flammarion. Flammarion's tale, though, was about a comet set to collide with the earth, and had no more pretentions than being just another 'end of the world' fantasy – Wells, for his part, turned the idea into a brilliant allegory. Once again, too, it was not long before someone produced a parody of 'The Star', and perhaps appropriately it was a Frenchman, Jules Castier, who achieved this with 'The Finding of Laura'. As both a parody of Wells and an ingenious piece of science fiction it is well worth reprinting today.*

Chapter 1 – The New Planet

I

Of course, it is all very obvious and quite natural to us who live in the 22nd century, but to the primitive men and women who existed about 2050, over a hundred years ago, the whole thing bordered on the marvellous – that obsolescent realm of fuzzy-headed ignorance and fungoid growth of erroneous learning.

That would be just about the time that Ferrers had created his first model of hyper-atomic motor, bringing the long and laborious researches of Lesage, Tomkins, and Guglielmo to a sound, if unexpected, conclusion. The presumptuous men of those early days would, of course, be inordinately proud of a machine that gave them about six million HP to the gramme; (it is useful to remember that the first motor founded on atomic dispersion barely gave a thousandth part of that, and yet our distant ancestors went clean head over heels with the joy of possessing what was, to them, such a condensed form of energy). Zuccolo, I believe, was the first to make use of the Ferrers motor for any really original purpose, and he constructed an antiquated species of self-propelling sphere, that just managed to defeat the acceleration of gravity in the atmosphere of the earth, pursued its puny course through ether, and was eventually attracted by the power of gravity towards some other celestial globe. . . . But this bold outline of facts is by now known to everyone with the slightest taste for historical erudition, and I need not dwell on it further than by mentioning that Harvey and Jones were the first two Telluric men who set foot on another globe than theirs, the former on the moon, the latter on Mars. . . .

II

Little by little, our ancestors discovered the less near planets, and even ventured to some of the most visible stars. It is difficult for us to comprehend the extraordinary enthusiasm that our grandfathers evidenced for the exploration of the cosmic bodies; now that we have a thrice daily service from our

North Pole to the Equator of Neptune (with restaurant accommodation), such nonsensical emotion seems altogether out of place. But let us not forget that we are looking at the past from the angle of the present times; if we try to focus our spiritual lens at the correct distance of time, all these things become clearer.

Little by little, as I remarked, all the globes became known to our race – not without difficulty, of course, on account of the feeble speed that could be extracted from the Ferrers-Zuccolo shooting sphere. Those were the days of compressed oxygen, and albumin tabloids. . . . Still, our ancestors mastered most of the planets, including Uranus and Neptune, and their satellites; one audacious man of those days (I forget his name for the moment) was even so fortunate (aided by a happy fluke in ethereal trade-vibrations) as to drop clean on to Sirius.

III

Then it was that H. G. Laurence, FTSS – (those were the openings days of the Telluric Science Society) made his discovery of a new planet. He founded his calculations on the perturbations of Uranus, and was rewarded just as his erstwhile predecessor Leverrier, a now forgotten astronomer who flourished in the nineteenth century, had been – with the exact coordinates of his perturbing body. All the observatories were turned toward the spot located by Laurence, and sure enough, at the appointed hour, there appeared the newcomer in our little collection of planets. I say "at the appointed hour", but that is not strictly correct, the new planet as a matter of fact putting in its appearance about seven minutes later than the scheduled time. The fact was overlooked, of course, and simply put down to a slight error in Laurence's computations, though he always maintained them to be strictly accurate. Anyway, his planet was named Laura, and he was immensely proud of his discovery, and full of a spirit of benevolent waggery towards

anyone who had appeared to doubt his assertions. He was elected PTSS for ten years, because his achievement was considered to be quite the highest thing that could possibly be done in that period of time, and he was awarded the first solid helium medal the Telluric Science Society ever gave any of its members.

Of course, Laurence had not only calculated the coordinates of his planet for a given time, but he had also computed its distance, diameter, specific weight, age, chemical constitution, and so on. There seemed to be nothing ostensibly remarkable or irrationally novel in all these figures – beyond the fact that its average distance from the earth was something over double that of Neptune.

IV

There was something tragically humorous in the endeavours made to explore Laura, as all the other planets had been explored. Of course, the distance was great (for the time: remember all that is more than a hundred years ago), but the fact of Sirius having been reached laid aside *that* objection before it was even formulated.

All the keenest cosmic explorers of the day set out, in what was then the latest cry of Ferrers-Zuccolo shooting spheres; men like Gerald Brown and Leon Lambert, the most foolhardy and enterprising of their kind, made attempt on attempt. Some of them even took Neptune as a secondary starting point; some tried Uranus instead, as nearer the new planet's latest position; they perfected their motors, and dropped every milligramme of superfluous weight; but it remains a fact that they never reached the planet Laura. Somehow, when they got within anything like reasonable distance of it, they regularly had a break-down in their motors, or some petty disturbance stopped their further advance; one of these would-be explorers even goes to the length of saying that he was beginning to see the mountains and lakes on Laura's surface (through his wireless optoscope, of course), when a gust of swelling ether forced him back again, and he had to take refuge on one of the secondary satellites of Jupiter.

And just at the same time there began to be greater errors in the locating of the new planet. It became more and more in advance over its scheduled time, and the fact, of course, drew attention to the initial seven minutes lateness when it had first been discovered. And then, suddenly, it seemed to disappear: however sharp the observatories proved themselves to be, Laura was sharper still, as if it took pleasure in mocking both the astronomers and the explorers.

Everybody felt the keenest interest in the mystery, and Laurence himself was clean baffled by it. He did all his calculations over and over again, and had them looked through by his most eminent colleagues; but they found no trace of an error – and Laura continued to be as unfindable and unapproachable as ever.

Chapter 2 – The Counter-gravity

I

It will be remembered Green's anti-gravity screen was discovered in the opening months of 2051. The principle of the apparatus was not unlike Faraday's classic electric screen (Faraday was a primitive 19th

Above and facing page: Two illustrations from
Camille de Flammarion's 'La Fin du Monde' (1893)
about a star on a collision course with the Earth.

Wells used this same idea for his own highly-
praised short story, 'The Star'.

CHRISTINA ALBERTA'S FATHER

by H.G. WELLS

JOHN · AVETEN ·

H. G. Wells' strange later novel about the retired
laundryman, Mr Preemby, who becomes involved
in spiritualism and dreams of ruling the world.
This cover for 'Christina Alberta's Father' was
drawn by John Aveten in 1925.

century scientist, now hardly remembered, but fairly well-known in his day); by means of a wire netting through which an alternative electro-telluric current was switched on and off, the effects of gravity were more or less completely counterbalanced – sufficiently so, at all events, for the men of those days to be quite proud of the discovery. Of course, they had not yet mastered the correct nature of the force of gravity, and still clung to Newton's obsolete views on the subject.

With the aid of Green's rudimentary apparatus, it at all events became possible to experiment upon what were then new and undreamt-of sensations. Non-gravity aviation became an everyday matter, and travel over the surface of the earth mere child's play. The idea was, of course, for the aviator to ascend to some distance from terra-firma (any distance, though greater than the altitude of the highest mountains), and then to switch on his Green anti-gravity screen. When, in the course of its customary rotation, the earth had turned beneath him so as to present him with a view of his destination, he switched off the screen and suffered gravity to put him down where he wanted to go. There was hardly any expenditure of energy, and the entire process was so gluckingly simple, that it always remains a mystery that it had not been thought of earlier.

But it is hardly useful dwelling on so well-known a subject.

II

Of course everyone still remembers the sensation that arose from the flights of R. W. Rugban. He was a simple bottle-washer in Green's laboratory, and a man without any special scientific culture. Nevertheless, it is to a lucky freak of his that the men of those days owed the clearing up of the mystery that flocculated around the planet Laura.

Rugban conceived the idea of adapting an anti-gravity screen to one of the Ferrers-Zuccolo shooting spheres, the hyper-atomic motor producing the electro-telluric current necessary to the mechanism of the screen. There was no ultimate motive about this idea of the bottle-washer's – it was simply one of those lucky flukes without which all the genius of our greatest scientists can but produce rudimentary results, without obtaining objective certainty.

Naturally, the adapting of the Green Screen to the shooting sphere entailed no gain of motive power, the expenditure in electro-telluric current being far greater than the gain due to the annihilation of gravity near our planet. That is probably why no scientific man had thought of the combination. But the fact remains that Rugban actually landed on Laura on his fourteenth flight.

He proved his assertion beyond a shadow of a doubt, by bringing back with him a fragment of Laura soil – which contained the (then) unknown body of Laurium, characterised by Laurence's statement, and located in Laura's spectrum, while the planet had been visible. Further, he was able to give the accurate distances between Laura, Uranus and the earth, and the observatories were thus enabled to hit upon the mysterious planet once more. That, however, was not for any considerable length of time. Laura still kept ahead of its computed position, and it was at last ascertained that its trajectory could not possibly be the one Laurence had assigned

it in accordance with all the astronomical laws then known.

The revelation came with Rugban's fifteenth flight, when he set foot on Laura for the second time, and triumphantly brought back one of the inhabitants of the elusive planet. It was a curiously shaped creature, with three legs and five arms, a head of sorts, and a body not unlike those that populate the smaller satellites of Neptune. The curious and salient fact about the Lauran, however, was that it insisted on standing *on its hands*, that were provided with a species of vacuum-sucking-knobs, and thus got so firm a grip of everything it was put upon that it became well-nigh impossible to move it. The Lauran explained by signs how anxious it was not to be shot out of the terrestrial atmosphere, and when Rugban started the anti-gravity screen above the creature's feet, it began to quake and shiver with terror. It calmed down as soon as the current was switched off, and again lost itself in voluble, if incomprehensible, explanations.

They tried to grasp the meaning of the Lauran's torrent of words, but it was impossible to make anything of them without the help of a proper interpreter. Green called Lug-Hsn, the ex-Neptune native, who seemed to catch the gist of what was being said. And then the explanation came, perfectly simple and convincing.

On the planet Laura, said the new-brought creature, *weight was a negative force*; everything was attracted *into space*, away from the planet's atmosphere. Of course, all the living species had to be provided with vacuum-sucking-knobs in order to remain on the planet at all – and that was why the Lauran had been so frenzied lest he should lose hold of the earth. The law of inverse ratio to the square of the distance had been proved to exist by the Lauran scientists, but this was a centrifugal, and not centripetal, force on their planet.

Naturally, the whole aspect of the case was completely changed; Laurence immediately resumed his computations (founding them upon a change of sign in his equations). It was child's play to deduce the true trajectory of the new planet – a hyperbola, of course, instead of the customary ellipse. It had been an astounding stroke of good luck that Laura had been discovered at all; it was just in the region of the curve's centre when Laurence had made his sensational discovery; but now it was already speeding through ether along one of its asymptotic branches.

Laura became the converging focus of all the observatories once more, and they were able to trace its flight nearer and nearer its located asymptote, till at last its distance became greater than the power of even the greatest equatorials then existing, and the new planet disappeared for ever from our field of vision. . . .

The First Men in the Moon

Ever since his childhood discovery of moon travel in the adventures of Baron Munchausen, Wells had never lost the desire to write a book about a journey to earth's neigh-

Above: The two astronauts, Bedford and Cavor, enter their space ship as they set out to become 'The First Men in the Moon'. This illustration, and all those in this section, are by Claude A. Shepperson, who drew them for the first serialisation of the story in 'The Strand Magazine', 1900-1.

Below: Bedford, the narrator of 'The First Men in the Moon', watches fascinated as the space ship flies him to the moon.

Facing page: Safely landed on the moon, Bedford watches his companion discover the change in gravity as he makes prodigious leaps.

bouring planet. When, at the turn of the new century, he set about this, he abandoned much of the fantasy which had featured so prominently in his earlier works, and tried to make The First Men in the Moon *as realistic and factually correct as possible. Perhaps no other review quite expressed so well what Wells had achieved in this, the other of his most enduring books, than the highly regarded journal,* Nature, *in its issue of 9 January 1902. And as this was a publication written by scientists and scholars for scientists and scholars, its considered opinion is all the more important.*

A LUNAR ROMANCE.
The First Men in the Moon. By H. G. Wells. Pp. 312. (London: George Newnes, 1901.) Price 6s.

It is many years now since Jules Verne wrote his imaginary account of a journey to the moon. He supposed a party of three men enclosed in a projectile shot by a huge gun towards the moon, which they never reached; they fell back to earth and escaped in a marvellous manner to tell the tale. The work was imaginative enough to hold the attention, but full of scientific blunders and improbabilities of the most glaring character. Mr. Wells has produced a book of a very different character; he has made himself master of the little we know about the moon, and thought out the possibilities with the greatest care, and the result is a narrative which we will venture to say is not only as exciting to the average reader as Jules Verne's, but is full of interest to the scientific man. We do not mean that the astronomer is likely to learn any new facts from this *résumé*, for which he himself furnished the material; but he will be astonished to find how different the few scientific facts with which he is familiar look in the dress in which a skilful and imaginative writer can clothe them, and it is worth reading the book with minute care to see if one cannot catch Mr. Wells in any little scientific slip. Some writers are so easy to catch that the game is not worth playing; but Mr. Wells is a worthy opponent, and we are glad to see that his scientific rank has been recognised by the Royal Institution, who have invited him to lecture.

The visit to the moon is made possible by the discovery of a substance (cavorite) impervious to gravitation. This interesting property comes to

cavorite only at a critical temperature (60° F.), after "the paste has been heated to a dull red glow in a stream of helium," and the suddenness with which the imperviousness arrives causes interesting events at first. When the new conditions are better realised, a glass sphere is built and covered with cavorite blinds which can be put up or down. When all are down the sphere is entirely free from attraction, and when any particular blind is up it is only attracted by the stars or planets seen in that direction. It is obvious that in these circumstances a comfortable voyage through space is manageable. The two occupants of the sphere journey to the moon and land upon it near the terminator, on a snow drift of frozen air. With sunrise they find that the air melts and evaporates, and there is enough for them to breathe, so that they emerge from the sphere. They find their weight a trivial matter and leap twenty or thirty yards at a step, and a

Bedford and Cavor get their first sight of a moon creature.

Below: The intrepid explorers come face to face with the inhabitants of the moon, the Selenites.

speckled green mossy plant. The cowherd was a "mere ant" by comparison, and the intelligent Selenites generally turn out to be a sort of insect, varied physically in a grotesque manner at will. After various adventures in and on the moon, one of the voyagers recovers the sphere and gets back to earth; the other stays in the moon and sends messages by ethereal telegraphy describing it more fully; and the interest never flags throughout. Following similar writings, Mr. Wells sometimes allows himself a sly hint at terrestrial matters in describing lunar affairs. He describes a lunar artist thus (p. 302):—

"Love draw. No other thing. Hate all who not draw like him. Angry. Hate all who draw like him better. Hate most people. Hate all who not think all world for to draw."

Bedford battles against the attacking ranks of Selenites.

wonderful fungus vegetation springs up before their eyes. In the exhilaration of exploring they lose their sphere and are thus thrown on their own resources. Presently they come across the Selenites, who emerge from the interior of the moon, where they have been spending the lunar night. The first to emerge are those herding the moon calves – great beasts 200 feet long, that browse in a vividly described and rather disgusting manner ("like stupendous slugs") on a

And two pages on there is a similar burlesque description of a mathematician. It is even easier to see the point than to find the pun in the following:—

"And since the density of the moon is only three-fifths that of the earth, there can be nothing for it but that she is hollowed out by a great system of caverns. There was no necessity, said Sir Jabez Flap, F. R. S., that most entertaining exponent of the facetious side of the stars, that we should ever have gone to the moon to find out such easy inferences, and points the pun with an allusion to Gruyère . . ."

**Top left: Cavor is seized by a group of Selenites
and carried off to their dwelling place.**

**Bottom left: Cavor conversing with the leaders of
the moon people about their way of life.**

**Above: An unhappy end for the luckless Cavor. The
final moments of 'The First Men in the Moon'.**

Of a book so full of unfamiliar things it is impossible
to give a complete account. We will conclude this
notice by heartily recommending the book to readers
both scientific and unscientific, and by giving, with a
triumph not free from trepidation, an instance where
we think Mr. Wells has been caught napping. When
the cavorite blinds are closed and the sphere starts on
its journey, he describes the curious effects of the
absence of external gravitational attraction – all the
material occupants of the sphere slowly collect in the
interior by their *mutual* attractions, and there is no
"up" or "down." Then a window is opened towards
the moon and promptly everything gravitates towards the moon – the direction towards the moon is
downwards, though the attraction is slight. Surely this
is a slip? With bodies moving freely in space only the
differential attraction would be felt, and this would be
negligible compared with the mutual attraction of the
occupants of the sphere. Even if it were not so small it
could not act in the manner specified; its tendency
would be to *separate* bodies (as in the case of the tides),
not to bring them together, and thus a man near a
"floor" would not fall towards it but would rise from
it. But Mr. Wells is so wonderfully careful in general
that we make this criticism with far less confidence
than we should have felt in another case; we have an
uneasy feeling that he may dexterously transfer the
supposed slip from his account to ours.

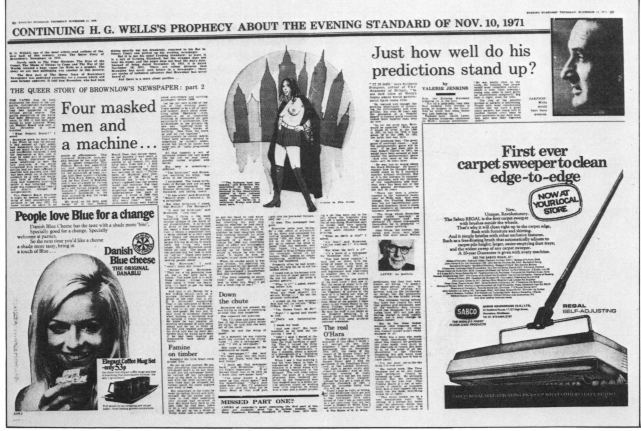

The forgotten H. G. Wells' story which featured the London newspaper, the 'Evening Standard', and which that paper especially revived on 10 and 11 November 1971. 'The Queer Story of Brownlow's Newspaper' described a man receiving a copy of the 'Standard' in 1931 dated forty years ahead and picturing the world as it then was. These illustrations show how the 'Standard' presented the tale of prophecy, and the full version of the text is printed on the pages which follow . . .

The Queer Story of Brownlow's Newspaper

H. G. WELLS

Once the twentieth century had arrived, Wells was busy in other fields as a writer of serious novels and delivering his essays on social conditions, and sadly there was no time for more works like The War of the Worlds *and* The First Men in the Moon. *When, in 1929,* The Collected Stories of H. G. Wells *was published it seemed that the great man had even turned his back on this form, too. But not so – for in 1931 he wrote one more short story which has never been included in any collection of his works and is virtually unknown to all but Wells' enthusiasts. The tale is called 'The Queer Story of Brownlow's Newspaper' and deals with one of Wells' favourite themes – a man glimpsing what the future holds for humanity. Wells added authenticity to his tale by choosing his own favourite newspaper, the London* Evening Standard, *as the medium by which his reader 'sees' into the future. By a twist of time, the reader of 1931 is delivered a copy of the* Evening Standard *for forty years hence and reads of a world as Wells thought it might be. Just how accurate he was you can judge for yourself. The story made its original appearance in an American publication,* Ladies' Home Journal *in 1932 (a surprising choice!) and was then completely forgotten until the* Evening Standard *itself was reminded of the tale and published a cut version on exactly the day forty years hence that Wells had selected – 10 November 1971. For its republication here, though, we have returned to the first and full version. (It is perhaps sad to have to add by way of a postscript that the* Standard *could not find the Mr Evan O'Hara of Sussex Court who should have received a forty-year-old copy of the paper that 10 November. But then of such are mysteries made!)*

I call this a Queer Story because it is a story without an explanation. When I first heard it, in scraps, from Brownlow I found it queer and incredible. But – it refuses to remain incredible. After resisting and then questioning and scrutinizing and falling back before the evidence, after rejecting all his evidence as an elaborate mystification and refusing to hear any more about it, and then being drawn to reconsider it by an irresistible curiosity and so going through it all again, I have been forced to the conclusion that Brownlow, so far as he can tell the truth, has been telling the truth. But it remains queer truth, queer and exciting to the imagination. The more credible his story becomes the queerer it is. It troubles my mind. I am fevered by it, infected not with germs but with notes of interrogation and unsatisfied curiosity.

Brownlow is, I admit, a cheerful spirit. I have known him to tell lies. But I have never known him to do anything so elaborate and sustained as this affair, if it is a mystification, would have to be. He is incapable of anything so elaborate and sustained. He is too lazy and easy-going for anything of the sort. And he would have laughed. At some stage he would have laughed and given the whole thing away. And after all there is his bit of newspaper in evidence – and the scrap of an addressed wrapper. . . .

I realized it will damage this story for many readers

An evocative painting by Dudley Tennant for one of Wells' best short stories, 'The Country of the Blind'.

that it opens with Brownlow in a state very definitely on the gayer side of sobriety. He was not in a mood for cool and calculated observation, much less for accurate record. He was seeing things in an exhilarated manner. He was disposed to see them and greet them cheerfully and let them slip by out of attention. The limitations of time and space lay upon him. It was after midnight. He had been dining with friends.

I have inquired what friends – and satisfied myself upon one or two obvious possibilities of that dinner party. They were, he said to me, "just friends. They hadn't anything to do with it." I don't usually push past an assurance of this sort, but I made an exception in this case. I watched my man and took a chance of repeating the question. There was nothing out of the ordinary about that dinner party, unless it was the fact that it was an unusually good dinner party. The host was Redpath Baynes, the solicitor, and the dinner was in his house in St. John's Wood. Gifford, of the *Evening Telegraph*, whom I know slightly, was, I found, present, and from him I got all I wanted to know. There was much bright and discursive talk and Brownlow had been inspired to give an imitation of his aunt, Lady Clitherholme, reproving an inconsiderate plumber during some re-building operations at Clitherholme. This early memory had been received with considerable merriment – he was always very good about his aunt, Lady Clitherholme – and Brownlow had departed obviously elated by this little social success and the general geniality of the occasion. Had they talked, I asked, about the Future, or Einstein, or J. W. Dunne, or any such high and serious topic at that party? They had not. Had they discussed the modern newspaper? No. There had been nobody

THE STOLEN BACILLUS

A Tale of Anarchy.

BY H. G. WELLS.

Above: 'The Stolen Bacillus' the first of what Wells called his 'single sitting stories' here published in 'Pearson's Magazine' in 1905. Of these tales, Wells later wrote, 'After a time I became quite dexterous in evolving incidents and anecdotes from little possibilities of a scientific or quasi-scientific sort.'

Below: F. G. Moorsom's illustration for Wells' delightful story 'The Inexperienced Ghost' published in a 1936 anthology of supernatural tales.

whom one could call a practical joker at this party, and Brownlow had gone off alone in a taxi. That is what I was most desirous of knowing. He had been duly delivered by his taxi at the main entrance to Sussex Court.

Nothing untoward is to be recorded of his journey in the lift to the fifth floor of Sussex Court. The liftman on duty noted nothing exceptional. I asked if Brownlow said, "Good night." The liftman does not remember. "Usually he says Night O," reflected the liftman – manifestly doing his best and with nothing particular to recall. And there the fruits of my inquiries about the condition of Brownlow on this particular evening conclude. The rest of the story comes directly from him. My investigations arrive only at this: he was certainly not drunk. But he was lifted a little out of our normal harsh and grinding contact with the immediate realities of existence. Life was glowing softly and warmly in him, and the unexpected could happen brightly, easily, and acceptably.

He went down the long passage with its red carpet, its clear light, and its occasional oaken doors, each with its artistic brass number. I have been down that passage with him on several occasions. It was his custom to enliven that corridor by raising his hat gravely as he passed each entrance, saluting his unknown and invisible neighbours, addressing them softly but distinctly by playful if sometimes slightly indecorous names of his own devising, expressing good wishes or paying them little compliments.

He came at last to his own door, number 49, and let himself in without serious difficulty. He switched on his hall light. Scattered on the polished floor and invading his Chinese carpet were a number of letters and circulars, the evening's mail. His parlourmaid-housekeeper, who slept in a room in another part of the building, had been taking her evening out, or these letters would have been gathered up and put on the desk in his bureau. As it was, they lay on the floor. He closed his door behind him or it closed of its own accord; he took off his coat and wrap, placed his hat on the head of the Greek charioteer whose bust adorns his hall, and set himself to pick up his letters.

This also he succeeded in doing without misadventure. He was a little annoyed to miss the *Evening Standard*. It is his custom, he says, to subscribe for the afternoon edition of the *Star* to read at tea-time and also for the final edition of the *Evening Standard* to turn over the last thing at night, if only on account of Low's cartoon. He gathered up all these envelopes and packets and took them with him into his little sitting-room. There he turned on the electric heater, mixed himself a whisky-and-soda, went to his bedroom to put on soft slippers and replace his smoking jacket by a frogged jacket of llama wool, returned to his sitting-room, lit a cigarette, and sat down in his arm-chair by the reading lamp to examine his correspondence. He recalls all these details very exactly. They were routines he had repeated scores of times.

Brownlow's is not a preoccupied mind; it goes out to things. He is one of those buoyant extroverts who open and read all their letters and circulars whenever they can get hold of them. In the daytime his secretary intercepts and deals with most of them, but at night he escapes from her control and does what he pleases, that is to say, he opens everything.

He ripped various envelopes. Here was a formal acknowledgement of a business letter he had dictated the day before, there was a letter from his solicitor asking for some details about a settlement he was making, there was an offer from some unknown gentleman with an aristocratic name to lend him money on his note of hand alone, and there was a notice about a proposed new wing to his club. "Same old stuff. What bores they all are!" He was always hoping, like every man who is proceeding across the plain of middle-age, that his correspondence would contain agreeable surprises – and it never did. Then, as he put it to me, *inter alia*, he picked up the remarkable newspaper.

The first publication of 'The Story of the Inexperienced Ghost' in the 'Strand' in March 1902. The illustration was by W. G. Stacey.

It was different in appearance from an ordinary newspaper, but not so different as not to be recognizable as a newspaper, and he was surprised, he says, not to have observed it before. It was enclosed in a wrapper of pale green, but it was unstamped; apparently it had been delivered not by the postman, but by some other hand. (This wrapper still exists; I have seen it.) He had already torn it off before he noted that he was not the addressee.

For a moment or so he remained looking at this address, which struck him as just a little odd. It was printed in rather unusual type: "Evan O'Hara Mr., Sussex Court 49."

"Wrong name," said Mr. Brownlow; "Right address. Rummy. Sussex Court 49 . . . 'Spose he's got *my Evening Standard* . . . 'Change no robbery.' "

He put the torn wrapper with his unanswered letters and opened out the newspaper.

The title of the paper was printed in large slightly ornamental black-green letters that might have come from a kindred fount to that responsible for the address. But, as he read it, it was the *Evening Standard!* Or, at least, it was the "Even Standrd." "Silly," said Brownlow. "It's some damn Irish paper. Can't spell – anything – these Irish . . ."

He had, I think, a passing idea, suggested perhaps by the green wrapper and the green ink, that it was a lottery stunt from Dublin.

Still, if there was anything to read he meant to read it. He surveyed the front page. Across this ran a streamer headline: "WILTON BORING REACHES SEVEN MILES: SUCCESS ASSURED."

"No," said Brownlow. "It must be oil . . . Illiterate lot these oil chaps – leave out the 's' in 'success.' "

He held the paper down on his knee for a moment,

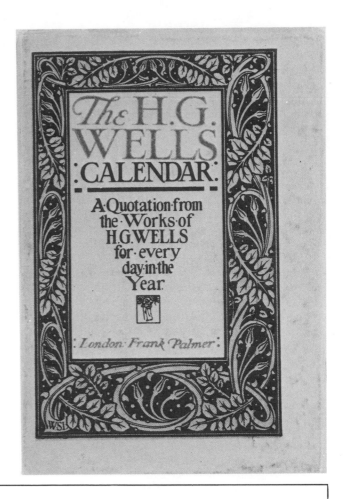

Right: Cover of a rare Wells item published in 1911 which drew extensively on his early novels and short stories for quotations – 'The H. G. Wells Calendar' published by Frank Palmer.

H. G. WELLS

Four

Scientific prophecy will not be fortune-telling, whatever else it may be.

Five

The world has a purpose greater than happiness ; our lives are to serve God's purpose, and that purpose aims not at man as an end, but works through him to greater issues.

Six

Life is morality ; life is adventure. Squire and master. Adventure rules, and morality—looks up the trains in the Bradshaw. Morality tells you what is right, and adventure moves you.

Seven

Women, I am convinced, are as fine as men ; they can be as wise as men ; they are capable of far greater devotion than men.—Remington in *The New Machiavelli.*

24

MARCH

Eight

True brotherhood is universal brotherhood.

Nine

We think, because things have been easy for mankind as a whole for a generation or so, we are going on to perfect comfort and security in the future. We think that we shall always go to work at ten and leave off at four, and have dinner at seven for ever and ever.

Ten

After thirty there are few conversions and fewer fine beginnings ; men and women go on in the path they have marked out for themselves.

Eleven

Ideals are not the easiest possessions to have and manage, and they may even rise to the level of serious inconveniences. —My Uncle in *Select Conversations.*

25

reinforced himself by a drink, took and lit a second cigarette, and then leant back in his chair to take a dispassionate view of any oil-share pushing that might be a foot.

But it wasn't an affair of oil. It was, it began to dawn upon him, something stranger than oil. He found himself surveying a real evening newspaper, which was dealing so far as he could see at the first onset, with the affairs of another world.

He had for a moment a feeling as though he and his arm-chair and his little sitting-room were afloat in a vast space and then it all seemed to become firm and solid again.

This thing in his hands was plainly and indisputably a printed newspaper. It was a little odd in its letter-press, and it didn't feel or rustle like ordinary paper, but newspaper it was. It was printed in either three or four columns – for the life of him he cannot remember which – and there were column headlines under the page streamer. It had a sort of art-nouveau affair at the bottom of one column that might be an advertisement (it showed a woman in an impossibly big hat), and in the upper left-hand corner was an unmistakable weather chart of Western Europe, with *coloured* isobars, or isotherms, or whatever they are, and the inscription: "Tomorrow's Weather."

And then he remarked the date. The date was November 10th, 1971!

"Steady on," said Brownlow. "Damitall! Steady on."

He held the paper sideways, and then straight again. The date remained November 10th, 1971.

He got up in a state of immense perplexity and put the paper down. For a moment he felt a little afraid of it. He rubbed his forehead. "Haven't been doing a Rip Van Winkle, by any chance, Brownlow, my boy?" he said. He picked up the paper again, walked out into his hall and looked at himself in the hall mirror. He was reassured to see no signs of advancing age, but the expression of mingled consternation and amazement upon his flushed face struck him suddenly as being undignified and unwarrantable. He laughed at himself, but not uncontrollably. Then he stared blankly at that familiar countenance "I must be halfway *tordu*," he said, that being his habitual facetious translation of "screwed." On the console table was a little respectable-looking adjustable calendar bearing witness that the date was November 10th, 1931.

"D'you see?" he said, shaking the queer newspaper at it reproachfully. "I ought to have spotted you for a hoax ten minutes ago. Moosing trick, to say the least of it. I suppose they've made Low editor for a night, and he's had this idea. Eh?"

He felt he had been taken in, but that the joke was a good one. And, with quite unusual anticipations of entertainment, he returned to his arm-chair. A good idea it was, a paper forty years ahead. Good fun if it was well done. For a time nothing but the sounds of a newspaper being turned over and Brownlow's breathing can have broken the silence of the flat.

Regarded as an imaginative creation, he found the thing almost too well done. Every time he turned a page he expected the sheet to break out into laughter and give the whole thing away. But it did nothing of the kind. From being a mere quip, it became an immense and amusing, if perhaps a little over-elaborate, lark. And then, as a lark, it passed from stage to stage of incredibility until, as anything but the thing it professed to be, it was incredible altogether. It must have cost far more than an ordinary number. All sorts of colours were used, and suddenly he came upon illustrations that went beyond amazement; they were in the colours of reality. Never in his life had he seen such colour printing – and the buildings and scenery and costumes in the pictures were strange. Strange and yet credible. They were colour photographs of actuality, forty years from now. He could not believe anything else of them. Doubt could not exist in their presence.

His mind had swung back, away from the stunt-number idea altogether. This paper in his hand would not simply be costly beyond dreaming to produce. At any price it could not be produced. All this present world could not produce such an object as this paper

'The Trick of the Mirror' picture by Edmund J. Sullivan which Wells considered the best illustration of his work.

he held in his hand. He was quite capable of realizing that.

He sat turning the sheet over and – quite mechanically – drinking whisky. His sceptical faculties were largely in suspense; the barriers of criticism were down. His mind could now accept the idea that he was reading a newspaper of forty years ahead without further protest.

It had been addressed to Mr. Evan O'Hara, and it had come to him. Well and good. This Evan O'Hara evidently knew how to get ahead of things. . . .

I doubt if at that time Brownlow found anything very wonderful in the situation.

Yet it was, it continues to be, a very wonderful situation. The wonder of it mounts to my head as I write. Only gradually have I been able to build up this picture of Brownlow turning over that miraculous sheet, so that I can believe it myself. And you will understand how, as the thing flickered between credibility and incredibility in my mind, I asked him, partly to justify or confute a vast expanding and, at last, devouring curiosity: "What was there in it? What did it have to say?" At the same time, I found myself trying to catch him out in his story, and also asking him for every particular he could give me.

What was there in it? In other words, what will the world be doing forty years from now? That was the

POLLOCK AND THE PORROH MAN
by H. G. Wells

Author of "The Time Machine," "A Story of the Stone Age," etc.

But he was not quick enough to prevent the man, who was anxious to get to Pollock's side of the bargain, from opening the cloth and throwing the head of the Porroh man upon the table. It bounded from there onto the floor, leaving a red trail on the cards, and rolled to the side, where it came to rest upside down, but glaring hard at Pollock.

stupendous scale of the vision, of which Brownlow was afforded a glimpse. The world forty years from now! I lie awake at nights thinking of all that paper might have revealed to us. Much it did reveal, but there is hardly a thing it reveals that does not change at once into a constellation of riddles. When first he told me about the thing I was – it is, I admit, an enormous pity – intensely sceptical. I asked him questions in what people call a "nasty" manner. I was ready – as my manner made plain to him – to jump down his throat with "But that's preposterous!" at the very first slip. And I had an engagement that carried me off at the end of half an hour.

But the thing had already got hold of my imagination, and I rang up Brownlow before tea-time, and was biting at this "queer story" of his again. That afternoon he was sulking because of my morning's disbelief, and he told me very little. "I was drunk and dreaming, I suppose," he said. "I'm beginning to doubt it all myself." In the night it occurred to me for the first time that, if he was not allowed to tell and put on record what he had seen, he might become both confused and sceptical about it himself. Fancies might mix up with it. He might hedge and alter to get it more credible. Next day, therefore, I lunched and spent the afternoon with him, and arranged to go

The pioneer American Science Fiction magazine, 'Amazing Stories', and its Editor, Hugo Gernsback, were great enthusiasts of Wells short stories. Here are just two of the many tales they reprinted: (facing page) 'Pollock and the Porroh Man' from the February, 1928 issue, and (below) 'The Remarkable Case of Davidson's Eyes' from April, 1927.

down into Surrey for the weekend. I managed to dispel his huffiness with me. My growing keenness restored his. There we set ourselves in earnest, first of all to recover everything he could remember about his newspaper and then to form some coherent idea of the world about which it was telling.

It is perhaps a little banal to say we were not trained men for the job. For who could be considered trained for such a job as we were attempting? What facts was he to pick out as important and how were they to be arranged? We wanted to know everything we could about 1971; and the little facts and the big facts crowded on one another and offended against each other.

The streamer headline across the page about that seven-mile Wilton boring, is, to my mind one of the most significant items in the story. About that we are fairly clear. It referred, says Brownlow, to a series of attempts to tap the supply of heat beneath the surface of the earth. I asked various questions. "It was *explained*, y'know," said Brownlow, and smiled and held out a hand with twiddling fingers.

"It was *explained*, all right. Old system, they said, was to go down from a few hundred feet to a mile or so and bring up coal and burn it. Go down a bit deeper, and there's no need to bring up and burn anything. Just get heat straightway. Comes up of its own accord – under its own steam. See? Simple.

"They were making a big fuss about it," he added. "It wasn't only the streamer headline; there was a leading article in big type. What was it headed? Ah! The Age of Combustion Has Ended!"

Now that is plainly a very big event for mankind, caught in midhappening. November 10th, 1971. And the way in which Brownlow describes it as being

handled, shows clearly a world much more preoccupied by economic essentials than the world of today, and dealing with them on a larger scale and in a bolder spirit.

That excitement about tapping the central reservoirs of heat, Brownlow was very definite, was not the only symptom of an increase in practical economic interest and intelligence. There was much more space given to scientific work and to inventions than is given in any contemporary paper. There were diagrams and mathematical symbols, he says, but he did not look into them very closely because he could not get the hang of them. "*Frightfully* highbrow, some of it," he said.

A more intelligent world for our grandchildren evidently, and also, as the pictures testified, a healthier and happier world.

"The fashions kept you looking," said Brownlow, going off at a tangent, "all coloured up as they were."

"Were they elaborate?" I asked.

"Anything but," he said.

His description of these costumes is vague. The people depicted in the social illustrations and in the advertisements seemed to have reduced body clothing – I mean things like vests, pants, socks and so forth – to a minimum. Breast and chest went bare. There seem to have been tremendously exaggerated wristlets, mostly on the left arm and going as far up as the elbow, provided with gadgets which served the purpose of pockets. Most of these armlets seem to have been very decorative, almost like little shields. And then, usually, there was an immense hat, often rolled up and carried in the hand, and long cloaks of the loveliest colours and evidently also of the most beautiful soft material, which either trailed from a sort of gorget or were gathered up and wrapped about the naked body, or were belted up or thrown over the shoulders.

There were a number of pictures of crowds from various parts of the world. "The people looked fine," said Brownlow. "Prosperous, you know, and upstanding. Some of the women – just lovely."

My mind went off to India. What was happening in India?

Brownlow could not remember anything very much about India. "Ankor," said Brownlow. "That's not India, is it?" There had been some sort of Carnival going on amidst "perfectly lovely" buildings in the sunshine of Ankor.

The people there were brownish people but they were dressed very much like the people in other parts of the world.

I found the politician stirring in me. Was there really nothing about India? Was he sure of that? There was certainly nothing that had left any impression in Brownlow's mind. And Soviet Russia? "Not as Soviet Russia," said Brownlow. All that trouble had ceased to be a matter of daily interest. "And how was France getting on with Germany?" Brownlow could not recall a mention of either of these two great powers. Nor of the British Empire as such, nor of the U.S.A. There was no mention of any interchanges, communications, ambassadors, conferences, competitions, comparisons, stresses in which these governments figured, so far as he could remember. He racked his brains. I thought perhaps all that had been going

on so entirely like it goes on today – and has been going on for the last hundred years – that he had run his eyes over the passages in question and that they had left no distinctive impression on his mind. But he is positive that it was not like that. "All that stuff was washed out," he said. He is unshaken in his assertion that there were no elections in progress, no notice of Parliament or politicians, no mention of Geneva or anything about armaments of war. All those main interests of a contemporary journal seemed to have been among the "washed out" stuff. It isn't that Brownlow didn't notice them very much; he is positive they were not there.

Now to me this is a very wonderful thing indeed. It means, I take it, that in only forty years from now the great game of sovereign states will be over. It looks also as if the parliamentary game will be over, and as if some quite new method of handling human affairs will have been adopted. Not a word of patriotism or nationalism; not a word of party, not an allusion. But in only forty years! While half the human beings already alive in the world will still be living! You cannot believe it for a moment. Nor could I, if it wasn't for two little torn scraps of paper. These, as I will make clear, leave me in a state of – how can I put it? – incredulous belief.

After all, in 1831 very few people thought of railway or steamship travel, and in 1871 you could already go around the world in eighty days by steam, and send a telegram in a few minutes to nearly every part of the earth. Who would have thought of that in 1831? Revolutions in human life, when they begin to come, can come very fast. Our ideas and methods change faster than we know.

But just forty years!

It was not only that there was this absence of national politics from that evening paper, but there was something else still more fundamental. Business, we both think, finance that is, was not in evidence, at least upon anything like contemporary lines. We are not quite sure of that, but that is our impression. There was no list of Stock Exchange prices, for example, no City page, and nothing in its place. I have suggested already that Brownlow just turned that page over, and that it was sufficiently like what it is today that he passed and forgot it. I have put that suggestion to him. But he is quite sure that that was not the case. Like most of us nowadays, he is watching a number of his investments rather nervously, and he is convinced he looked for the City article.

November 10th, 1971, may have been Monday – there seems to have been some readjustment of the months and the days of the week; that is a detail into which I will not enter now – but that will not account for the absence of any City news at all. That also, it seems, will be washed out forty years from now.

Is there some tremendous revolutionary smash-up ahead, then? Which will put an end to investment and speculation? Is the world going Bolshevik? In the paper, anyhow, there was no sign of, or reference to, anything of that kind. Yet against this idea of some stupendous economic revolution we have the fact that here forty years ahead is a familiar London evening paper still tumbling into a private individual's letter-box in the most uninterrupted manner. Not much suggestion of a social smash-up there. Much stronger

is the effect of immense changes which have come about bit by bit, day by day, and hour by hour, without any sort of revolutionary jolt, as morning or springtime comes to the world.

These futile speculations are irresistible. The reader must forgive me them. Let me return to our story.

There had been a picture of a landslide near Ventimiglia and one of some new chemical works at Salzburg, and there had been a picture of fighting going on near Irkutsk. (Of that picture, as I will tell presently, a fading scrap survives.) "Now that was called – " Brownlow made an effort, and snapped his fingers triumphantly. " – 'Round-up of Brigands by Federal Police.' "

"*What* Federal Police?" I asked.

"There you have me," said Brownlow. "The fellows on both sides looked mostly Chinese, but there were one or two taller fellows, who might have been Americans or British or Scandinavians.

"What filled a lot of the paper," said Brownlow, suddenly, "was gorillas. There was no end of fuss about gorillas. Not so much as about that boring, but still a lot of fuss. Photographs. A map. A special article and some paragraphs."

The paper had, in fact, announced the death of the last gorilla. Considerable resentment was displayed at the tragedy that had happened in the African gorilla reserve. The gorilla population of the world had been dwindling for many years. In 1931 it had been estimated at nine hundred. When the Federal Board took over it had shrunken to three hundred.

"*What* Federal Board?" I asked.

Brownlow knew no more than I did. When he read the phrase, it had seemed all right somehow. Apparently this Board had had too much to do all at once, and insufficient resources. I had the impression at first that it must be some sort of conservation board, improvised under panic conditions, to save the rare creatures of the world threatened with extinction. The gorillas had not been sufficiently observed and guarded, and they had been swept out of existence suddenly by a new and malignant form of influenza. The thing had happened practically before it was remarked. The paper was clamoring for inquiry and drastic changes of reorganization.

This Federal Board, whatever it might be, seemed to be something of very considerable importance in the year 1971. Its name turned up again in an article of afforestation. This interested Brownlow considerably because he has large holdings in lumber companies. This Federal Board was apparently not only responsible for the maladies of wild gorillas but also for the plantation of trees in – just note these names! – Canada, New York State, Siberia, Algiers, and the East Coast of England, and it was arranged for various negligences in combating insect pests and various fungoid plant diseases. It jumped all our contemporary boundaries in the most astonishing way. Its range was world-wide. "In spite of the recent additional restrictions put upon the use of big timber in building and furnishing, there is a plain possibility of a shortage of shelter timber and of rainfall in nearly all the threatened regions for 1985 onward. Admittedly the Federal Board has come late into its task, from the beginning its work has been urgency work; but in view of the lucid report prepared by the James Commission, there is little or no excuse for the inaggressiveness and over-confidence it has displayed."

I am able to quote this particular article because as

a matter of fact it lies before me as I write. It is indeed, as I will explain, all that remains of this remarkable newspaper. The rest has been destroyed and all we can ever know of it now is through Brownlow's sound but not absolutely trustworthy memory.

My mind, as the days pass, hangs on to that Federal Board. Does that phrase mean, as just possibly it may mean, a world federation, a scientific control of all human life only forty years from now? I find that idea – staggering. I have always believed that the world was destined to unify – "Parliament of Mankind and Confederation of the World," as Tennyson put it – but I have always supposed that the process would take centuries. But then my time sense is poor. My disposition has always been to underestimate the pace of change. I wrote in 1900 that there would be airplanes "in fifty years' time." And the confounded things were buzzing about everywhere and carrying passengers before 1920.

Let me tell very briefly of the rest of that evening paper. There seemed to be a lot of sport and fashion; much about something called "Spectacle" – with pictures – a lot of illustrated criticism of decorative art and particularly of architecture. The architecture in the pictures he saw was "towering – kind of magnificent. Great blocks of buildings. New York, but more so and all run together" . . . Unfortunately he canot sketch. There were sections devoted to something he couldn't understand, but which he thinks was some sort of "radio programme stuff."

All that suggests a sort of advanced human life very much like the life we lead today, possibly rather brighter and better.

But here is something – different.

"The birth-rate," said Brownlow searching his mind, "was seven in the thousand."

I exclaimed. The lowest birth-rates in Europe now are sixteen or more per thousand. The Russian birth-rate is forty per thousand, and falling slowly.

"It was seven," said Brownlow. "Exactly seven. I noticed it. In a paragraph."

But what birth-rate, I asked. The British? The European?

"It said the birth-rate," said Brownlow. "Just that."

That I think is the most tantalizing item of all this strange glimpse of the world of our grandchildren. A birth-rate of seven in the thousand does not mean a fixed world population; it means a population that is being reduced at a very rapid rate – unless the death-rate has gone still lower. Quite possibly people will not be dying so much then, but living very much longer. On that Brownlow could throw no light. The people in the pictures did not look to him an "old lot." There were plenty of children and young or young-looking people about.

"But Brownlow," I said, "wasn't there any crime?"

"Rather," said Brownlow. "They had a big

Left: Cosmo Rowe provided this dramatic illustration for Wells' 'Stories of the Stone Age' which appeared in 'The Idler', June 1897.

Facing page: The luckless policeman who encounters 'The Man Who Could Work Miracles' and finds himself whisked away from rural England to the San Francisco waterfront! From 'The Illustrated London News', 1913.

confused. The stick receded at a considerable velocity, and incontinently came a cry of anger and a bad word from the approaching person. "Who are you throwing brambles at, you fool?" cried a voice. "That got me on the shin."

"I'm sorry, old chap," said Mr. Fotheringay, and then realising the awkward nature of the explanation, caught nervously at his moustache. He saw Winch, one of the three Immering constables, advancing.

"What d'yer mean by it?" asked the constable. "Hullo! It's you, is it? The gent that broke the lamp at the Long Dragon!"

analogy, perhaps, quite as much as the feeling that he would be unwelcome in the Long Dragon, that drove him out after supper into the lane beyond the gas-works, to rehearse a few miracles in private.

There was possibly a certain want of originality in his attempts, for apart from his will-power Mr. Fotheringay was not a very exceptional man. The miracle of Moses' rod came to his mind, but the night was dark and unfavourable to the proper control of large miraculous snakes. Then he recollected the story of "Tannhäuser" that he had read on the back of the Philharmonic programme. That seemed to him singularly attractive and harmless. He stuck his walking-stick—a very nice Poona-Penang lawyer—into the turf that edged the footpath, and

Struck by a happy thought, he transferred the constable to San Francisco.

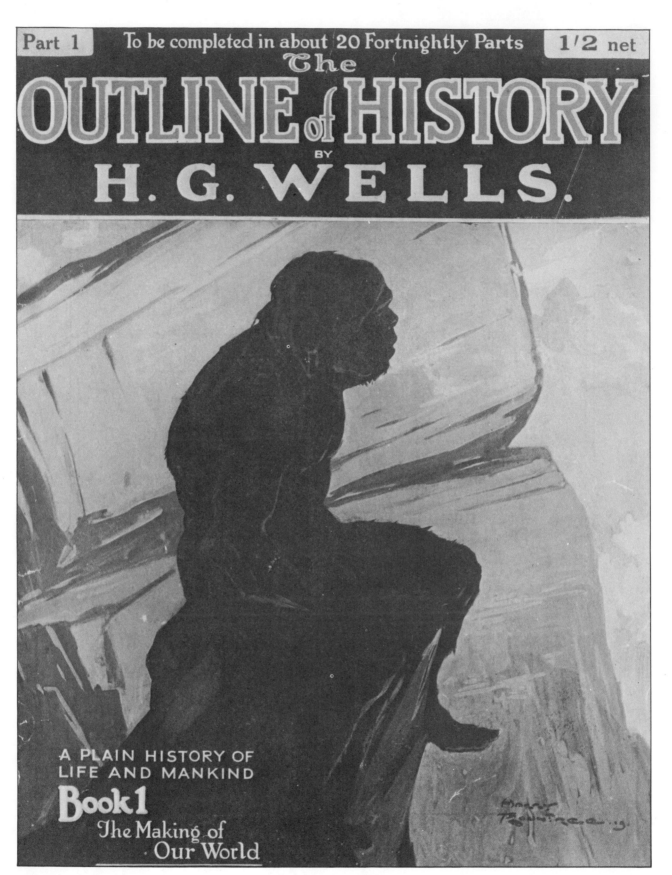

Part 1 To be completed in about 20 Fortnightly Parts **1/2 net**

The

OUTLINE of HISTORY

BY

H.G. WELLS.

A PLAIN HISTORY OF
LIFE AND MANKIND

Book 1

The Making of
Our World

poisoning case on, but it was jolly hard to follow. You know how it is with these crimes. Unless you've read about it from the beginning, it's hard to get the hang of the situation. No newspaper has found out that for every crime it ought to give a summary up-to-date every day – and forty years ahead they hadn't. Or they aren't going to. Whichever way you like to put it.

"There were several crimes and what newspapermen call stories," he resumed; "personal stories. What struck me about it was that they seemed to be more sympathetic than our reporters, more concerned with the motives and less with just finding someone out. What you might call psychological – so to speak."

"Was there anything about books?" I asked him.

"I don't remember anything about books," he said. . . .

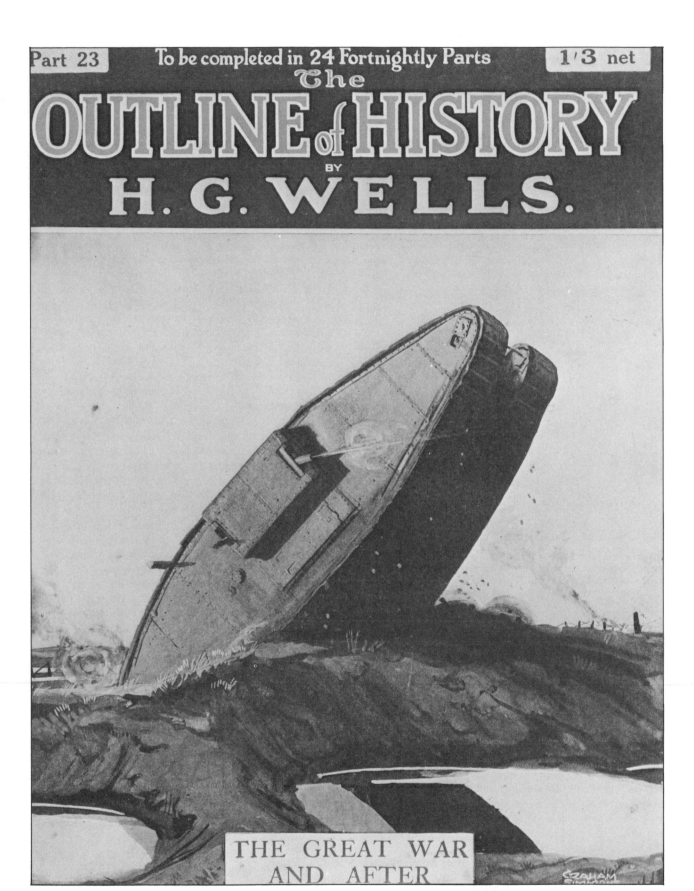

Part 23   To be completed in 24 Fortnightly Parts   1/3 net

The OUTLINE of HISTORY
BY H. G. WELLS.

THE GREAT WAR
AND AFTER

And that is all. Except for a few trifling details such as a possible thirteenth month inserted in the year, that is all. It is intolerably tantalizing. That is the substance of Brownlow's account of his newspaper. He read it – as one might read any newspaper. He was just in that state of alcoholic comfort when nothing is incredible and so nothing is really wonderful. He knew he was reading an evening newspaper of

Above and facing page: Two issues of the famous 'part-work' which H. G. Wells wrote for George Newnes and was published in 1920. Despite the enormous range of material that had to be covered, and the necessary generalisations, the work was a great success with the public: indeed the early intention for it to run for 20 issues was extended to 24 as these front pages show!

forty years ahead and he sat in front of his fire, and smoked and sipped his drink and was no more perturbed than he would have been if he had been reading an imaginative book about the future.

Suddenly his little brass clock pinged Two.

He got up and yawned. He put that astounding, that miraculous newspaper down as he was wont to put any old newspaper down; he carried off his correspondence to the desk in his bureau, and with the swift laziness of a very tired man he dropped his clothes about his room anyhow and went to bed.

But somewhere in the night he woke up feeling thirsty and grey-minded. He lay awake and it came to him that something very strange had occurred to him. His mind went back to the idea that he had been taken in by a very ingenious fabrication. He got up

A humorous moment from Wells' 'The New Accelerator' another of the short stories which appeared in 'The Strand', 1901.

for a drink of Vichy water and a liver tablet, he put his head in cold water and found himself sitting on his bed towelling his hair and doubting whether he had really seen those photographs in the very colours of reality itself, or whether he had imagined them. Also running through his mind was the thought that the approach of a world timber famine for 1985 was something likely to affect his investments and particularly a trust he was setting up on behalf of an infant in whom he was interested. It might be wise, he thought, to put more into timber.

He went back down the corridor to his sitting-room. He sat there in his dressing-gown, turning over the marvelous sheets. There it was in his hands complete in every page, not a corner torn. Some sort of auto-hypnosis, he thought, might be at work, but certainly the pictures seemed as real as looking out of a window. After he had stared at them some time he went back to the timber paragraph. He felt he must keep that. I don't know if you will understand how his mind worked – for my own part I can see at once how perfectly irrational and entirely natural it was – but he took this marvellous paper, creased the page in question, tore off this particular article and left the rest. He returned very drowsily to his bedroom, put the scrap of paper on his dressing-table, got into bed and dropped off to sleep at once.

When he awoke again it was nine o'clock; his morning tea was untasted by his bedside and the room was full of sunshine. His parlormaid-house-keeper had just re-entered the room.

"You were sleeping so peacefully," she said; "I couldn't bear to wake you. Shall I get you a fresh cup of tea?"

Brownlow did not answer. He was trying to think of something strange that had happened.

She repeated her question.

"No. I'll come and have breakfast in my dressing-gown before my bath," he said, and she went out of the room.

Then he saw the scrap of paper.

In a moment he was running down the corridor to the sitting-room. "I left a newspaper," he said. "I left a newspaper."

She came in response to the commotion he made.

"A newspaper?" she said. "It's been gone this two hours, down the chute, with the dust and things."

Brownlow had a moment of extreme consternation.

He invoked his God. "I wanted it *kept!*" he shouted. "I wanted it *kept.*"

"But how was *I* to know you wanted it kept?"

"But didn't you notice it was a very extraordinary-looking newspaper?"

"I've got none too much time to dust out this flat to be looking at newspapers," she said. "I thought I saw some colored photographs of bathing ladies and chorus girls in it, but that's no concern of mine. It didn't seem a proper newspaper to me. How was I to know you'd be wanting to look at them again this morning?"

"I must get that newspaper back," said Brownlow. "It's – it's vitally important. . . . If all Sussex Court has to be held up I want that newspaper back."

"I've never known a thing come up that chute again," said his housekeeper, "that's once gone down it. But I'll telephone down, sir, and see what can be done. Most of that stuff goes right into the hot-water furnace, they say. . . ."

It does. The newspaper had gone.

Brownlow came near raving. By a vast effort of self-control he sat down and consumed his cooling breakfast. He kept on saying, "Oh, my God!" as he did so. In the midst of it he got up to recover the scrap of paper from his bedroom, and then found the wrapper addressed to Evan O'Hara among the overnight letters on his bureau. That seemed an almost maddening confirmation. The thing *had* happened.

Presently after he had breakfasted, he rang me up to aid his baffled mind.

I found him at his bureau with the two bits of paper before him. He did not speak. He made a solemn gesture.

"What is it?" I asked, standing before him.

"Tell me," he said. "Tell me. What are these objects? It's serious. Either – " He left the sentence unfinished.

I picked up the torn wrapper first and felt its texture. "Evan O'Hara, Mr.," I read.

"Yes. Sussex Court, 49. Eh?"

"Right," I agreed and stared at him.

"*That's* not hallucination, eh?"

I shook my head.

"And now this?" His hand trembled as he held out the cutting. I took it.

"Odd," I said. I stared at the black-green ink, the unfamiliar type, the little novelties in spelling. Then I turned the thing over. On the back was a piece of one of the illustrations; it was, I suppose, about a quarter of the photograph of that "Round-up of Brigands by Federal Police" I have already mentioned.

When I saw it that morning it had not even begun to fade. It represented a mass of broken masonry in a sandy waste with bare-looking mountains in the distance. The cold, clear atmosphere, the glare of a cloudless afternoon were rendered perfectly. In the foreground were four masked men in a brown service uniform intent on working some little machine on wheels with a tube and a nozzle projecting a jet that went out to the left, where the fragment was torn off. I cannot imagine what the jet was doing. Brownlow says he thinks they were gassing some men in a hut. Never have I seen such realistic colour printing.

"What on earth is this?" I asked.

"It's *that*," said Brownlow. "I'm not mad, am I? It's really *that*."

"But what the devil is it?"

"It's a piece of a newspaper for November 10th, 1971."

"You had better explain," I said, and sat down, with the scrap of paper in my hand, to hear his story. And, with as much elimination of questions and digressions and repetitions as possible, that is the story I have written here.

I said at the beginning that it was a queer story and queer to my mind it remains, fantastically queer. I return to it at intervals, and it refuses to settle down in my mind as anything but an incongruity with all my experience and beliefs. If it were not for the two little bits of paper, one might dispose of it quite easily. One might say that Brownlow had had a vision, a dream of unparalleled vividness and consistency. Or that he had been hoaxed and his head turned by some elaborate mystification. Or, again, one might suppose he had really seen into the future with a sort of exaggeration of those previsions cited by Mr. J. W. Dunne in his remarkable "Experiment with Time." But nothing Mr. Dunne had to advance can account for an actual evening paper being slapped through a letter-slit forty years in advance of its date.

The wrapper has not altered in the least since I first saw it. But the scrap of paper with the article about afforestation is dissolving into a fine powder and the fragment of picture at the back of it is fading out; most of the colour has gone and the outlines have lost their sharpness. Some of the powder I have taken to my friend Ryder at the Royal College, whose work in micro-chemistry is so well known. He says the stuff is not paper at all, properly speaking. It is mostly aluminum fortified by admixture with some artificial resinous substance.

Though I offer no explanation whatever of this affair I think I will venture on one little prophecy. I have an obstinate persuasion that on November 10th, 1971, the name of the tenant of 49 Sussex Court, will be Mr. Evan O'Hara. (There is no tenant of that name now in Sussex Court and I find no evidence in the Telephone Directory, or the London Directory, that such a person exists anywhere in London.) And on that particular evening forty years ahead, he will not get his usual copy of the *Even Standrd*: instead he will get a copy of the *Evening Standard* of 1931. I have an incurable fancy that this will be so.

There I may be right or wrong, but that Brownlow really got and for two remarkable hours, read, a real newspaper forty years ahead of time I am as convinced as I am convinced that my own name is Hubert G. Wells. Can I say anything stronger than that?

Scientific Romances

In this leading article from The Times Literary Supplement *of 3 August 1933, the paper considers half a century of the scientific romance, and in particular the impact of H. G. Wells on the now flourishing genre. In reviewing Wells' own stories, it also examines both the influences on him, and some of his contemporaries who have taken up the cause of speculation.*

Scientific romances are looked down on from two sides. Scientific men pronounce their science fallacious. Admirers of the purely human novel condemn the intrusion of any interest which is not part of individual life and character. The proper interest of mankind is man, say they; or at least the only satisfying food for his imagination is men and women.

Corgi Paperback edition of Wells' prophetic vision of the future published in 1967, 'The Shape of Things to Come'.

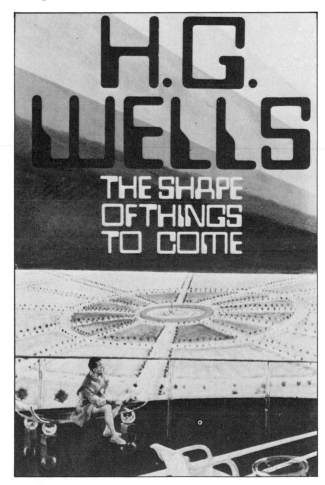

Above: Space travellers seemingly unaffected by the lack of air as they make 'Our Second Voyage to Mars', an anonymous tale from 'Cassell's Magazine' of 1887. Paul Hardy was the artist.

Right: The French writer, J. H. Rosny's novel of half-human creatures which has been seen as an influence on Wells. This illustration by Mittis was for the 1896 edition.

Man's interests are not really quite so limited, nor even his emotions. It is possible, although not easy, to write very good stories in which human beings and their feelings, and even their adventures, are secondary. Mr. H. G. Wells has so far excelled most other experimenters in this art that, when one attempts a general view of it, Mr. Wells fills most of that view.

This refers of course to the Wells of 1895-1907, not to the author of countless society novels, political essays, and Outlines of most things, who, after about 1905, gradually ousted his predecessor from the use of brain and pen, and took over his vivid style (slightly blunted) and his scalding and scolding scorn for our stupidity and wastefulness (slightly sharpened). It is the earlier Wells of whose romances eight have been reprinted in an omnibus volume, with a few omissions (some of them regrettable, even though they are probably the author's own) and a four-page introduction by the author. (*The Scientific Romances of H. G. Wells.* Victor Gollancz. 8s. 6d.).

Authors are not always the best critics of their own works, even long-ago works; and there are parts of this preface with which most admirers of the stories concerned are likely to disagree. It is a modest preface – in a sense; but the Wells who wrote the romances and the Wells who describes them with depreciatory half-tolerance are really rivals, and the latter has the same impatient scorn for the former as for most other people. His criticisms of the earlier and younger Wells sometimes betray the growth of kinks in his critical faculty. "The living interest," he says, "lies in the non-fantastic element, not in the inventions": the fantastic element is a mere "intensifier." If that was so, the relative attractiveness of these stories would be very different from what most readers assign to them. The "Days of the Comet" would be read chiefly as a story of poverty and jealousy in Burslem.

Yet it is almost certain that most of those who read the story in 1906, and wish to reread it now, will hurry to the two middle chapters, that in which the comet "spread its shining nets" over the sky and that which describes with infectious delight the waking in the dawn of a new world. In the "Time Machine," which first gave Mr. Wells his well-deserved rank as an author, and whose merits can be best appreciated after reading a few other books whose central idea is similar, the non-fantastic hardly exists. Of the two best chapters, one, the visit to the Palace of Green Porcelain, followed by the death of Weena in the wood, owes its effectiveness to the weirdness of the prowling Morlocks. The other, the extraordinarily lifelike account of the journey through time ("night followed day like the flapping of a black wing") is wholly outside daily life, and is in fact one of the best examples of Mr. Wells's chief talent, the ability to make us feel and see things wholly unlike anything we ever have felt or seen. And, although the "Star" is not included in this volume, it must be mentioned here as the best refutation of its author's own preface. For Mr. Wells himself twice selected it as his best short story, and probably all his most admiring readers will agree. Yet it has no human character at all, and not even a political or social interest. So far as it has a hero, the moon is hero (or heroine); it is she who at the critical moment shelters her half-scorched and tide-swept parent, the earth, from the blaze of the "great white star" whose headlong fall to the sun took it across our orbit within a few hours before our arrival at the same point. (Or a few hours after; the story is inconsistent on that detail.)

In some other ways, however, the comments of the later Wells on the earlier one are just. The popular comparisons of him to Verne have very little base, though it is an exaggeration to say there is "no literary resemblance whatever." In at least one story, "Dr. Ox's Experiment," Verne did follow, or rather anticipate, the Wells formula, "bring in one marvel and no more, and let us see how it affects ordinary life." Dr. Ox saturated with oxygen the air of the Flemish village of Quiquendone, with remarkable effects on the phlegmatic Flemings. This one story is enough to show that Verne might have been a gentler, less Swiftian and much less political Wells; but in fact Verne's own usual formula was "take some interesting and unfamiliar part of earth (or sea, or sky) and travel there." The submarines and projectiles were incidental. The difference from Wells is conspicuous, for none of the Wells books is a voyage – at least in space. The seeming exception, the "First Men in the Moon," only proves the rule, for if we compare it with Verne's voyage to the moon, we find Verne full of details and

The effects of saturating the village of Quiquendone with oxygen – an illustration by Leon Bennett for Jules Verne's 'Dr Ox's Experiment' (1875).

interest in the voyage, Wells in what came before and after. A momentary glimpse by the light of a bursting meteor was all Verne allowed his travellers to see of life on the moon; while Mr. Wells's two friends, after a bare four pages of voyage, were plunged amid a complex society of overgrown insects, moon-calves and cactus.

When Mr. Wells goes on to say that his own stories are impossible and Verne's possible, he does injustice both to his own plausibility and to Verne's audacity. Few things could defy possibility more completely than Verne's comet in "Hector Servadac," which picked up a bit of Algeria and put it back in the same place two years later, right way up and unhurt. On the other hand, only one of these eight Wells romances can be proved impossible – namely, the "Food of the Gods." For, as someone pointed out nearly two hundred years ago in commenting on Gulliver's Brobdingnag, multiplying length by six means multiplying weight by 216 and cross-section of muscles by only thirty-six, so that the giant could not even stand unless his material was six times as hard as human flesh and bone. The difficulty about the refraction index of the Invisible Man's eyes might be overcome by giving him slightly abnormal adjusting muscles. As for the Time Machine and the Fourth Dimension (the latter gives access to Utopia in "Men Like Gods"), they are outside our reason rather than against it. After Mr. J. W. Dunne's work on Time we

framework for inexplicable things (including apparent contradictions in atomic theory), that it will not readily be consigned to the lumber room of the purely fantastic.

However it does not really much matter whether the central feature of a story of this kind will stand *aqua regia*, provided the author has the skill to make it plausible at first sight, a skill which Mr. Wells never lacks. The essential condition, as he quite rightly insists, is to have only one abnormal condition. The reader is willing to take one flying leap from the solid ground of the familiar world, across a gulf without visible bottom, to a new ledge beyond; but, having arrived there, he will want to be shown over that ledge step by step. Ask him to take more flying leaps, and he will probably leap home again – in other words, shut the book in disgust. In this respect the

are obliged to admit that a backward movement in time does sometimes happen, even if we cannot conceive it, nor even name it without dropping into contradictions. And the Fourth Dimension, even if equally inconceivable, is so convenient as a theoretic

Left: Two men find themselves weightless when a comet tears off a bit of the Earth's surface in 'Hector Servadac' by Jules Verne (1882).

Below: A battle between two of the flying men in Robert Paltock's novel, 'The Adventures of Peter Wilkins' (1763).

Facing page: Cyrano de Bergerac lifted above the Earth in his glass bubble by the heat of the sun's rays. An illustration from de Bergerac's 'A Comical History of the States and Empires of the Moon' (1687).

modern reader has a fastidious consecutiveness of mind unknown to previous ages. The savage, like the Red Queen, can believe three impossible things before breakfast, and, as any one can see by a very short study of negro or Eskimo folklore, does not expect the third to be a result of the first two. In medieval romances, enchanters could upset the natural sequence of things and send the story flying onto a new ledge every tenth sentence. Giants were elastic enough to take seven-league strides on page one, woo a normal-sized princess on page two, and shovel the Isle of Man out of Lough Neagh in one spadeful on page three. The assortment of miraculous weapons, fruits, tools and salves which the Sons of Tuireann gained in successive fights must have pleased the medieval Gaelic listener, but their very number makes the story dull to a modern reader. One miracle is impressive, twenty disconnected ones are tedious.

Things were not quite so bad a thousand years earlier. Lucian and Apuleius had some regard for moderation in their miracles. Still, it is hardly fair for Mr. Wells of 1933 to call the earlier Wells a follower of Apuleius, or even of Lucian. To find even the dawn of scientific romance we must leave the Greco-Roman world, skip the Middle Ages, glance at More's Utopia and Bacon's New Atlantis, pause a moment over Cyrano de Bergerac, and alight at the feet of Swift, by whom Mr. Wells admits himself deeply influenced. By that time there was already a considerable public to whom (as to Cervantes) enchanters and dragons were a source of amusement rather than materials for an absorbing temporarily-believed story. But the map of the earth still had big blanks, and Swift could annex most of the Pacific Ocean for Brobdingnag and Laputa without repelling many readers; and Paltock in "Peter Wilkins" could put his winged men in a still unknown south. But progress in geography and astronomy closed realm after realm to imaginations whose owners wished their excursions to be plausible. Even the moon, offered "rivers and mountains on its spotted globe" to Milton, offered no possibility of romance later, at least on its visible surface. Science passed through a stage in which it killed old romance and did not yet offer its own. After Swift, it is difficult to name a romancer before Verne to whom science gave any inspiration. "Frankenstein" is a forerunner of "Dracula" and Algernon Blackwood's books, not of Verne's, nor even of "Dr. Moreau" except superficially. Lytton's "Coming Race" and Edward Maitland's "Story of the Future" are also works of men with little real taste for the semi-scientific machinery they found useful. A real forerunner of Wells appeared in the eighties, Dr. Abbott's "Flatland," reprinted not long ago. Camille Flammarion's fiction about the far-future earth is also good work; but he did not, as Wells did, give the reader the feeling that the things were happening just outside the window. Perhaps Mark Twain's "Yankee at the Court of King Arthur" deserves mention here, for one imagines King Arthur regarding it exactly as we regard "When the Sleeper Wakes." Bellamy and William Morris produced Utopias comparable with the "Days of the Comet" and "Men Like Gods" (in which Morris's "News from Nowhere" is quoted); but they did not take the trouble to demand from science a plausible way of

Facing page and top: Two more of T. Morten's outstanding illustrations for 'Gulliver's Travels', showing the inside and outside of the fabulous 'Flying City'.

Above: Considered one of the real forerunners of Wells was Dr E. A. Abbott's 'Flatland', written and illustrated by the author and published in 1884.

reaching their Utopias, and Morris quite ostentatiously avoided the mechanical and inventive side of his Paradise.

So we come to Mr. Wells himself and the eight stories here reprinted. Eight is not a high percentage of the eighty-nine volumes which had come from the same pen by 1925 (and several have come since), but they include a much higher percentage of his best work than those figures imply. First of the eight is the "Time Machine," earliest and best of them all. We have Mr. Wells's word that it was re-written four or five times before it appeared in 1895. Probably no later book was so lovingly treated. Then come "Dr. Moreau" and the "Invisible Man," with which Mr. Wells in his preface recommends the new reader to begin, perhaps because it is the only one in which not even the author's later self can discover an allegory nor a "purpose." The reviewers at its birth all called it "humorous," despite its tragic end. (The misprint of Manchester for Winchester (c. 26, p. 290) is not in the original yellow-paper-covered edition.) Then come the "War of the Worlds" and the "First Men in the Moon," from which one entire page (p. 32) of the original *Strand Magazine* issue has vanished, seemingly by accident. Next comes the "Food of the Gods," still with its clumsy title. For gods are usually non-material, while young Caddles suffered from too much material. The title had been used before, with about equal inappropriateness, for a book on cocoa (least ethereal of drinks), so Mr. Wells had a good excuse to drop it, but he only lengthened it. The year before it appeared (1903) Professor Hatai, of Chicago, was said to have

Lord Lytton (above) whose novel 'The Coming Race' (1888) was a precursor of Wells' stories. It details the adventures of a man who discovers a race of people living inside the Earth, and receives instructions as to their habits and customs from a tall, beautiful woman (below).

Right: A delightful illustration by Albert Levering for Mark Twain's 'Extract From Captain Stormfield's Visit to Heaven' (1909).

produced rats near double-size by lecithin. Like many such paragraphs, it has had no sequel, but "Lecithin, or the Wolf-rats" might have been a good title for the story. The full moon on page 673, which rises at midnight on page 675, behaves as eccentrically as in the original edition.

The remaining two stories are the two Earthly Paradise stories, the "Days of the Comet" and "Men like Gods." The latter appeared in 1923, seventeen years after the last of the others; but in both Mr. Wells almost abandons the field in which he has few serious rivals, and challenges comparison in the open field where half the novelists of the world are his rivals. This article is a survey of the former field, but it is amusing to note how Mr. Wells answered the prurient people to whom the one interesting thing in the "Days of the Comet" was a dim hint of free love in the epilogue. Father Amerton in the later book is a not-unfair caricature of that type of one-idea'd critic. It is also worth noting that Mr. Barnstaple, through whose eyes we see the later Paradise, is a much less impatient and irritable man than the Time Traveller, the Woking man who recorded the Martian invasion, or the Invisible Man. These three are one, though that one man was rather fiercer when invisible than in his other two incarnations. He does not seem to have reappeared in any later novel, though Mr. Wells's cast of over 359 characters is so large that it would be rash to assert a positive negative. Other characters appear twice; the tame tiger in the "Door in the Wall" is the tame leopard in "Men like Gods."

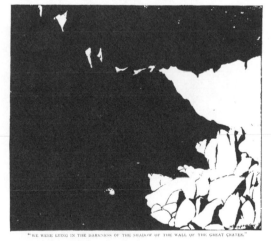

smeared puzzle of the glass and stared at his face. "Yes," I said, "I am hungry. I feel somehow enormously disappointed. I had expected——. I don't know what I had expected, but not this."

I summoned my philosophy, and, rearranging my blanket about me, sat down on the bale again and began my first meal on the moon. I don't think I finished it—I forget. Presently, first in patches, then running rapidly together into wider spaces, came the clearing of the glass, came the drawing of the misty veil that hid the moon-world from our eyes.

We peered out upon the landscape of the moon.

CHAPTER VII.
SUNRISE ON THE MOON.

As we saw it first it was the wildest and most desolate of scenes. We were in an enormous amphitheatre, a vast circular plain, the floor of the giant crater. Its cliff-like walls closed us in on every side. From the westward the light of the unseen sun fell upon them, reaching to the very foot of the cliff, and showed a disordered escarpment of drab and greyish rock, lined here and there with banks and crevices of snow. This was, perhaps, a dozen miles away, but at first no intervening atmosphere diminished in the slightest the minutely-detailed brilliancy with which these things glared at us. They stood out clear and dazzling against a background of starry blackness that seemed to our earthly eyes rather a gloriously-spangled velvet curtain than the spaciousness of the sky.

The eastward cliff was at first merely a starless selvedge to the starry dome. No rosy flush, no creeping pallor, announced the commencing day. Only the Corona, the Zodiacal light, a huge, cone-shaped, luminous haze, pointing up towards the splendour of the morning star, warned us of the imminent nearness of the sun.

Whatever light was about us was reflected by the westward cliffs. It showed a huge, undulating plain, cold and grey—a grey that deepened eastward into the absolute raven darkness of the cliff shadow, innumerable rounded grey summits, ghostly hummocks, billows of snowy substance, stretching crest beyond crest into the remote obscurity, gave us our first inkling of the distance of the

Left: The page from the 'Strand' magazine serialisation of 'The First Men in the Moon' which the writer claims has disappeared from the published novel.

Above: S. Fowler Wright has been hailed as 'the new Wells' and this Stephen Lawrence illustration was for the 'Famous Fantastic Mysteries' publication of his story, 'The Island of Captain Sparrow' (April, 1946).

Those with little taste for scientific romance often say science puts it out of date too soon. It is true our methods of flight or of radio transmission are not exactly those foreseen by any novelist. But the technical weak points are usually discoverable by a carping reader when the book is new. Experience has not yet shown that time makes them worse, at least not in these eight. It is disputed whether cavorite implies a possibility of getting something out of nothing, but it was disputed as soon as cavorite was heard of. It is unlikely that the Martians or any other organic being could stand being fired from a cannon at the necessary speed; but the unlikelihood was seen as soon as Verne fired his moon-tourists from the big cannon in Florida, with a waterbed under them to meet that very objection. Often indeed reality fulfils romance; sometimes reality parodies romance. The Martian fighting machines are now visible to all of us as the pylons of the grid. The book-burnings after the comet have been realized in Nazi Germany; probably Mr. Wells's own works have gone into the fire as *nicht-deutsch*. It is only in trifles that these eight stories "date"; a hatless man on an open moor would not cause remark now as in Comet 3.3.2 (p. 1,008).

evidently read the Wells romances. He quotes the "Food of the Gods" and the "First Men in the Moon," and his catastrophe owes much to the "Star." He seems to have asked himself "If the Earthlings in 'Men like Gods' had gained Utopia's physical advantages without any change in mind or heart, what would happen?" The story is a good answer to that question, but, as a story, it resembles the medieval romances in having too many miracles; and its point of view, always above, never inside nor below, gives less vivid pictures than Wells's.

Sir Conan Doyle's excursions into scientific fiction, such as the "Lost World" and the "Maracot Deep," were on a high level of scientific plausibility, combined with exciting adventure; but one felt that the author was writing to please the public rather than from an inward impulse such as the "Time Machine" betrays. Mr. Kipling has made an excursion or two into the future's inventions, and then retired to his own sufficiently extensive domain. Joseph Delmont, as far as his translated works show, is a successor of Verne rather than of Wells. Mr. Aldous Huxley's "Brave New World" ranks not so much with Wells as with Professor Leacock's excellent caricatures of

Left and below: Two fine illustrations from Frank R. Stockton's 'The Great Stone of Sardis' (1898) about a multi-talented inventor who perfects a flying 'saucer' and a burrowing machine which enables him to reach the Earth's core. The pictures are by Peter Newell Harper.

Facing page: Another Stephen Lawrence illustration for M. P. Shiel's nightmare story of a world devastated, 'The Purple Cloud', published in 'Famous Fantastic Mysteries', June, 1949.

It is as difficult to find successors to Mr. Wells as predecessors. Many hasty reviewers have hailed many new writers as "new Wellses," but on scrutiny they prove different or inferior, often both. Mr. Fowler Wright has received the compliment many times (though it is not always meant as a compliment). But Mr. Fowler Wright, versatile as he is, has only once attempted a really Wellsian book; and the "World Below," an avowed descendant of the "Time Machine," is not a book in which subject and author seem made for each other. He is much happier when, as in "Deluge," he can dismiss a geological catastrophe in a page and thenceforward devote himself wholly to the mutual reactions of the survivors. Indeed, it is with the later Wells, the severe schoolmaster of our stupidity and perverseness, that Mr. Fowler Wright has more in common than with the earlier Wells.

If Mr. J. F. Sullivan, author of two extremely good short stories in the *Strand Magazine* about 1897. "Impossibility" and the "Thinner-out," had pursued his vein further, Mr. Wells might have had a rival fully his equal. Mr. J. D. Beresford showed in "Goslings" and elsewhere that he might succeed in the Wellsian field; but his little study of Wells (published 1915) showed that he considered work in that field "mere exuberance". Most literature is; it pleases by lending wings to the reader's exuberance; but different kinds of reader are lifted by different kinds of wing. The author of the "Seventh Bowl" has

Utopias in general, Wellsian and other. If only the Time Machine would give us a glimpse of 1970 we might see which, if any, of these works are then reprinted. Few indeed are the scientific fictions of 1895-1905 that are reprinted now. Besides the Wells books, the only visible instance is the "Purple Cloud," Mr. M. P. Shiel's startling but nightmarish story of wholesale slaughter, illustrating Mr. Wells's remark that "horror stories are easier to write than gay and exalting stories." It is not likely that any one will reprint George Griffith's "Honeymoon in Space," although that and his other stories were in the later

An illustration from George Griffith's 'Honeymoon in Space' drawn by the talented Stanley L. Wood (1899). For a few years Griffith's books were every bit as popular with readers as those of Wells – though today he is forgotten.

nineties fully as popular as the Wells books, and had a superficial likeness to them. But Mr. Griffith's science was as elastic and mystic as witchcraft; indeed, he had so little faith in his ability to interest his public in it that he peopled most of his planets with near-men (his Martians spoke English as "the best language"), and also filled half his space with honeymoon love-making – even in Space with a big S.

We have left to the end mention of two recent books of first-rate quality which are closely akin to the Wells romances. Mr. Olaf Stapledon's "Last and First Men" might be described as ten successive sequels to the "Time Machine." And Mr. Stapledon can touch

emotion as well as curiosity. He has passages nearly as good as Wells's best. Perhaps they would seem quite as good to a young reader who came first to them and then to Wells. In praising the "End of the World" by Mr. Geoffrey Dennis, there is no need for even the foregoing slight qualification. It is that rare combination, a scientific book and a prose poem. Mr. Dennis has felt the poetry of science as keenly as ever the Wells of 1895 felt it, and he has equal ability to make his readers feel it too. If the Wells scientific romances are to have any more worthy successors Mr. Stapledon and Mr. Dennis are the only men visible who can write them. The field is not half explored yet. The late Dr. Fournier d'Albe's Infra-world tempts one to romance about it. So does any slave-holding anthill. So do several of the ten or fifteen theories which account for the Great Ice Age, especially Mr. W. Clark's smashed-up planet whose fragments shut off the sun for three months, destroyed prehistoric civilization, and originated the myth of Lucifer.

Mr Wells Apocalypse

GERALD HEARD

A British writer deeply impressed by Wells' speculations about the future in both fact and fiction was Gerald Heard (1889-1971), who himself wrote pessimistically about the 'things to come'. He was indeed one of a whole school of writers who, beginning in the early years of the century, had predicted conflict between nations, and dissatisfaction among mankind. (Wells' own book, The War in the Air *written in 1908, was an outstanding example of these 'Future War' stories.) In this important essay from the October 1933 issue of* Nineteenth Century, *Gerald Heard examines the questions posed by Wells about the future and their likelihood of being resolved.*

In pre-scientific ages men said the future will be even as the past. They did not concern themselves with forecasting because they did not believe they could change their surroundings or their fate. During the mechanistic period of science, which is closing today, men believed that the future would go on continu-

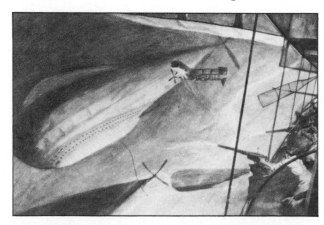

An American aeroplane attacks one of the marauding airships in Wells' 'The War in the Air' (1908). A. C. Michael drew this illustration for the 'Pall Mall Magazine' serialisation of the novel.

ously yielding more and more effective results. And they knew in the main what those results would be. They would not be qualitatively different. They would yield only a vast quantative increase of all the things men had always wanted. To plot the future you had therefore only to 'extrapolate' – to draw out the present lines of discovery and research into the future and so see to what degree of power and comfort and enjoyment humanity would be brought.

No man has done more to make this the faith, hope, and happiness of mankind than has H. G. Wells. When forty years ago he began to construct this

distinctive scientific Utopianism he found such forecasts immature, tentative and vague. Those behind cried forward and those in front cried back. Morris was a Socialist, but his *News from Nowhere* told of a revived mediaevalism with the inspiration of mediaevalism (religion) left out – a shell without nacre-secreting mollusc. At the other extreme Jules Verne saw science being used, always for childish private ends, whether by the super-submarine of Captain Nemo for the pettiness of romantic revenge, by the atomic physicist of the pirates of 'Backup' for loot, or by the 'Clipper of the Clouds' for aimless wanderings. Wells gave scientific speculation clear outline and vivid colour. He linked up scientific finds into a whole of consistent social consequences and presented us with a future which was, both from the point of view of physical science credible and from the social aspect ethically coherent and to many attractive. But 'nothing fails like success,' the final and sad wisdom of the sad Dean of St. Paul's. Not only was it probably impossible for Wells to have achieved so much (he has written sixty-five volumes – many, such as *The Science of Life*, very large and thorough) and won so great a public – *The Outline of History* was read by more people than have ever read a new book before – if he himself was not the summing up of an epoch, if he did not stand at the moment when the unreflective methods of science were about to undergo a revolution; but it may also be that the very effectiveness of his presentation, the powers of his peculiar genius, by giving a coherent picture of the present and the future, themselves helped to precipitate the revolution which threatens him with elimination. Because he believed in science so strongly and had such creative imagination he may have helped to bring on the next epoch of science, and, though his works as a novelist and a creator of character may last to delight many generations, his prophecies and scientific forecasts may

become nothing but speculations explored by such curious examiners into the history of ideas as study the Rosicrucians and the alchemists. Whether this is true or not, it is clear that the phase of 'extrapolation,' the sure and certain hope that scientific progress would go straight ahead and the parallel straight lines of its advance never meet, overlap or collide, is rapidly disappearing and must soon be gone.

It is the realisation of this fact that makes the reading of Mr. Wells' latest book, *The Shape of Things to Come*, unusually interesting. For in it we see how the author has lived right through the crisis in modern

Above left: 'As the airships sailed along they smashed up the city as a child will shatter its cities of brick and card.' Another illustration from 'The War in the Air'.

Above: 'The Battle of the North Atlantic' – one of the climactic moments in 'The War in the Air'.

thought – noting, reacting, making his deduced reckonings and calculating his land-fall all the time. We see in his huge life's output perhaps the most vivid illustration of this the most unsettling fact in all our unsettled lives – that whereas in all previous ages at least several generations lived within the span of one culture, now more than one culture may be lived through by a single generation. *The Shape of Things to Come* is half diary of the last thirty years and half prophecy – made as plain and ordinary as the diary – of the next 200 years. Indeed, reading straight on, so well is the effect of historical narrative kept up that

Three illustrations from H. G. Wells' story, 'The Land Ironclads' which appeared in the 'Strand' in 1903. This tale predicted the tank and although Wells offered his services when the first such mechanical contrivances were being devised under the instructions of Winston Churchill, he was turned away: a rebuff that embittered him towards the Army for the rest of his life.

the reader hardly notices when he passes from yesterday to to-morrow. There are the same references to authorities and diarists as there are in the first half, and it is with something of the same shock that an antiquarian realises that part of a façade which he took to be original is really a clever restoration, that the sociological treatises and economic works, which thickly adorn the later pages, as they do the earlier, are realised to be all fakes. The picture, however, which is built up is the same original Wellsian picture. Mr. Wells sticks to his guns in shooting at the future, and after all he has no reason to doubt them. No man has prophesied so much and made so many hits. Unfortunately, as we have seen, the penalty of such rightness is to be eliminated. From the beginning in the long-ago 'nineties, when men were hardly aware that art for art's sake was about to be pushed aside by science for man's sake, he began prophesying that man's powers would grow out of all expectation. They have grown. At first Mr. Wells was undoubtedly safe in not aiming too high; it was hard enough to get people to believe in the most modest extrapolation of their present scientific equipment.

As Professor J. B. S. Haldane pointed out as far back as 1923 in his *Daedalus, or The Future of Science*, Mr. Wells in his 1902 *Anticipations* dared foretell that heavier-than-air flying machines would be used, at

least in war, by 1950. That was as much as he dared tell the dawning century about its future and not be branded a charlatan. Yet it is obvious that, shooting ahead, Mr. Wells' fancy was certainly firing well behind that particular bird. What his caution and his wish to be considered a reliable forecaster kept him from realising was that the discoveries that he foresaw would not stay still – each golden egg neatly laid awaiting the smelters. These eggs hatch themselves and out of them come some phoenixes and some basilisks, but all heavy layers and all capable of giving rise to broods of still more disconcerting creatures still more fertile and stronger on the wing. So it is that this prophet has suffered the opposite fate of Jonah, for by his very success, by the fact that the future he foretold has come even more true than he dared say, he has put himself out of business – he has lived to find himself too fully fulfilled. Had he been more often wrong in the beginning there might be a few more guesses left him for the future, a few more clear and open lines to be followed up. As it is, he has been right: the world has become as fabulously inventive as he warned us it would; and we laughed and read him as a fairy tale. Indeed, so vast has been the change, and so menacing the futher changes set in motion, that he and we many rather sigh and say with that other remarkably accurate forecaster the prophet Balaam, 'Who shall live when God doeth these things?' We are lost in a maze of possibilities and do not know our way out. For, to turn to another Semitic story, what has happened to scientific forecasting is what happened to Ali Baba's door. In both cases where the breakers-through were to press was at first quite clear. The one door had on it a plain white cross. But now all the doors appear marked and we are just as much at a loss as to which leads to the future as if they all had no marks. And further, as we peer ahead, the unsettling doubt rises in our minds, Are they *real* crosses we see on all the doors, or are we 'projecting' them? Are we, like people who have looked too long at the sun, seeing the mark wherever we look? Certainly if we look to-day across the course of invention no one can be sure what dark horse, what absurd and unnoticed outsider, will not suddenly rush ahead like a nightmare, dash across the steady gallop of all the known entrants, and not only outpace them all but head off the whole field so that it will never turn up at the winning-post. Inventions have this power of cutting out each other. The history of discoveries is littered with ingenious devices which were rendered obsolete, undercut and cast aside long before they had developed, because a more radical discovery supplanted them.

So, though Mr. Wells' invention is probably as great as ever it was, he is embarrassed by the very riches which are now rightly his. This his latest book would be important if only for the signs it shows of this and for the manner in which he tries to struggle against the walls of the tunnel of the future falling in on him and so shutting off his view, or, perhaps we might say, the way in which he tries to prevent from vanishing away those clear rails which he taught us stretch out into the future. And without them, how are we to find our way across the waste to Utopia? So he has to be impatient with too fertile invention, knowing that now the danger is, not inability to believe wonders, but the even deeper scepticism, that final scepticism which realises that absolutely anything may happen. He therefore chides Michael Arlen's *Man's Mortality* for 'unbounded' belief in the possibilities of invention and 'preposterous' exaggeration. Aldous Huxley's *Brave New World* is 'an alarmist fantasy,' and Olaf Stapleton's epic *Last and First Men* does not even get a mention. It is a real danger, this, that speculation will flood the market and men lose, by sheer surfeit of possibilities, all interest in the future. 'Scepticism has to present a hard face to greedy superstition,' he makes his *persona*-in-chief say at the beginning of this chronicle. It is truer to say that the diamonds of scientific finds have to be hoarded, or they will swamp the market and men lose all interest in discovery.

The sobriety of the book is then deliberate. We learn that the next 200 years discover how to make new trees and new animals, but not even then by the present method of radiation with weak gamma-rays, but by using a powder made by a certain Pabst which has certain radioactive qualities. There are aeroplanes, but no stratosphere rocket-planes. There are roads still constructed of that rubber-glass which the Wells of the 'nineties made to make the fortune of the Sleeper, who woke, in consequence, to find himself financial owner of the world. There are super-submarines (but very faintly seen) grubbing up wealth from the Atlantic floor. Some inheritable types of disease have been bred out, but eugenics are kept as 'negative' as the most orthodox could wish. For it is sociology and politics that this Wells – now almost qualified to be a Shavian ancient – thinks really matter, and he is not going to have our attention during sermon time running off after fairy stories and asking for romances when we should be attending to the moral. Certainly this book deserves, and in the noblest sense, the title 'sermon.' It is not to amuse, but to instruct and to warn us, that it is written.

Almost as soon as the time-machine carries us over the frontier from past to future it swoops, and by 1940 we are down again in a very nasty war. Mr. Wells will not, however, creep our flesh any more than he will sicken us with scientific lollypop powers. The war will be very nasty, dirty, mean and exhausting, but,

'Pearson's' magazine which carried Wells' 'The War of the Worlds' also featured his controversial attack on religion in February 1923 – an article which provoked furious denunciations from several Bishops and Sir Arthur Conan Doyle.

H. G. WELLS' GREAT INDICTMENT OF THE CHURCH.

" The Archbishop of York, I think, was quite right when he said that the Church of England has lost its power in the daily lives of the people, and I do not think that he need have confined his remark to his own Church.

" It is almost equally true of the Nonconformist Churches, and much more true of the Roman Catholic Church.

Photo: Beresford.
MR. H. G. WELLS.

" Roman Catholics nowadays are born, not made; the adolescents leak away, and the small power for good of the Roman Church even over those who are still its nominal adherents has had the most startling demonstration during the last year of the brigandage and murder in Ireland.

" This increasing moral impotence is a phenomenon common to all the organised Christian Churches, not only in Britain, but throughout the world.

" But it does not follow that there has been a decline in religious feeling and aspiration.

" The world is now a very tragic and anxious world, and the desire for a peace of mind and a courage such as only deep and pure convictions can supply has never been so strong and so widespread.

" More people are asking to-day, and asking with a new intensity : ' What must I do to be saved ? ' The trouble with the Christian Churches is that they give a confused, unconvincing, and unsatisfying answer.

" This is an age of great distresses but it is also an age of cold, abundant light. People know more than was ever known before of the history of life in space and time, of the origins of the creeds and symbols of Christianity, of the possibilities of human existence.

" They are, as the Archbishop says, ' repelled ' when, in answer to that passionate inquiry for salvation, the Christian exponent, dressed up like an Egyptian priest of three thousand years ago, performs mysterious chants and motions and offers incomprehensible sacraments.

" They are equally ' repelled ' when he embarks upon tedious explanations of the multiplicity and unity of the Deity.

" Within a few score years of the Crucifixion, Christianity had become hopelessly involved with ceremonies and superstitions of immemorial antiquity and with a theology embodying the imperfectly embalmed philosophy of Alexandria. In a less critical age it was possible for many to live holy and noble lives within the terms of these old formulæ, but to-day when intellectual integrity is being recognised as a primary moral obligation this can be done no longer.

" Until Christianity sheds these priestly and theological encumbrances it will encounter greater and greater difficulty in serving Him it claims as its Founder, the Son of Man.

as the Hebrew prophets used always to conclude after the worst of threats, 'a remnant shall be saved.' Indeed, we learn that the war will kill so few, comparatively speaking, that it will not even get down the population to the level to which Mr. Wells has long considered it should be pruned. So – and this is the one stroke in the book in the grand old manner – 'maculated fever,' issuing from a baboon in the London Zoo, wipes out half the human race. Thereafter things creep up again. A skeleton air service, having resumed world air communications, holds a World Conference as early as 1965 at, of all the unhealthy places, Basra – a conference of technicians just to make their world-wide flying arrangements. 'Technicians unite!' They issue an 'air dollar' – its recipe is given so precisely that it is evidently for use. By 1978 (second Basra Conference) they definitely assume world power. There is a clear and ample description of their faith. It is to be based on a book written by an alien in the British Museum, a book vast and exhaustive which very few people actually read, but which forms minds and makes them, as it teaches, 'nucleate' – for the salvation of the world is to lie in group psychology. Here again we recognise,

Two illustrations for Wells' prophecy of the future, 'A Story of the Days to Come'. Below: Edmund J. Sullivan's picture of a Transatlantic aircraft arriving at London from New York in the original 'Pall Mall' publication in 1899, and (opposite page) Frank Paul's idea of Wells' city of the future in the 'Amazing Stories' serialisation, April 1928.

not wild speculation, but extrapolation from the late history of Socialism. The world rulers proceed to proclaim an Edict of Intoleration. They get rid of religion – that again has revolutionary precedent. They execute, by tabloid, one of their members who is evidently getting king-conscious about himself. In their turn they give way to a generation of quite Platonic – the Plato of the *Laws* – guardians who are of an emotional and intellectual plainness to which only the style of Plato himself could give any life. They are as Puritan as, we are told, a five-year-planned commissar must be, and they dread and restrain social and scientific experiments equally. The last phase of perfection is when this council is gently dismissed by the philosophic anarchy of its various sub-boards, and Man, at last properly tamed – even children no longer fight, and though it is not clear that women are fully recognised as equal, they are at last content – Man strolls off with the next twenty million years seen clearly in front of him, to experiment a bit, to make love a little, and to enjoy the scenery quite a great deal – not himself quite perfect, but as perfect as makes no difference; 'and after that the dark.'

On the last page it seems to cross Mr. Wells' mind that he may have ridden our fancies on too tight a rein. Perhaps he sees in the faces of his huge congregation not somnolence – he cares too much for us to go to sleep – but doubt, doubt as to whether this great darer has not been a little too cautious. 'Is that All?' Does the future hold only such long levels sloping to the ultimate sunset? Are there no peaks, no Pisgahs, or must the future, because it will have peace, exchange for that blessing our great gift of hope? And is it for such a conclusion that we must all die in faith, and many in such pain and personal defeat that only a blaze of faith can save their end from squalor? Mr. Wells hesitates as he turns to dismount from the secular pulpit. 'Eye hath not seen, nor ear heard, neither hath it entered into the mind of man,' we hear him murmur almost to himself; but the surging asterisks, like a death-rattle, drown his voice. And this sense that there is something beyond – that, though speculation has jammed itself, some future worthy of all our imagination does lie ahead, will open out if we believe it will – keeps on, like the cheerfulness that would attack the young Johnsonian philosopher, breaking in. The very cast of the story is strange. Far more wonderful than the revelation (which, indeed, is flat beside it) is the way it comes. It is granted to a League of Nations official – which means in Wellsian much the same thing as though the Grail came to a scullion – through a series of Dunne dreams, true dreams of the future. Mr. Wells has written a note which appears at the beginning of Mr. Dunne's remarkable book. His mind has faced this oddest of finds. He uses it here as the fictional device so as to get information about the future, or rather, to make pretence that what he thinks should happen will happen. And yet, having done this, having started with a find which may quite possibly be true and, if true, makes the future obviously very much more puzzling than we ever have thought, Mr. Wells does nothing more with it. Will not all the future be Dunning? we cannot help asking. And what about its elder and more active brother Telepathy? If you

ULTIMO RESTAURANT

The middle space was immovable and gave access by staircases descending into subterranean ways. Right and left were an ascending series of continuous platforms, each of which traveled about five miles an hour faster than the one internal to it. The establishment of the Suzanna Hat Syndicate projected a vast facade upon the outer way, sending overhead an overlapping series of huge white glass screens, on which gigantic animated pictures of the faces of well-known beautiful living women wearing novelties in hats were thrown.

can Dunne your way into the future, will not the future where you take an inch take an ell? And when you start to rally mankind and you find social psychology and the influence of group nucleation is essential, will not you be using psychic fields and be strengthening each other with such fertile silences and communions that can reach round the world?

Mr. Wells talks of even the first world Government's need to 'clean up the racial mind' and rid it of 'animal individualism.' But he falters. He is afraid to shock us, to shock his own conservative biologists. In the old days it was plain sailing. There was good, clean physical science cutting its way out from the social superstitious tangle into the good, clean outer world, so that in the end you might live and die as good, clean animals. But now physical science is not enough. You have got to have psychology, sociology, nucleation – and yet 'Scepticism must present' that 'hard face to greedy superstition, and it is one's public duty to refrain from rash statements about these flimsy intimations.' So there is the dilemma. Physical speculation is no longer possible, because we now know that the human mind has so grown, has now come to such a sudden revolution of knowledge, that it knows it can make any universe if only it understands itself. The wider the mind expands, the more reality can come in. As an eminent astro-physicist has said, 'the universe will give you just as many geometries as you have the mental power to make.' The deeper you advance in self-knowledge, in psychology, the deeper can be your knowledge of the universe of physics, for the two are complementary aspects of reality. You cannot advance the one without advancing the other. Physical speculation – just as much as social order – depends on our exploring our minds. Can anyone, then, doubt, watching science to-day, that it is in such a direction that the future advance of science must lie – that a future society will push its researches into completely new worlds, those 'possible worlds' about which Professor Haldane has written?

But, then, such speculation breaks the smooth tunnel that points good scientists, who have become socially conscious, through sane money, air dollars and air power and world committees, to a humanity which has ceased to ask what life is for and why mind appeared. The roof breaks through: the stars appear hanging far above it enigmatically. The old questions rise: Can a man serve humanity as it must be served, without fanatic dogma, with endless patience, understanding, selflessness and charity, unless he knows that it is not to end with a lot of super-healthy animals put out to grass until the night cuts them off? Does not the future point, quite as much if science continues to advance as if civilisation is to hold together, to some discovery which will reveal the super-field of which our individual consciousnesses are only waves on its deep? Yet how, at present, can we make out of these psychological elements those vivid fully materialised romances which are rightly called Wellsian? Modern physics has had to abandon all models and all images of the facts with which it deals. It is bound to do so, because it is feeling its way out into a universe which our present senses have never experienced and for which, therefore, they can give us no words or pictures. Is not the Utopianism which was based on the elder physics being driven, by this

George Inness Jr's picture for 'The World Set Free: A Prophetic Trilogy' which Wells wrote in 1914 and which appeared in the American magazine, 'The Century'. The other two articles in the series were 'A Trap to Catch the Sun' and 'The Last War in the World'.

change in its foundation, itself to become immaterial? It does grow increasingly certain as science advances that there lies in front of it a future more wonderful than any material phrase, any symbol taken from our past experience, can render. But, to requote Mr. Wells' final quotation, 'Eye has not seen, nor ear heard, neither has it entered into the mind of man.'

Fantastic though Wells' story The War of the Worlds *is, even more fantastic were the events which followed the broadcasting of a dramatisation of the novel over American radio on the evening of 30 October, 1938. It was perhaps appropriate that the then unknown young actor, Orson Welles, picked the story for the night before Halloween, but he and his fellow players could have had no idea that their realistic treatment of the invasion story (relocated from Woking to New Jersey for the benefit of local audiences) was to create a real panic among American listeners who actually believed that Martians were landing among them! Even as the broadcast went out, people were jamming the telephone lines in their fright to find out what they should do to escape from the terrible invaders, or else fleeing into the countryside leaving their possessions behind them. . . . That night has now gone down in radio history, but this contemporary report from the* New York Times *of Monday, 31 October brings every panic-stricken moment vividly back to life again.*

Radio Listeners in Panic— War Drama Taken as Fact!

Many Flee Homes to Escape 'Gas Raid From Mars'
Phone Calls Swamp Police at Broadcast of Wells Fantasy

A wave of mass hysteria seized thousands of radio listeners throughout the nation between 8.15 and 9.30 last night when a broadcast of a dramatization of H. G. Wells' fantasy, "The War of the Worlds", led thousands to believe that an interplanetary conflict had started with invading Martians spreading wide death and destruction in New Jersey and New York.

The broadcast, which disrupted households, interrupted religious services, created traffic jams and clogged communications systems, was made by Orson Welles, who as the radio character, "The Shadow", used to give "the creeps" to countless child listeners. This time at least a score of adults required medical treatment for shock or hysteria.

In Newark, in a single block at Heddon Terrace and Hawthorne Avenue, more than twenty families rushed out of their houses believing a gas raid was on. Some even began moving household furniture.

Throughout New York families left their homes, some to flee to near-by parks. Thousands of persons called the police, newspapers and radio stations here and in other cities of the United States and Canada seeking advice on protective measures against the raids.

The programme was produced by Mr. Welles and the Mercury Theatre on the Air over station WABC and the Columbia Broadcasting System's coast-to-coast network from 8 to 9 o'clock.

The radio play, as presented, was to simulate a regular radio programme with a "break in" for the material of the play. The radio listeners, apparently, missed or did not listen to the introduction, which was: "The Columbia Broadcasting System and its affiliated stations present Orson Welles and the Mercury Theatre on the Air in 'The War of the Worlds' by H. G. Wells."

They also failed to associate the programme with the newspaper listing of the programme, announced as "Today: 8.00-9.00 Play: H. G. Wells's 'War of the Worlds' – WABC." They ignored three additional announcements made during the broadcast emphasizing its fictional nature.

Mr. Welles opened the programme with a description of the series of which it is a part. The simulated programme began. A weather report was given prosaically. An announcer remarked that the programme would be continued from a hotel, with dance music. For a few moments a dance programme was given in the usual manner. Then there was a "break in" with a "flash" about a professor at an observatory noting a series of gas explosions on the planet Mars.

News bulletins and scene broadcasts followed reporting, with the technique in which the radio had reported actual events, the landing of a "meteor" near Princeton, N. J., "killing" 1,500 persons, the discovery that the "meteor" was a "metal cylinder" containing strange creatures from Mars armed with "death rays" to open hostilities against the inhabitants of the Earth.

Despite the fantastic nature of the reported "occurrences", the programme, coming after the recent war scare in Europe and a period in which the radio frequently had interrupted regularly scheduled programmes to report developments in the Czechoslovak situation, caused fright and panic throughout the area of the broadcast.

Soon the stations taking the programme were getting calls from listeners or persons who had heard of the broadcasts. Many sought first to verify the reports. But large numbers, obviously in a state of terror, asked how they could follow the broadcast's advice and flee from the city, whether they would be safer in the "gas raid" in the cellar or on the roof, how they could safeguard their children, and many of the questions which had been worrying residents of London and Paris during the tense days before the Munich agreement.

So many calls came to newspapers and so many newspapers found it advisable to check on the reports despite their fantastic content, that the Associated Press sent out the following at 8.45 p.m.:

"Note to Editors: Queries to newspapers from radio listeners throughout the United States tonight, regarding a reported meteor fall which killed a number of New Jerseyites, are the result of a studio dramatisation. The A.P."

One of the many headline stories generated by Orson Welles' broadcast – from the New York 'Daily News', 31 October 1938.

2 ★★★★★ DAILY NEWS, MONDAY, OCTOBER

Fake 'War' On Radio Spreads Panic Over U.S.

By GEORGE DIXON.

A radio dramatization of H. G. Wells' "War of the Worlds"—which thousands of people misunderstood as a news broadcast of a current catastrophe in New Jersey—created almost unbelievable scenes of terror in New York, New Jersey, the South and as far west as San Francisco between 8 and 9 o'clock last night.

The panic started when an announcer suddenly interrupted the program of a dance orchestra—which was part of the dramatization—to "flash" an imaginary bulletin that a mysterious "meteor" had struck New Jersey, lighting the heavens for miles around.

A few seconds later, the announcer "flashed" the tidings that weird monsters were swarming out of the mass of metal—which was not a meteor but a tube-like car from Mars—and were destroying hundreds of people with death-ray guns.

1,100 Call News.

Thousands Flee.

Without waiting for further details, thousands of listeners rushed from their homes in New York and New Jersey, many with towels

across their faces to protect themselves from the "gas" which the invader was supposed to be spewing forth.

Simultaneously, thousands more in states that stretched west to California and south to the Gulf of Mexico rushed to their telephones to inquire of newspapers, the police, switchboard operators, and electric companies what they should do to protect themselves. The "space cartridge" was supposed to have struck at Grover's Mills, an actual town near Princeton. Names of well-known highways were used in describing the advance of the monsters. The "Governor of New Jersey" declared martial law and the "Secretary of the Interior" tried to calm the people.

Eleven hundred calls flooded the switchboard at The News—more than when the dirigible Hindenburg exploded.

Occupants of Park Ave. apartment houses flocked to the street.

In Harlem excited crowds shouted that President Roosevelt's

(Continued on page 6, col. 1)

Senator Maps Bill to Censor Air Waves

Des Moines, Oct. 30 (P).—Senator Clyde L. Herring (Democrat, Iowa) said tonight he planned to introduce a bill in the next session of Congress "controlling just such abuses as was heard over the radio tonight." He said the bill would propose a censorship board to which all radio programs must be submitted.

Frank R. McNinch, chairman of the Federal Communications Commission, in Washington, said that an investigation would be held at once by the FCC. He would not predict what action might be taken, but said a thorough probe would be made.

115

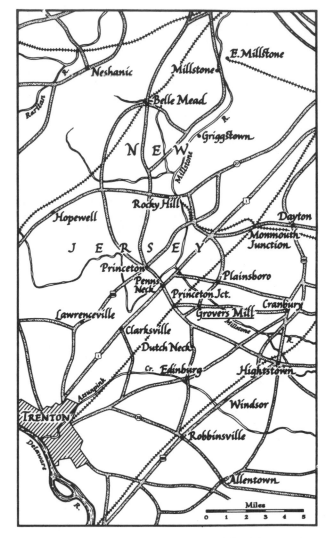

The American location for Orson Welles' 'War of the Worlds'.

Similarly, police teletype systems carried notices to all stationhouses, and police short-wave radio stations notified police radio cars that the event was imaginary.

MESSAGE FROM THE POLICE
The New York Police sent out the following:

"To all receivers: Station WABC informs us that the broadcast just concluded over that station was a dramatization of a play. No cause for alarm."

The New Jersey State Police teletyped the following:

"Note to all receivers – WABC broadcast as drama re this section being attacked by residents of Mars, Imaginary affair."

From one New York theatre a manager reported that a throng of theatre-goers had rushed from his theatre as a result of the broadcast. He said that the wives of two men in the audience, having heard the broadcast, called the theatre and insisted that their husbands be paged. This spread the "news" to others in the audience.

The switchboard of THE NEW YORK TIMES was overwhelmed by the calls. A total of 875 were received. One man who called from Dayton, Ohio

asked, "What time will it be the end of the world?" A caller from the suburbs said that he had had a houseful of guests and they had all rushed out to the yard for safety.

Warren Dean, a member of the American Legion living in Manhattan, who telephoned to verify the "reports", expressed indignation which was typical of that of many callers.

"I've heard a lot of radio programmes, but I've never heard anything as rotten as that," Mr. Dean said. "It was too realistic for comfort. Everybody in my house was agitated by the news."

At 9 o'clock a woman walked into the West 47th Street police station dragging two children, all carrying extra clothing. She said she was ready to leave the city. Police persuaded her to stay.

A garbled version of the reports reached the Dixie Bus Terminal, causing officials there to prepare to change their schedule on confirmation of "news" of an accident at Princeton on the New Jersey route. Miss Dorothy Brown at the terminal sought verification, however, when the caller refused to talk with the dispatcher, explaining to her that "the world is coming to an end and I have a lot to do."

HARLEM SHAKEN BY THE "NEWS"
Harlem was shaken by the "news". Thirty men and women rushed into the West 123rd Street police station and twelve into the West 135th Street station saying they had their household goods packed and were ready to leave Harlem if the police would tell them were to go to be "evacuated". One man insisted he had heard "the President's voice" over the radio advising all citizens to leave the cities.

The parlour churches in the Negro district, congregations of the smaller sects meeting on the ground floors of brownstone houses, took the "news" in their stride as less faithful parishioners rushed in with it, seeking spiritual consolation. Evening services became "end of the world" prayer meetings in some.

One man ran into the Wadsworth Avenue Police Station in Washington Heights, white with terror, shouting that enemy planes were crossing the Hudson River and asking what he should do. A man came into the West 152nd Street Station, seeking traffic directions.

The broadcast became a rumour that spread through the district, and many persons stood on street corners hoping for a sight of the "battle" in the skies.

In Queens the principal question asked of the switchboard operators at Police Headquarters was whether "the wave of poison gas will reach as far as Queens." Many said they were packed and ready to leave Queens when told to do so.

Samuel Tishman of 100 Riverside Drive was one of the multitude that fled into the street after hearing part of the programme. He declared that hundreds of person evacuated their homes fearing that the "city was being bombed."

"I came home at 9.15 p.m. just in time to receive a telephone call from my nephew who was frantic with fear. He told me the city was about to be bombed from the air and advised me to get out of the building at once. I turned on the radio and heard the broadcast which corroborated what my nephew had said, so I gathered up a few personal belongings and ran to the elevator. When I got to the street there were hundreds of people milling about in panic. Most of us ran towards Broadway and it was not until we stopped taxi drivers who had heard the entire broadcast on their radios that we knew what it was all about. It was the most asinine stunt I ever heard of."

"I heard that broadcast and almost had a heart attack," said Louis Winkler of 1322 Clay Avenue, the Bronx. "I didn't tune it in until it was half over, but when I heard the names and titles of Federal, State and municipal officials, and when the 'Secretary of the Interior' was introduced, I was convinced it was the McCoy. I ran out into the street with scores of others, and found people running in all directions. The whole thing came over as a news broadcast and in my mind it was a pretty crummy thing to do."

The Telegraph Bureau switchboard at police headquarters in Manhattan, operated by thirteen men, was so swamped with calls from apprehensive citizens inquiring about the broadcast that police business was seriously interfered with.

Headquarters, unable to reach the radio station by telephone, sent a radio patrol car there to ascertain the reason for the reaction to the programme. When the explanation was given, a police message was sent to all precincts in the five boroughs advising the commands of the cause.

"THEY'RE BOMBING NEW JERSEY!"
Patrolman John Morrison was on duty at the switchboard in the Bronx Police Headquarters when, as he

Orson Welles answering newspaper reporter's questions after his broadcast had created widespread panic and made national news.

afterwards expressed it. All the lines became busy at once. Among the first who answered was a man who informed him:

"They're bombing New Jersey."

"How do you know?" Patrolman Morrison inquired.

"I heard it on the radio," the voice at the other end of the wire replied. "Then I went to the roof and I could see smoke from the bombs, drifting over toward New York. What shall I do?"

The patrolman calmed the caller as well as he could, then answered other inquiries from persons who wanted to know whether the reports of a bombardment were true, and if so where they could take refuge.

At Brooklyn police headquarters, eight men assigned to the monitor switchboard, estimated that they had answered more than 300 inquiries from persons who had been alarmed by the broadcast. A number of these, the police said, came from motorists who had

"*This is Glub, sitting in for Tom Dunn on the 'Eleven O'Clock News,' and I wish to announce that there has been a rather sudden and sweeping change in your government.*"

The effect of Orson Welles' broadcast of the 'War of the Worlds' has continued to be felt long after it occurred – as this cartoon from 'The New Yorker' magazine in 1969 clearly demonstrates.

heard the programme over their car radios and were alarmed both for themselves and for persons at their homes. Also, the Brooklyn police reported, a preponderence of the calls seemed to come from women.

The National Broadcasting Company reported that men stationed at the WJZ transmitting station at Bound Brook, N.J., had received dozens of calls from residents of that area. The transmitting station communicated with New York and passed the information that there was no cause for alarm to the persons who inquired there.

Meanwhile the New York telephone operators of the company found their switchboards swamped with incoming demands for information, although the NBC system had no part in the programme.

RECORD WESTCHESTER CALLS
The State, county, parkway and local police in Westchester County were swamped also with calls from terrified residents. Of the local police departments, Mount Vernon, White Plains, Mount Kisco, Yonkers and Tarrytown, received most of the inquiries. At first the authorities thought they were being made the victims of a practical joke, but when the calls persisted and increased in volume, they began to make inquiries. The New York Telephone Company reported that it had never handled so many calls in one hour in years in Westchester.

One man called the Mount Vernon Police Headquarters to find out "where the forty policemen were killed"; another said his brother was ill in bed listening to the broadcast, and when he heard the reports he got into an automobile and "disappeared". "I'm nearly crazy!" the caller exclaimed.

Because some of the inmates took the catastrophic reports seriously as they came over the radio, some of the hospitals and the county penitentiary ordered that the radios be turned off.

Thousands of calls came into Newark Police Headquarters. These were not only from the terror stricken. Hundreds of physicians and nurses, believing the reports to be true, called to volunteer their services to aid the "injured". City officials also called in to make "emergency" arrangements for the population. Radio cars were stopped by the panicky throughout the city.

Jersey City police headquarters received similar calls. One woman asked Detective Timothy Grooty, on duty there, "Shall I close my windows?" A man asked, "Have the police any extra gas masks?" Many of the callers, on being assured the reports were fiction, queried again and again, uncertain in whom to believe.

Scores of persons in lower Newark Avenue, New Jersey, left their homes and stood fearfully in the street, looking with apprehension towards the sky. A radio car was dispatched there to reassure them.

The incident at Hedden Terrace and Hawthorne Avenue, in Newark, one of the most dramatic in the area, caused a tie-up in traffic for blocks around. The more than twenty families there apparently believed the "gas attack" had started, and so reported to the police. An ambulance, three radio cars, and a police emergency squad of eight men were sent to the scene with full inhalator apparatus.

They found the families with wet cloths on faces contorted with hysteria. The police calmed them' halting those who were attempting to move their furniture on their cars, and after a time were able to clear the traffic snarl.

At St. Michael's Hospital, High Street and Central Avenue, in the heart of the Newark industrial district, fifteen men and women were treated for shock and hysteria. In some cases it was necessary to give sedatives, and nurses and physicians sat down and talked with the more seriously affected.

While this was going on, three persons with children under treatment in the institution, telephoned that they were taking them out and leaving the city, but their fears were calmed when hospital authorities explained what had happened.

A flickering of electrical lights in Bergen County from about 6.15 to 6.30 last evening provided a build up for the terror that was to ensue when the radio broadcast started.

Without going out entirely, the lights dimmed and brightened alternately and radio reception was also affected. The Public Service Gas and Electric Company was mystified by the behaviour of the lights, declaring there was nothing wrong at their power plant or in their distributing system. A spokesman for the service department said a call was made to Newark and the same situation was reported. He believed, he said, that the condition was general throughout the State.

An old resident of New Jersey who was still taking no chances although the Martian invasion had long before been declared a hoax!

The New Jersey Bell Telephone Company reported that every central office in the State was flooded with calls for more than an hour and the company did not have time to summon emergency operators to relieve the congestion. Hardest hit was the Trenton toll office, which handled calls from all over the East.

One of the radio reports, the statement about the mobilization of 7,000 national guardsmen in New Jersey, caused the armories of the Sussex and Essex troops to be swamped with calls from officers and men seeking information about the mobilization place.

PRAYERS FOR DELIVERANCE

In Caldwell, N.J., an excited parishioner ran into the First Baptist Church during the evening service and shouted that a meteor had fallen, showering death and destruction, and that North Jersey was threatened. The Rev. Thomas Thomas, the pastor, quieted the congregation, and all prayed for deliverance from the "catastrophe".

East Orange Police Headquarters received more than 200 calls from persons who wanted to know what to do to escape the "gas". Unaware of the broadcast, the switchboard operator tried to telephone Newark, but was unable to get the call through because the switchboard at Newark headquarters was tied up. The mystery was not cleared up until a teletype explanation had been received from Trenton.

More than 100 calls were received at Maplewood Police Headquarters, and during the excitement, two families of motorists, residents of New York City, arrived at the station to inquire how they were to get back to their homes now that the Pulaski Skyway had been blown up.

The women and children were crying and it took some time for the police to convince them that the catastrophe was fictitious. Many persons who called Maplewood said their neighbours were packing their possessions and preparing to leave for the country.

In Orange, N.J., an unidentified man rushed into the lobby of the Lido Theatre, a neighbourhood picture house, with the intention of "warning" the audience that a meteor had fallen on Raymond Boulevard, Newark., and was spreading poisonous gases. Skeptical, Al Hochberg, manager of the theatre, prevented the man from entering the auditorium of the theatre and then called the police. He was informed that the radio broadcast was responsible for the man's alarm.

Emanuel Priola, bartender of a tavern at 442, Valley Road, West Orange, closed the place, sending away six customers, in the middle of the broadcast to "rescue" his wife and two children.

"At first I thought it was a lot of Buck Rogers stuff, but when a friend telephoned me that general orders had been issued to evacuate every one from the metropolitan area, I put the customers out, closed the place and started to drive home, " he said.

William H. Decker of 20 Aubrey Road, Montclair, N.J., denounced the broadcast as "a disgrace" and "an outrage", which he said had frightened hundreds of residents in his community, including children. He said he knew of one woman who ran into the street with her two children and asked for the help of neighbours in saving them.

"We were sitting in the living room casually listening to the radio," he said, "when we heard reports of a meteor falling near New Brunswick and reports that gas was spreading. Then there was an announcement of the Secretary of the Interior from Washington who spoke of the happening as a major disaster. It was the worst thing I ever heard over the air."

COLUMBIA EXPLAIN BROADCAST
The Columbia Broadcasting System issued a statement saying that the adaptation of Mr. Wells's novel which was broadcast, "followed the original closely, but to make the imaginery details more interesting to American listeners, the adapter, Orson Welles, substituted an American locale for the English scenes of the story."

Pointing out that the fictional character of the broadcast had been announced four times, and had been previously publicized, it continued:

"Nevertheless, the programme apparently was produced with such vividness that some listeners who may have heard only fragments, thought the broadcast was fact not fiction. Hundreds of telephone calls reaching CBS stations, city authorities, newspaper offices and police headquarters in various cities, testified to the mistaken belief.

"Naturally, it was neither Columbia's nor the Mercury Theatre's intention to mislead anyone, and when it became evident that a part of the audience had been disturbed by the performance, five announcements were read over the network later in the evening to reassure those listeners."

Expressing profound regret that his dramatic efforts should cause such consternation, Mr. Welles said, "I don't think we will choose anything like this again." He had hesitated about presenting it at all, he disclosed, because "it was our thought that perhaps people might be bored or annoyed at hearing a tale so improbable."

Stephen Lawrence's illustration of the invading Martians for 'Famous Fantastic Mysteries' publication of the story in July, 1951.

The Man Who Did Work Miracles—In the Movies

DENIS GIFFORD

The variety and brilliance of H. H. Wells novels and stories have naturally enough attracted film makers since the tales were first published – and already some of the titles are being remade for a second time, demonstrating further the timeless nature of their author's unique talent. In this survey, the leading British film historian, Denis Gifford, traces Wells in the cinema and brings his authoritative and perceptive judgement to bear on the films made from his work.

H. G. Wells and the movies were made for each other, the inventiveness of the man and the invention of the machine coinciding precisely in 1895 when Wells wrote and published *The Time Machine*, and Robert William Paul actually made one. Paul called his the Theatrograph, a working camera and projector that captured a minute of life upon a celluloid strip, pinning it down and playing it back for ever – or until the celluloid scratched into shreds. Working with scientist/photographer Birt Acres upon ideas pirated from Edison's Kinetoscope, engineer Paul made practical the imagination of writer Wells. And having captured the present and thus recorded the past, Paul saw how he could predict the future. And on 24 October 1895 he patented it:

A Novel Form of Exhibition or Entertainment, Means for Presenting the Same
My invention consists of a novel form of exhibition whereby the spectators have presented to their view scenes which are supposed to occur in the future or past, while they are given the sensation of voyaging upon a machine through time, and means for presenting these scenes simultaneously and in conjunction with the production of the sensations by the mechanism described below, or its equivalent.

The mechanism is detailed in less legal language in an interview Paul gave to *The Era*, the leading entertainment trade paper of the period, on 15 April 1896:

In a room capable of accommodating some hundred people, he would arrange seats to which a slight motion could be given. He would plunge the apartment into Cimmerian darkness, and introduce a wailing wind. Although the audience actually moved but a few inches, the sensation would be that of travelling through space. From time to time the journey would be stopped, and on the stage a wondrous picture be revealed – the Animatographe (Paul's new name for his Theatrograph), combined with panoramic effects. Fantastic scenes of future ages would first be shown. Then the audience would set forth upon its homeward journey.

At this point, Paul's inborn streak of showmanship

showed: 'The conductor would regretfully intimate that he had over-shot the mark.' This could be the cue for a series of historical scenes, then a sensation of forward travel, concluding with 'the rearrival notified by the representation on the screen of the place at which the exhibition is held, which by the movement forward of the lantern can be made to increase gradually in size as if approaching the spectator.'

This early exercise in mixed media (moving seats, sound effects, music, slides, models, films, lighting effects including 'Sunlight, darkness, moonlight, rain, etc') came to naught. Perhaps it was too ambitious, more likely it was too expensive. But for a moment it seemed as though the imagination of the artist and the engineer had made a perfect marriage. Paul would go on to produce many imaginative fantasies, directed for him by the professional conjurer Walter Booth, but none of them would match the imagination of the show that never was, the R. W. Paul-H. G. Wells *Time Machine*.

The First Men in the Moon was published by Wells in 1901, but the book had been serialised in the *Strand Magazine* the year before. It caused as great a sensation among its readers as had that famous monthly's earlier serials of Conan Doyle's Sherlock Holmes. George Newnes' distribution was world wide,

Left: H. G. Wells who always took a keen interest in the films based on his books is seen here on the set of 'Things to Come' with Raymond Massey and Margarita Scott (1936).

Two versions of H. G. Wells' 'Selenites', the creatures who feature in 'The First Men in the Moon'. Above: As they were portrayed by Georges Méliès in his 'A Trip to the Moon' (1902) and (facing page) another group make life equally difficult for Lionel Jeffries in the 1964 version, 'First Men on the Moon'.

and evidence suggests that copies not only reached Paris, France, but the hands of the city's foremost film-maker.

Georges Méliès had been both a conjurer and a cartoonist. One of the first to realise the potential in the new invention of the cinematograph, he had bought himself a projector/camera from, intriguingly enough, Robert Paul of London. With a studio designed and built by himself at Montreuil, Méliès went into the movie business, writing, directing, designing, and

starring in a series of magical entertainments the like of which the world had never seen. Using all the tricks in his magician's book, plus several created specifically for the new medium, he plundered literature and legend for ideas to use them in. Naturally, as a Frenchman, he was familiar with the fantasies of Jules Verne, and out of *From the Earth to the Moon* (1865) Méliès created the first science-fiction film. *A Trip to the Moon*, produced in 1902, followed Verne's plot closely, but as an added embellishment included crustaceous Selenites as the moon's inhabitants. These crab-clawed creatures came close to Wells' creations, but closer still to the drawings of Shepperson, the artist who illustrated *The First Men in the Moon* so brilliantly in the *Strand*.

It was the same Wells novel that became the first Wells film and, indeed, the first major science-fiction film. *The First Men in the Moon* was also the first production to be made at the Gaumont studio after its Great War shut-down. Unfortunately, when it was

THE KING WHO WAS A KING BY H·G·WELLS

THE BOOK OF A FILM

BENN

Right: Paul Rotha's dust jacket design for H. G. Wells' 'The Man Who Was A King' – 'The Book of a Film' as it was heralded but never actually got made. (1929).

Below and facing page: Two stills from 'The Island of Lost Souls' based on 'The Island of Dr Moreau' and starring Charles Laughton (1933).

unveiled in May 1919, it proved that British film-makers had also undergone a creative shut-down and were still making movies as if D. W. Griffith had never existed. The film, all nitrate prints of which were destroyed decades ago, is lost to us, but the few stills which remain, decorating a handsome hardback book issued as a souvenir to the trade, tell all. Ham actors grimace, tell-tale puckers betray the canvas structure of the Cavorite Sphere, comic extras load the space ship with tins of Jacobs Cream Crackers and H.P. Sauce, shadows loom large on the lunar landscape back-cloth. As Geoffrey H. Wells remarked, the film 'showed a few inadequate scenes of the moon's interior and depicted the Grand Lunar as a giant baby.' The director was J. L. V. Leigh, who as Jack Leigh had made many a comedy short for Cricks & Martin of Mitcham. Doing their patriotic utmost to boost the film, critics excused the poverty-stricken sets. 'It would have been possible to stage many of the mountain pictures against natural backgrounds, but the element of unreality introduced by artificial settings and lighting is by no means a disadvantage in a picture which aims at creating an extra-mundane atmosphere,' said *The Bioscope*. By way of conscience, the same paper felt compelled to note that 'one or two of the subtitles are grammatically unworthy of Mr. Wells, and in an early episode a trifling slip causes the inventor to change his headgear during the course of a short continuous walk.' Of those involved only Heather Thatcher survived to scale cinema stardom: she played Susan Cavor, added as love interest for Hannibal Hogben.

The experience failed to sour Wells. In 1929 he wrote, 'I believe that if I had my life to live over again I might devote myself entirely to working for the cinema.' And to back up his claim, he wrote three original comedies for the upcoming Miss Elsa Lanchester. Scripted by his son, Frank Wells, who was to find a career in British films, only one of these two-reelers might be considered a fantasy film: *Daydreams* (1928).

Wells continued to rhapsodise over the possibilities of cinema in the Introduction to his book, *The King Who Was a King* (1929). This novel was 'in the form of a model scenario for a film of the future', and was a follow-through to a fascination with film form that had come to Wells through his membership of the Film Society. This club for the furtherance of the art of silent cinema had been formed by the Hon Ivor Montagu, a noted left-winger of the period, and it was Montagu who produced Wells' Elsa Lanchester shorts.

Wells' hopes for 'a spectacle-music-drama greater, more beautiful, and intellectually deeper and richer than any artistic form humanity has hitherto achieved' were somewhat diminished when Paramount Pictures produced *The Island of Lost Souls*. This 1933 version of Wells' 1896 novel, *The Island of Dr Moreau*, was promptly banned by the British Censor. The growing audience of horror film fans were furious; Wells, reportedly, was delighted. When the film was finally unveiled in England by Eros Films, some quarter of a century later, its misty, sadistic brilliance proved that the fans were right and Wells was wrong.

Charles Laughton (in a curious Wellsian link: he was married to Elsa Lanchester and had played uncredited bit parts in those silent shorts) gave one of his finest character studies as the slippery vivisectionist who sought to speed evolution through surgery, and who ultimately died horribly at the hands . . . claws . . . of his experiments in his own 'House of Pain'. Star billing went to Kathleen Burke, who played Lota the Panther Girl after a nationwide search for a feline beauty, but more memorable was that old vampire Bela Lugosi, unrecognisably hirsute as The Sayer of the Law ('Not to spill blood, that is the Law . . .'). His make-up, as was that of all the other memorable menagerie of animal men, was created by Wally Westmore, labouring modestly

behind an uncredited bushel. The 1977 remake, *Island of Dr Moreau*, not only miscast muscular Burt Lancaster as the evil experimenter, and switched a sunlit shore for the misty mystery, but its 'humanimals' were created by twelve make-up men – *all* of them credited!

The high year for horror films was 1933, and its highest point was *The Invisible Man*. Wells' novel of 1897 had been promised for some time, ever since *Frankenstein* shot Boris Karloff to fame. R. C. Sherriff, who wrote the classic Great War play, *Journey's End*, had been shipped to Universal City to tailor the tale to Karloff's persona, but in the end the Monster had turned it down. Nobody wanted to play a hero who remained unseen until the climactic deathbed materialisation. Nobody, that is, except Claude Rains.

The English actor was long on experience but short in stature, always fatal for any hopeful Hollywood hero. However, inches mattered little in this case, and Rains had that vital horror-film ingredient, an English voice. It was a trend that began with Karloff, continued with Lionel Atwill, and ended with George

Zucco. Rains was also eager for stardom and knew that what horror films had done for Karloff and Lugosi they could do for him. Instead of agonising hours of make-up, he had equally agonising hours of acting for special effects. John P. Fulton, Universal's wizard of lens and laboratory, used every trick in the movie-magician's book, from those originally created by the master, Méliès, to some nobody had previously heard of, to depict the effect of 'monocaine' on Jack Griffin.

The Invisible Man was, is, a classic of the cinema. It stands as a tribute to Wells' originality, Sherriff's witty dialogue, James Whales' unique directorial talents, and Rains' brilliant acting as 'The Invisible One'. Rains was right: the film made him a star.

Left: H. G. Wells with Alexander Korda in 1935 during the planning of 'Things to Come'. Above: 'The Invisible Man' was one of the successful films cited by the science fiction magazine, 'Wonder Stories' when it ran a campaign to try and encourage film makers to produce more SF movies.

Opposite page: Claude Rains as 'The Invisible Man' – Universal Pictures classic film based on Wells' story and released in 1933.

Millions of picturegoers turned their heads sideways, the better to see his fading face in the ultimate moments. Even Wells was reasonably pleased. He told the press at a London launching party for the film:

Here I do find my narrative sequences respected and the interest gathered together and brought to a climax in competent story-telling style. That is, I suppose, because the synopsis was made by Mr R. C. Sherriff, himself a competent dramatist and story-teller. I am told that Mr Sherriff's version was the thirteenth prepared. I should be amused to see the other twelve versions.

'The Invisible Man' has been a favourite with film makers and audiences ever since his successful first appearance in 1933. Above: A still from 'The Invisible Man Returns' made by Universal in 1940; and (below) David McCallum in the TV serial version, 'The Invisible Man' (1975).

At this point James Whale revealed that 'one bright writer changed the character of the Invisible Man into a giant octopus which captured the heroine in its writhing tentacles!' Wells laughed, then criticised Sherriff for making Monocaine turn Griffin insane. 'If the man had remained sane, we should have had the inherent monstrosity of an ordinary man in this extraordinary position. But instead of an Invisible Man, we now have an Invisible Lunatic!' Whale had an easy rejoinder: If a man said to you that he was about to make himself invisible, wouldn't you think he was crazy already?' Even Wells joined in the lunch-time laughter.

How much of that laughter lingered later is left unrecorded, as Universal Pictures launched their sequence of spin-offs. Perhaps Wells followed the old precept of 'laughing all the way to the bank', as *The Invisible Man Returns* (1940) was followed by *The Invisible Woman* (1941), *Invisible Agent* (1942), *The Invisible Man's Revenge* (1944), and the ultimate degradation, *Abbott and Costello Meet the Invisible Man* (1951). The ultimate, *ultimate* degradation would come through television. Those who thought poorly of the British series of *The Invisible Man* (1958), in which a bit-player in a built-up padded suit spoke with the dubbed-on voice of *Look at Life* commentator Tim Turner, came to regard those shoddy little monochrome half-hours as classics when they saw the American *Invisible Man* (1975). And even David McCallum, ex-Man from UNCLE, in his rubber face-mask, would shine in superiority to the succeeding spin-off, *The Gemini Man* (1976).

In marked contrast to the ever-recycling *Invisible Man*, the next Wells film stands alone, unique, unequalled even in the age of *2001* and *Star Wars*. If the duty of science fiction is to predict as well as entertain, and the science-fiction movie is to visualise both prophecy and philosophy, then *Things to Come* must remain to tower over them all. 'It is a Leviathan among films. A stupendous spectacle staggering to the eye, mind and spirit, the like of which has never been seen and never will be seen again. It makes film history.' So wrote Sydney W. Carroll, film critic of the *Sunday Times*, back in 1935: words that hold true after more than forty years.

'Wells' Prophetic Spectacle', as one of the many publicity phrases put it, was conceived on the grand scale from the start. Alexander Korda, the Hungarian from Hollywood who had won England her first Oscar with *The Private Life of Henry VIII*, was determined to produce the biggest and best British film ever. Wells had all the prestige Korda could need, plus the popular touch: his latest book, more philosophy than fiction, was top of the best-seller lists – *The Shape of Things to Come* (1933). The publicity that followed Wells' agreement to adapt his book to the cinema was only the start. Treatment followed treatment, and the final one, together with Wells' notes and comments, was published as the Book of the Film. It shows Wells' involvement went deeper than the dialogue: music, costumes, design, everything is carefully thought out. The music became an instant classic, and Arthur Bliss's tremendous score became the first film music to be recorded as an album. The special effects were worked out by Ned Mann, the Hollywood ace from Douglas Fairbanks' unequalled

Thief of Bagdad. The director was William Cameron Menzies, again a Hollywood ace: director of *Chandu the Magician*, adaptor of *Alice in Wonderland*. Art director and designer was Korda's brother Vincent, assisted by H. G.'s son, Frank. Costumes were by John Armstrong, Rene Hubert and the Marchioness of Queensberry: 'The feminine ensemble consists of a flimsy one-piece garment, the skirt of which ends well above the knees, with a long cape surmounted by a wide stiff collar'. Actors were the pick of the London stage: Ralph Richardson as the Boss who would rise from the rubble of war; Sir Cedric Hardwicke as the philosopher Theotocopulos who would argue eloquently against man's voyage to the moon; Raymond Massey as John and Oswald Cabal, who would lead Wings Over the World to bring peace through science.

The film began scripting in March 1934, was costed

An advertisement for Alexander Korda's much vaunted production of 'Things to Come' (1936).

at £100,000, to complete by January 1935. By the time the cameras stopped turning in February 1936, £260,000 had been spent: a world record. The film itself opened in 1940 and ended in 2036 as mankind stepped into space. That Wells was one year out in his prediction of World War Two, eighty years out in his prediction of space flight, is a subject for the philosophers to discuss. In the history of the cinema it is of no importance. *Things to Come* is, and always will be, an experience.

The Man Who Could Work Miracles came in 1937 as Korda and Wells' follow-up, 'a film of imaginative comedy' as the author described it in a companion volume to his *Things to Come*. The foundation of the film was a short story he had written in 1898, with that favourite Wellsian character, the humble little shopman, as hero. George McWhirter Fotheringay was ideally cast: Roland Young, a Hollywood henpeck. This meek fellow is bestowed the power to work miracles by some heavenly elementals (including a young George Sanders). The results range from the hilarious to the epic, from a fat village Bobby sent to patrol the streets of San Francisco, to the stopping of the world. Again the effects were superb, by the expert Ned Mann, the acting of the finest, by Ralph Richardson again and Ernest Thesiger, and the whole a great popular success.

Facing page: One of the lavish sets designed for 'Things to Come'.

Left: A daring costume for Margarita Scott, one of the stars of 'Things to Come'.

Below: Raymond Massey, the star of 'Things to Come' in his futuristic aircraft which did actually fly!

The war Wells had predicted came true in 1939, and it was not until it had ended in 1945 that another of his fantasies was filmed. And again it was a short story, *The Inexperienced Ghost*, perfec stuff for fun in the special effects department. Basil Radford and Naunton Wayne, a ready-made team from Alfred Hitchcock's *The Lady Vanishes*, discarded their Charters and Caldicott characters and donned their Parratt and Potter hats. George Parratt it was who cheated at golf and was haunted ever after by Larry Potter, sacrificial suicide. The appearings and disappearings were in line with those established by *Topper* and *Hellzapoppin'*, thus making an oasis of laughter in the otherwise macabre omnibus that was *Dead of*

Night. The segment was directed by Charles Crichton who had been one of the film editors on *Things to Come*.

Paramount Pictures bought *The War of the Worlds*, which Wells had written in 1896, in 1926. The film did not emerge until 1953, but it was worth the wait. Technicolor was here, and George Pal, the Hungarian

A montage of films based on works by H. G. Wells. Far left: 'The Man Who Could Work Miracles' starring Roland Young, 1937. Left: Basil Radford haunted by the shade of his golf partner in 'The Inexperienced Ghost' segment of the film 'Dead of Night' (1945). Stephen Murray and Ian Hunter debate whether to go through the mysterious 'Door in the Wall' made in 1956 (below). A touch of beauty (right) as Yvette Mimieux wrestles with one of the Morlocks in 'The Time Machine' (1960).

puppet-master, had graduated from Horlicks commercials to the position of top science-fiction filmmaker with his epics *Destination Moon* and *When Worlds Collide*. Both those films had been box-office successes despite their stolid documentary styles, and Pal sought the imaginative sweep of Wells' ever-popular novel to add a new dimension to his fantasy film-making. The special effects department had a field day, bringing the honour of an Academy Award to Gordon Jennings, regrettably posthumously. As with most of George Pal's pictures, this one fell down in the casting. Going as usual for relative unknowns, on the theory that this created believability, Pal picked Gene Barry and Ann Robinson as his leads in the battle of Earth versus Mars. However, the choice

The making of 'The First Men in the Moon' in 1964.
Right: On the set of the lunar landscape, the two
astronauts, Edward Judd and Lionel Jeffries, take
their first tentative steps on the moon's surface.
Below: The special effects for the picture were in
the hands of the brilliant Ray Harryhausen who
used Dynamation, Panavision and Lunacolor to
achieve his ends: these are some of his sketches for
important scenes. Bottom: Harryhausen on the left
supervising the filming of his special effects.

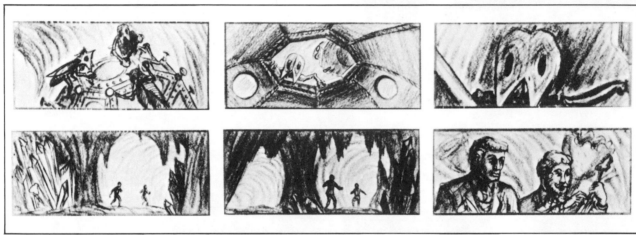

of Charles Gemora to play the only Martian seen on screen was not bad: Gemora specialised in supplying ape monsters to horror films! Barre Lyndon shifted his screenplay from Wellsian England of the 'Nineties to contemporary California, evidently under orders, for Lyndon was the English author Alfred Edgar who turned out thousands of 'tuppeny blood' tales in *Modern Boy* and many other boys' papers of the 'Thirties. Sir Cedric Hardwicke linked back to the pre-war Wells films by playing the voice that delivered the famous epilogue on how the Martians were finally defeated by the smallest creatures on God's Earth, bacteria. 'Nothing so Spectacular Ever put on Film Before!' screamed the posters, quite forgetting *Things to Come*.

Just as Wells had experimented with ideas, so cinema has experimented. Some catch on: Cinema-Scope, Stereoscopy, Cinerama. Some don't: Dynamic Frame. *The Door in the Wall* was a short film made in this process in 1956; it remains unique. Glenn H. Alvey Jr invented the system, adapted the Wells story of 1906, and directed it. Stephen Murray and Ian Hunter co-starred, with Kit Terrington as the young Murray who, as a boy, discovers an enchanted garden. The Dynamic Frame used a basic cinema-scope screen, masking off portions to make dramatic points. Thus the screen expands to reveal a dragon, contracts to close in on the boy to express his confinement.

At last, in 1960, *The Time Machine* came to the screen. George Pal produced and also directed, so the result was perhaps less than all R. W. Paul and H. G. Wells might have hoped for. Yankee Rod Taylor played Wells himself, in as unlikely a stroke of casting in screen history. At least, one may presume he played Wells, for although his name was never spoken in the story, a shot of the Time Machine itself, which he has constructed, bears the engraved abel: 'H. George Wells'. The Traveller's trip through the centuries to the far-flung future of the Eloi seemed cut-price after the excesses of *The War of the Worlds*. Curious, for the move of Pal from Paramount to MGM might have suggested the reverse. Yvette Mimieux played Weena the Eloi, happily amplified into a Hollywood-style love interest, while the Morlocks were monsters indeed. Pal's permanent failing, overbright Technicolor, brought back the usual memories of his *Puppetoons*. Nor was the time-lapse photography of the passing years without its careless faults.

A new version of *The First Men in the Moon* arrived in 1964, made in England, as was the original, but with American talent and money. Charles H. Schneer, a producer with a taste for fantasy, had his favourite effects man Ray Harryhausen animate the Selenites in Dynamation, Panavision and Lunacolor, and the *Quatermass* scriptwriter from BBC-TV, Nigel Kneale, adapt the screenplay. Cleverly cashing in on the nostalgic boom in Victoriana, Ameran Productions kept their film in 1899, framing the tale as a flashback through the investigations of United Nations astronauts of today. They even had Colonel John 'Shorty' Powers, voice of Mercury Control, give a testimonial. 'It's definitely All Systems Go!' said Shorty, characteristically. But despite all this, despite too an injected love interest in the shape of Martha Hyer, suffragette-astronaut, the film failed in its mission at the box-office.

Rod Taylor at the controls of 'The Time Machine' produced and directed by George Pal in 1960.

Most of the movie monsters of the outsize ilk owe their origins to Wells' novel *The Food of the Gods* (1904). This science-fantasy of Herakleophorbia, a growth-stimulant that creates giant insects and vermin, came to the screen twice, and each film seems to have devoured its own Herakleophorbia. Each pretended it was bigger and better than its budget allowed, and each died the death of the overblown quickie. *Village of the Giants* (1965) had teenagers eat the stuff for kicks and the resultant rock'n'roll riots tore up the town. The cast included Tommy Kirk, Freddie Cannon, Beau Bridges and the Beau Brummels, and the film was directed by Bert I. Gordon, something of a specialist in Z-grade B-movies built around his back-projection screen. *The Food of the Gods* (1976) was not much better, but was at least honest. The credits claimed it was 'based on a portion of the novel by H. G. Wells'. That portion was evidently the five words of the title. Wells' experimental growth-stimulant has become a strange substance oozing out of the earth, while the shakily-animated results have become a wasp, a cockerel, and some worms. The film was written, directed, and Special Visual Effect-ed by the same Bert I. Gordon, who provided a chill note of suspense at the end. Two jars of the Food escape and drift downstream towards some grazing cows . . . Will there be a sequel? Will Bert I. Gordon strike back? Coming Next Week: *The Milk of the Gods*? For the sake of H. George Wells and cinemagoers everywhere, one can only hope not.

Filming War of the Worlds

GEORGE PAL

Paramount Pictures 1953 version of The War of the Worlds *is still regarded in many quarters as one of the best interpretations of a Wells story on the screen – particularly because of the successful special effects it contained. In this article, written for* Astounding Science Fiction *magazine in October 1953, George Pal, the world-famous producer of the film, explains both how the project was assembled and the secrets behind achieving the realistic portrayal of the Martian invasion.*

Whenever a Hollywood producer brings out a new motion picture in which he has tampered with the plot of a well-known novel or play, he's inviting criticism.

We took that risk when we made the H. G. Wells classic, "War Of The Worlds," but inasmuch as none of us connected with it have been dodging any verbal tomatoes since, I take it that the audiences approve.

"War of the Worlds" was on my agenda of future projects almost since the day I arrived at Paramount Studio two and one half years ago after producing my first science-fiction venture, "Destination Moon" for Eagle-Lion release.

Paramount had owned the Wells story for some twenty-six years but no producer had ever tackled it, although it had been discussed several times. But now

with the big vogue for films of a science-fiction nature it seemed a logical choice.

So it was natural that I selected it as one of my first story properties for future production.

I was stimulated by the problems it posed. Although written fifty-six years ago, in many respects it had

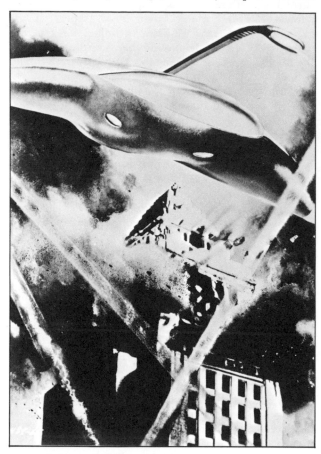

The Martian invader wrecks death and destruction – an exciting moment from the finished film of 'The War of the Worlds' (1953).

withstood the advances of time remarkably well and remained today an exciting and visionary story of the future.

It offered me my greatest challenge to date in figuring out how to film the Martian machines, their heat and disintegration rays and the destruction and chaos they cause when they invade Earth.

It ended up by being my most costly picture to date, $2,000,000, as contrasted with $586,000 for "Destination Moon," and $936,000 for "When Worlds Collide".

It also took the longest period of time to make. More than six months of special-effects work plus an additional two months for optical effects were needed after our regular shooting schedule with the cast was concluded; work with the cast took forty days at the studio and on location in Arizona.

More special-effects work went into "War of the Worlds" than any of my other pictures. More than four times as many, for instance, as went into "When Worlds Collide".

Actually one half of the final completed picture which you see on the screen consists of some form of special effects created by our exceptional department here at Paramount Studio.

It is my great sorrow that my good friend Gordon Jennings, Paramount Special-Effects Director for more than two decades, a multiple Academy Award winner and the recognized leader in his field, died of a heart attack shortly after we finished work on the picture and before it was shown publicly.

If for one moment you think the challenge of modernizing Wells' story was child's play, just take a scrap of paper and list the commonplace inventions and scientific discoveries which we utilize in our daily living that were utterly nonexistent when Wells wrote his story.

There were no airplanes, atom bombs or tanks with which to fight the Martian machines at the time he wrote his tale. His readers followed his story on a flight of imagination. Our audience comes to the theater today conversant with the terms: nuclear physics, atomic fission, gravitational fields and space platforms.

Even the children play with space helmets and ray guns and are even more familiar with such expressions as "blast off" than their elders.

It was exciting to take Wells' imaginative work and couple it with modern discoveries and come up with a film that would be entertaining, credible and believable to an audience geared to scientific awareness.

One of our first decisions was to move the setting from London and environs to Southern California. It was more practical to shoot in an easily accessible area. Also influencing our decision were the many stories of flying saucers in the last few years which have emanated from the western part of the United States.

George Pal, producer and director of 'The War of the Worlds'.

Our audiences might well believe that such a Martian invasion could take place in such a locale.

Los Angeles as the metropolis invaded by the Martians was a logical choice, too, because it was possible for us to arrange to actually clear a portion of the city streets of the populace for several of our scenes.

I'll wager that if I could climb into the Time Machine which Wells wrote about in another story and flash back fifty-six years for a conference with the gentleman, he'd have approved the changes.

Now how he would have taken our addition of a romantic interest I won't hazard a guess. But in the film business you have to be practical. No one is less interested in doing routine boy meets girl stories than I. But a boy-and-girl theme is necessary even in a science-fiction film of the scope of "War of the Worlds". Audiences want it.

So we introduced a young college scientist played by a talented newcomer named Gene Barry. As his companion we cast Ann Robinson, another bright new talent.

In one respect we hewed right to the Wells original. That was in his conception of a Martian being.

He dreamed up an octopuslike creature. We made ours a huge crablike being with one giant Cyclops eye with three separate lenses, a big head to hold its oversize brain, and long spindly tentacles with suckers on the end for arms.

The Martian was the handiwork of our talented young unit art director Albert Nozaki who worked throughout with us from start to finish under Paramount supervising art director Hal Pereira.

After Nozaki finished his design I called in a sculptor, make-up man and artist named Charles Gemora, who became famous as the gorilla in the film "Ingagi" years ago. I asked him to build the monster.

He built it out of papier-mâché and sheet rubber, created arms that actually pulsated – through the use of rubber tubing in them – and painted the whole thing lobster red. It was a startler all right – something right out of your worst nightmare.

Gemora is a short-statured man who could fit into the contraption too, so we hired him to operate it. When he got inside he moved around on his knees, holding his arms hunched out. His hands came just to the elbows of the Martian's formidable-looking tentacles.

Then we showed only one fleeting glimpse of the creature in the final picture! All that effort, money and time for a few seconds on the screen.

Why? Naturally there was an argument on how much the Martian was to be shown in the finished picture. But we decided that a hint of horror is often more effective than a large dose. And anyway, would you have wanted to know this thing intimately?

Our greatest special-effects problem in the production was building and operating the warlike Martian machines which land on Earth to destroy its inhabitants. We came close to electrocuting our crew in designing this one.

We went back to the original Wells book for inspiration. My first edition is illustrated with scenes of a huge, disklike object on giant stilts.

However, Wells' conception of the machines was

A technician supervising the building of one of the Martian space craft on the set of 'The War of the Worlds'.

mechanical. In this era we decided ours should be electrical.

I wish we'd never seen the illustrations of the stiltlike legs at all! We'd have saved a lot of grief. For the original plan, worked out by the special-effects people, was to have the machines – which were to be miniatures – rest on three pulsating beams of static electricity serving as legs.

The idea was to use a high-voltage electrical discharge of some one million volts fed down to the legs from wires suspended from an overhead rig on the sound stage. A high velocity blower was used from behind to force the sparks down the legs.

We made tests under controlled conditions on our special-effects stage and they were spectacular. I couldn't have been more delighted.

But there was one great problem. It was dangerous to generate a million volts on a regular sound stage. It would be too easy for the sparks to jump to damp, dirt, metal, or what have you. It could have killed someone, perhaps set the studio on fire.

So after the test opening scene we reluctantly gave up the electrical legs for the machine, although a great deal of hard work had already been expended on them.

It was in actuality as dangerous as we had wanted it to be on the screen!

The Martian machine and its destructive rays, although looming large on the screen, in reality were scaled down to one sixth real size when we filmed it.

We built three miniature machines, forty-two inches in diameter and made out of copper to maintain the reddish hue always identified with Mars, the red planet.

They were flat, semi-disk shaped objects. We gave them three distinctive features, a long cobra neck which emitted a disintegrating ray, an electrical TV camera type scanner on the end of a snakelike metal coil which emerged from the body of the machine, and wing-tip flame throwers.

Each machine was operated by fifteen hair-fine wires connected to a device on an overhead track. By means of these wires we carried the electrical controls to make the cobra neck, the scanning eye and other portions operate properly.

This was indeed puppetry on a huge scale!

Here is another trade trick on how we made the triple-lensed scanner:

It was actually thick plastic with hexagonal holes cut in it. Behind these, rotating light shutters gave a flickering effect.

But in creating the flicker we got into fresh trouble. We got a strobotach effect, the sort of thing you see in a movie of wagon wheels in which the turning spokes seem to go faster, then slower when they are in conflict with the camera shutter speed. Our answer was to very carefully regulate the shutter speed behind the head.

Those vicious-looking fire rays emanating from the machines were burning welding wire. As the wire melted, a blow torch set up behind, blew the wire out. The finished result looked highly realistic.

Before we ever started shooting the picture, more than one thousand sketches were prepared by Nozaki supervised by Art Director Pereira, working in close collaboration with Director Byron Haskin. These showed their conception of how combined live action and special effects, or each of them separately, would look.

Originally, they were rough sketches but by the time we were ready to begin shooting in January, 1952, detailed drawings were completed and inserted at the proper places in the script to guide Director Haskin, Cameraman George Barnes, A.S.C., and the rest of the crew.

It isn't customary to detail so carefully what each scene and camera setup will look like but in a science-fiction film of this type, it is vitally necessary to hold down costs and production time.

Nozaki's drawings were especially valuable in the extensive sequence showing the evacuation of Los Angeles and the attack on the city by the Martian machines. Both live action and special- and optical-effects were extensively mixed in these complex scenes.

In addition to shooting the downtown section of Los Angeles in real life, we created it in miniature on a Paramount sound stage.

Miniatures are becoming a worse headache with each picture made. I've learned that even the bobby-soxers can spot them in most films these days.

We absolutely had to maintain an aura of credibility and authenticity for our story. This tends to give those expensive ulcers to special-effects men and producers you read about.

As a result we built miniatures more carefully than ever before. We strove for lifelike authenticity by distinguish between the miniatures and the real thing making them larger. Our Los Angeles City Hall miniature, for example, was eight feet tall.

Quite a few experts told me that they couldn't

which really made me feel proud.

A check was made with Civil Defense Authorities before staging the evacuation scenes in order to incorporate the latest techniques for such an emergency.

Automobiles, rather than tuxedos, were the requirements for the nine hundred extras hired for the sequence. We wanted a traffic jam.

One of the scenes turned out to be unrehearsed real life. During the filming we heard one day that there had been a crash on the new Hollywood Freeway which had caused a bad traffic tie-up. A camera crew was rushed to the spot like a newsreel staff and caught the scene.

We needed a deserted city. Ours was Los Angeles at 5:00 a.m. on a Sunday morning. Its normally clear streets at that hour were enforced by police outposts hooked up with our company by walkie-talkie.

It was hard work to frame a panic evacuation scene – but even more work to clean up the fallen masonry, rubble, papers, and trash scattered for blocks up and down the center of one of America's largest cities afterwards.

Here's an example of how we tied in special-effects with the real-life evacuation:

We photographed a street on our back lot. With this we matched four by five ectachrome still shots of Bunker Hill in downtown Los Angeles. These were rephotographed on Technicolor film.

A hand-painted matte, done on an eight by ten inch blowup, then reduced to regulation 35 mm. film frame size, of the sky, background, flame-effects and the Martian machines was then matched with the live action.

This complicated business is accomplished in the special-effects camera department with large, expensive, custom-built, optical printers under the direction of Paul Lerpae, a veteran in the business.

He has optical printer cameras mounted on lathes with adjustments calibrated down to 1/10,000 of an inch.

It has to be in that great detail. The tiniest mistake made on a single film frame is magnified two hundred times on a average-sized screen, even more on the new wide screens now coming into vogue.

For "War of the Worlds," the optical-effects department painted between three thousand to four thousand celluloid frames for us.

In one brief flash in the picture an army colonel is disintegrated by a Martian machine. It took exactly one hundred forty-four mattes of his inked-in figure to accomplish this illusion.

But everything I've described so far was just a practice session for the biggest hurdle of them all. The single, most difficult sequence to create in the entire picture was when the United States Army attacked the Martian machines and they fought back.

First we did the easy part – the live action with our cast and the National Guard on location near Phoenix, Arizona. For two days the outfit went through maneuvers while our cameramen shot scenes of them defending our country against Martians.

Then the special-effects boys went to work. First, matte shots of trees and a command post were made. Then miniatures of a gully where the actors could hide, and the approaching three Martian machines were photographed.

Next the rays and explosions were inserted. After that came the bright yellowish foreground explosions.

In all we had five complicated processes to contend with. At times we made as many as twenty-eight different exposures to get one single final color scene.

For a scene where an attacking tank is disintegrated, we inked in the tank outline on an opaque matte. Then we changed the color to red, then to red-blue. We got a flaring out of sudden flame from the tank by using diffusion glasses. Here was the spot where we switched from red to yellow. Afterwards we photographically "dodged in" the burnt areas around the area where the tank had been.

When the United States forces drop an atom bomb on the Martians we had to come up with a gimmick to protect the invaders in this crisis. Special-effects devised a large, plastic bubble, five feet in diameter.

First, the machine was filmed alone. The we photographed the explosion and the bubble and superimposed that negative over the first to get the final result.

There was no clearance needed for the facsimile of the atom bomb we used. It was a stunt engineered right on our own sound stage by Paramount's eighty-one-year-old powder expert, Walter Hoffman.

He got his effect by putting a collection of colored explosive powders on top of an air-tight metal drum

Technicians creating one of the miniature houses to be 'destroyed' by the Martian space craft – another photograph taken on the set of 'The War of the Worlds'.

filled with an explosive gas. Rigged up with an electrical remote control, its second try reached a height of seventy-five feet with the mushroom top of the real thing.

Getting Army clearance was not a major concern in producing "War of the Worlds". We did use a few stock shots from the Northrop and North American Aviation Companies which had to be submitted to the Department of Defense, but it was minor. One of these was a shot of the Flying Wing which we used to carry the atom bomb against the Martians.

While producing both "Destination Moon" and "When Worlds Collide," I had employed the unique talents of artist Chesley Bonestell. I naturally wanted him back for "War of the Worlds". When he came, he served a double role.

A series of his paintings of the planets in our solar system were shown during the prologue with the voice of Sir Cedric Hardwick impersonating that of H. G. Wells in describing why the Martians were forced to migrate from their planet. He explains why Earth was the only one that would do.

Most of Bonestell's paintings were made on canvas of standard size but in the case of Jupiter he painted on glass. He created a mural seven by four feet showing Jupiter's ragged terrain leaving cut-out areas in order that the special-effects department could insert lifelike looking streams of molten lava coursing down the mountainsides.

Bonestell was also our trouble shooter in his role of technical adviser. He's the one who questioned accuracy when screenwriter Barre Lyndon gave the night temperature on Mars. As Dr. Robert Richardson, Mount Wilson Observatory solar specialist affirmed, we have never seen the night side of Mars through telescopes so we can only guess at the temperature. Better cut it out.

Then there was the Saturn incident. The script had presented the planet as peaceful and quiet. Bonestell advised that the bands around Saturn – not the famous rings – appear stormy.

As contact man between us and Mount Wilson and scientists at California Institute of Technology – which we call Pacific Tech in the picture – Bonestell kept us on the right track.

Unfortunately for the straining ingenuity of the creators, you aren't through with a science-fiction film when it looks right. It's got to sound right, too.

Just what does an out-of-this-world cry or noise sound like? Gene Garvin, our dubbing mixer, took on this problem and pondered and tested it for three months.

How would a Martian scream sound? The boys thought a long time on that one. Finally they arrived at the unusual conclusion of scraping dry ice across a

microphone and combining it with a woman's high scream recorded backwards.

It was the weirdest sound anyone has yet come up with for one of my pictures.

The vibrating, almost singing noise of the machines themselves was a magnetic recorder hooked up to send back an oscillation sound.

The eerie sound of the Martian's death ray was chords struck on three guitars, the sounds amplified,

then played backwards and reverberated.

Although it took months to come up with the sounds, once we had them it was a simple matter to record them in the picture.

The nerve strain or co-ordination in a film like "War of the Worlds" is tremendous. Let one department fluff off and the whole result goes flooey no matter how the others have knocked themselves out for perfection. You get so wrapped up in your own particular problems and your part of the teamwork that by the time the film is in the can, the whole thing is sort of a haze.

You've knocked yourself out on details and technicalities so that when someone asks you, "Is it good," you can't answer "yes" or "no" for sure. The whole thing is a blur. A conventional picture is considerably easier to produce and judge.

That's why the first sneak preview at the Paradise Theater in Westchester, a Los Angeles suburb, last November had all those who worked on the film slightly off this world's gravity. We'd used our imagination and ingenuity – given it everything we had. Was it good or was it ripe for blasé teenagers' laughter?

It was a fine feeling which the cast and creators shared when the preview cards came in "good." Just to make sure that this favorable audience wasn't an exception, we staged a second sneak preview in Santa Monica. Another top response. Then we really relaxed.

Those Friday night audiences of youths from twelve to twenty-five in jeans and leather jackets are the toughest audiences in the world to please. We were satisfied that, if they took our version of H. G. Wells, we'd made the grade.

Uncurling our fingers, almost arthritic with crossings, the print was shipped to New York. But was it time to vacation? Not by a planetful. Now let's see: If we got disintegration in "War of the Worlds," can we create artificial satellites in "Conquest of Space"? I hope so. It's the next science-fiction film on the agenda, you know.

Wells the Science Fiction Fan!

In the 1920's and 30's, many of H. G. Wells's scientific novels and short stories were published in the American 'pulp' magazines which flourished at this time. The pioneer science-fiction magazine, *Amazing Stories*, edited by the great Hugo Gernsback, reprinted twenty-six of his tales, and several reprints also appeared in *Science Wonder Stories*, *Ghost Stories* and the legendary horror magazine, *Weird Tales*. Wells received copies of some of these, and on a number of occasions expressed interest in the illustrations which accompanied his work. (A selection of some of the best of these drawings from *Amazing Stories* are reproduced in this book.)

Many of the stories which were appearing all the time in these magazines were clearly influenced by Wells, but one man who went further than most to show his debt was the British writer, Festus Pragnell,

who contributed to several of the pulps, and in particular the Gernsback publications. Other than *Amazing Stories*, Gernsback also edited *Wonder Stories*, and it was for this that Pragnell wrote a serial in 1933 entitled, "The Green Men of Graypec" with a leading character called . . . H. GeeWells (see illustration).

Shortly afterwards, the serial was republished in book form in Britain with the revised title, "The Green Men of Kilsona", and the publishers sent a

Facing page: The cameras roll as the technicians set the Martian invader in motion on the set of 'The War of the Worlds'.

This page: Advertisements for the latest of H. G. Wells' stories to be turned into films. Top: 'Food of the Gods', 1977; (left) Man-into-animal motif for 'The Island of Dr Moreau', 1977; (above) paperback tie-in edition for 'Empire of the Ants' (1978).

copy to Wells in the hope that he might comment on it. A few weeks later, and much to his delight, Festus Pragnell, received the following letter from Wells:

Dear Mr. Pragnell,
I wanted something to read last night and I found your book on a table in my study. I think it's a very good story indeed of the fantastic-scientific type, and I was much amused and pleased to find myself figuring in it.

Wells could not resist signing himself: 'H. GeeWells'. It seemed from this that the man who had pioneered science fiction had himself become a fan of the genre!

Science Fiction Times, 1959

H. GeeWells, the hero of 'The Green Men of Graypec' by Festus Pragnell, which Wells read and enjoyed. This illustration by Saaty was for its publication in 'Wonder Stories', 1933.

Science Fiction That Endures

HUGO GERNSBACK

H. G. Wells, of course, played no part in giving the scientific romance type of story the popular name it now enjoys – Science Fiction – although his importance in helping establish it is undeniable. The man who actually evolved the words which now sum up this whole area of speculative writing was Hugo Gernsback (1884-1967) the legendary 'Father of the

Science Fiction Magazine'. As a child, Gernsback read both Jules Verne and Wells and they so fired his imagination that he vowed one day to launch a magazine full of such material. On 5 April 1926 he finally published Amazing Stories – The Magazine of Scientifiction *and in the first issue defined what he meant by his title. 'By "scientifiction",' he wrote, 'I mean the Jules Verne, H. G. Wells and Edgar Allan Poe type of story – a charming romance intermingled with scientific fact and prophetic vision.' The publication was an immediate success, and it was only a short while before the somewhat clumsy 'Scientifiction' had evolved into science fiction. Throughout his long and influential life, Gernsback saw science fiction develop from a quirky minority interest into one of the most popular of all literary forms. But throughout all this time, he never forgot the debt he and all other admirers of the genre owed to the men who sparked all their interests – Jules Verne and H. G. Wells. And shortly before his death, he paid a final tribute to both of them in this special article for* Amazing Stories. *Once again it underlines the richness and importance of the inheritance Wells' gave us with his works.*

As we look back over the vista of modern science fiction, we are struck by the fact that the outstanding stories in the field – the ones that endure – are those that almost invariably have as their wonder ingredient true or prophetic science.

It is these stories that arouse our imagination and make a lasting impression on us which succeeding years do not seem to obliterate.

Let us take only two authors, Jules Verne (1828-1905) and H. G. Wells (1866-1946), as an example. Both authors had a considerable output of true *science* fiction, with the accent on science. In the *Encyclopaedia Britannica*, top billing is given to only these Verne stories: *Voyage to the Centre of the Earth* (1864); *From the Earth to the Moon* (1865); *20,000 Leagues Under the Sea* (1869); *The English at the North Pole* (1870); *Around the World in 80 Days* (1872). All of these highly imaginative tales concern themselves with science, and, as the *Britannica* says: "The novels of Jules Verne are dreams come true, dreams of submarines, airplanes, television; they look forward, not backward. Therefore they are still the books of youth."

Wells' best and most enduring stories, too, were comparatively few of a large list. To quote the *Britannica* once more: "He was to clothe scientific speculation in the form of fiction." Here are some of Wells' outstanding science-fiction efforts, both novels and short stories: *The Time Machine* (1895); *The Stolen Bacillus* (1896); *The Invisible Man* (1897); *The War of the Worlds* (1898); *The Sleeper Awakes* (1899); *Tales of Space and Time* (1899); *The First Men in the Moon* (1901).

Both Verne and Wells wrote a large variety of other stories, yet in my opinion and that of many authorities it is the science-fiction content that makes them enduring and historic – deservedly so.

Both of these illustrious authors had succumbed to the phenomenon of science fiction fatigue – the creative science distillate of the mind had been exhausted. New prophetic visions could no longer be generated.

Science fiction exhaustion is well known to every author of the genre; some succumb to it early, others late in their careers. It is a phenomenon only too well understood by all editors and publishers, who must cope with it. Nor is it any wonder that the science output of nearly all authors who have ever tried it is so limited. Only those who have attempted it can know how difficult and exhausting the subject can become.

Verne and Wells continued writing until advanced ages, after they had written themselves out in science-fiction themes. They then went into many other avenues of literature. To mention only one: Wells' famous *The Outline of History* (1920).

The true science-fiction author must have a high order of inventiveness; he must have constant inspiration, intuitive and prophetic insight of the future; and, above all, he must know his science. No wonder that there are only a handful of first-rate science-fiction authors.

When I brought out AMAZING STORIES monthly in 1926, I had accumulated considerable experience in science fiction. I had been publishing what I called "Scientifiction" in my various earlier magazines off and on, but not in a periodical entirely devoted to it.

In 1911 for my pioneer magazine MODERN ELECTRICS, I wrote a serial, *Ralph 124C 41+*. Then came *The Scientific Adventures of Mr. Fosdick*, by Jacque Morgan, who lasted for five stories. Later, in the ELECTRICAL EXPERIMENTER magazine, I wrote *Baron Munchhausen's New Scientific Adventures*, which went through 13 instalments. Very good authors in the same magazine were George Frederic Stratton, Charles M. Adams, Charles S. Wolfe, all of whom wrote occasional stories.

Next to arrive was the celebrated Clement Fezandié, a most talented French-American who invented the famous humorous science fiction stories under the all-encompassing title of *Dr. Hackensaw's Secrets*, each with a fresh scientific concept. The first one, in the ELECTRICAL EXPERIMENTER for July, 1920, was entitled *My Message to Mars*. This titan of science fiction ended his output with story No. 43 – a four-part serial which he called *A Journey to the Center of the Earth*, in my former magazine, SCIENCE AND INVENTION, September, 1925, issue. Fezandié avowedly was an idea genius. In the color-powder-pigment business, he wrote for fun *only* and religiously sent back all checks in payment of his stories! He also wrote two more stories for AMAZING STORIES in 1926. I doubt if any science fiction author today can match his voluminous output for pure science fiction stories and unusual ideas.

There was also a nine-part serial, *Tarrano the Conqueror*, by Ray Cummings, in the same magazine, as was *The Metal Emperor* by A. Merritt, which ran from 1927 to 1928 through eleven installments.

Finally, we printed the *Ark of the Covenant*, by Victor MacClure, a serial published in 15 parts in PRACTICAL ELECTRICS from Nov. 1924, to Jan. 1926.

From the short history above it will be seen that the concept of AMAZING STORIES in 1926 was not a haphazard undertaking. Its groundwork had been well prepared for 15 years! Few modern magazines that have endured were rehearsed so well and so long!

What is the future of science fiction in this country? For one who has been closely allied with it for 50

Top: Hugo Gernsback, the 'Father of Scientifiction'.

Above: Cover of the April 1928 issue of Gernsback's 'Amazing Stories' which contained his own story 'Baron Munchhausen's Scientific Adventures' and H. G. Wells' 'A Story of the Days to Come'.

years, I would venture the opinion that, like the stock market, it has its ups and downs, its peaks and its valleys – yet, it, too, for the long pull, advances steadily over the years.

Because of the present unusual interest in science by our young generation, it would seem certain that there will be far more science-fiction authors in the future than there ever were in the past. Hence there should be more and better stories, too.

I was much encouraged last October when, invited to speak on science fiction at the Massachusetts Institute of Technology, I noted the profound interest of the students in the subject. My talk lasted only 30 minutes, but the question and answer period took nearly 2 hours!

But what impressed me most was that a university of the calibre of MIT took science fiction so seriously. If now all other seats of learning will inaugurate science-fiction societies, I can see only a vast and steady increase in this, the most exciting facet of literature in modern times.

And now a thought from our a-pun-sor. It may NOT be welcomed in certain quarters: There will come the future amazing day – now don't all laugh at once – when AMAZING STORIES will be

The influence that H. G. Wells had over Hugo Gernsback was perhaps nowhere more evident than in the 'Superworld Comics' he published in 1940. This now extremely rare collectors' item was illustrated by Frank Paul who had been Gernsback's leading artist on 'Amazing Stories'. Above: Mitey Powers who was sent to the Moon to battle with some hostile Martians ensconsed there and planning to invade the Earth. Top: Buzz Allen, 'The Invisible Avenger', who put his special powers to work in fighting crime. Right: Illustration from a special article by Gernsback himself entitled 'Humans and Martians' complete with a sketch of Wells' Martian!

Facing page, left: The stories of H. G. Wells are now favourite material for comic strip publishers, as these four examples from the 'Marvel Comics' range show.

Facing page, right: Even some of the slightest of Wells' novels with elements of fantasy or science fiction about them are being republished in the current SF boom. 'Star Begotten', which Wells wrote in 1937 and dedicated to Winston Churchill, came out in this edition from Sphere Books in 1975.

composed, or perhaps outlined in detail, not by human authors, but by an *electronic biocomputer-menograph* (*menos*-mind). I also predict that this *Autocerebration* wonder is not likely to suffer from Science-Fiction Fatigue nor Exhaustion.

Mars Probe Furrows Scientists' Brows

This report from The Times *of 18 June 1977 makes a most appropriate final item, as it details some of the most recent discoveries about Mars. I wonder what the creator of* The War of the Worlds *would have made of it?*

Mars has been having a spell of typically English weather lately; but that intelligence has done nothing to help to clear up the mystery of the ploughed fields.

The areas of immaculate, championship-standard furrowing were shown in some of the 12,000 photographs of the red planet sent back by the American Viking space probe between its launching in June last year and the recent arrival of a large bank of thick cloud. Members of the Viking team, reporting progress at a Royal Society lecture in London yesterday, confessed that they were puzzled.

Photographs of the Martian landscape taken by the orbiting spacecraft from a height of 1,500 km and resembling extreme close-ups of the hide of a particularly pimply elephant, show the southern hemisphere of Mars to be heavily cratered like the Moon, and the northern hemisphere to be a lava plain with much sparser cratering.

Scientists are taking a close interest in the gullies and channels, which were once thought to be canals but which, it is now considered certain, were created by the action of water.

Dr. Michael Carr, of the United States Geological Survey, said he had detected from the pictures integrated drainage systems, which he concluded had been caused by "early fluvial episodes".

Dr. Carr said that some of the channels were about 1 km deep, suggesting enormous flows of water; other features of the terrain, too, suggested the passage of huge floods. Some of the drainage systems, however, showed little or no sign of erosion, suggesting that they were either recent or had been short-lived.

What the scientists cannot determine at this stage is where such large quantities of water came from. The surface of Mars is as dry as dust, except for large ice caps at its poles. The theory carrying most weight is that water came from the condensation of gases and vapour emitted by the planet's many gigantic volcanoes.

Dr. Carr also said there were grounds for believing

that the apparently dry surface held large quantities of interstitial ice in the fissures and pores of the rock.

Even more puzzling is where all that water has gone. Clouds do develop in low-lying areas of the surface, but as Dr. Carr admitted "it is a puzzle".

The Viking photographs have also shown hitherto unknown details of some of the largest volcanoes on Mars, some of which display lava flows running for 800 km from the vent, causing speculation that the lava is of low viscosity. By plotting the number of subsequent craters on the rims of the volcanoes the scientists conclude that some have been active for at least 2,000 million years.

Several of Wells novels have been made into long playing records which are enthusiastically collected on both sides of the Atlantic.

Viking is expected to continue taking pictures until December, a time span the scientists hope will enable them to detect any seasonal changes in the Martian weather.

While the Viking spacecraft has been taking black and white pictures in orbit, the landing craft has been sending back colour pictures from the surface, showing a chaotic reddish-brown terrain, strewn with boulders.

The Scientific Romances and Prophecies of H. G. Wells

A Select Guidelist

The Time Machine (1895)
The Wonderful Visit (1895)
The Stolen Bacillus and Other Incidents (1895)
The Island of Dr Moreau (1896)

The Plattner Story and Others (1897)
The Invisible Man (1897)
Certain Personal Matters (1897)
Thirty Strange Stories (New York) (1897)
The War of the Worlds (1898)
When the Sleeper Wakes (1899)
Tales of Space and Time (1899)
The First Men in the Moon (1901)
Anticipations (1901)
The Discovery of the Future (1902)
Mankind in the Making (1903)
Twelve Stories and a Dream (1903)
The Food of the Gods (1904)
A Modern Utopia (1905)
In The Days of the Comet (1906)
The War in the Air (1908)
First and Last Things (1908)
The Country of the Blind and Other Stories (1911)
Men Like Gods (1923)
Short Stories of H. G. Wells (1927)
The Shape of Things to Come (1933)
The Scientific Romances of H. G. Wells (1933)
Things to Come (1935)
Star Begotten (1936)

Neil Austin's commemorative drawing of H. G. Wells published in 1946 shortly after the great prophet's death.